OXFORD
SLAVONIC PAPERS

Edited by

I. P. FOOTE   G. S. SMITH

and

G. C. STONE

General Editor

NEW SERIES
VOLUME XXII

OXFORD
AT THE CLARENDON PRESS
1989

Oxford University Press, Walton Street, Oxford OX2 6DP

Oxford New York Toronto
Delhi Bombay Calcutta Madras Karachi
Petaling Jaya Singapore Hong Kong Tokyo
Nairobi Dar es Salaam Cape Town
Melbourne Auckland

and associated companies in
Berlin Ibadan

Oxford is a trade mark of Oxford University Press

Published in the United States
by Oxford University Press, New York

British Library Cataloguing in Publication Data
Oxford Slavonic Papers: new series.
Vol. 22
1. Eastern Europe
I. Foote, I. P. (Irwin Paul), 1926–
II. Smith, G. S.   III. Stone, G. C.
947.0008
ISBN 0–19–815668–5

Typeset by Joshua Associates Ltd., Oxford
Old Church Slavonic setting by
Oxford University Computing Service
Printed in Great Britain by
Bookcraft (Bath) Ltd.
Midsomer Norton, Avon

THE editorial policy of the New Series of *Oxford Slavonic Papers* in general follows that of the original series, thirteen volumes of which appeared between the years 1950 and 1967. It is devoted to the publication of original contributions and documents relating to the languages, literatures, culture, and history of Russia and the other Slavonic countries, and appears annually towards the end of the year. Reviews of individual books are not normally included, but bibliographical and review articles are published from time to time.

The British System of Cyrillic transliteration (British Standard 2979: 1958) has been adopted, omitting diacritics and using -y to express -й, -ий, -ій, and -ый at the end of proper names, e.g. Sergey, Dostoevsky, Bely, Grozny. For philological work the International System (ISO R/9) is used.

Editorial correspondence and typescripts should be addressed to Dr G. C. Stone at Hertford College, Oxford. Copies of the rules for style and presentation of typescripts will be supplied on request.

I. P. FOOTE
G. S. SMITH
G. C. STONE

Hertford College, Oxford

CONTENTS

Two for the Price of One:
the Psalter MS Peć 68

By C. M. MACROBERT

THE medieval scribe's request that his readers should correct his errors is a commonplace; and the complex textual traditions that could result from such correction have long been evident. Among possible examples, the investigations of Jagić[1] and Pogorelov,[2] and more recently of Karačorova,[3] into the textology of the early Church Slavonic Psalter illustrate with discouraging clarity the difficulties in textual criticism which are caused by probable wholesale or piecemeal correction and conflation. It is less usual, though, to be able to observe the process of correction at first hand, in a MS which has been subjected to systematic alteration to bring it in line with a current received version of a text.

Such an opportunity is presented by the Church Slavonic Psalter MS No. 68 in the Monastery of the Patriarchate in Peć (south-east Yugoslavia).[4] This MS comprises Ps. 33 v. 7 to Ps. 149 v. 9 and the Old and New Testament Canticles normally appended to the Psalter in the Eastern Orthodox tradition. As is usual, the Psalter itself is divided into twenty sections, called *kathismata*. After every third *kathisma*, short hymns (penitential *troparia*) and prayers are inserted, and at the end of the MS prayers to be recited in case of temptation in one's dreams are appended (i.e. an embryonic *posledovanie*).

Brief paleographical descriptions have been given by Vuksan[5] and Mošin.[6] The latter ascribes the MS to the first half of the fourteenth century. The leaves of parchment are clean, cream-coloured and

[1] I. V. Jagič, 'Četyre kritiko-paleografičeskie stat'i', *Priloženie k otčetu o prisuždenii Lomonosovskoj premii za 1883 god*, *Sbornik Otdelenija russkogo jazyka i slovesnosti Imperatorskoj Akademii nauk*, xxxiii (1884), 37–73.

[2] V. A. Pogorelov, 'O redakcijach slavjanskogo perevoda Psaltyri', in *Psaltyri*, Biblioteka Moskovskoj Sinodal'noj Tipografii, čast' 1, vyp. 3 (M., 1901).

[3] E. Koceva, I. Karačorova, and A. Atanasov, 'Nekotorye osobennosti slavjanskich psaltyrej na materiale XI–XVI vv.', *Polata knigopisnaja 14–15* (1985), 25–75, especially 26–38.

[4] My work on this MS was made possible by a series of visits to the Serbian Academy of Sciences and Arts under the exchange agreement between the British Academy and the Yugoslav Council of Academies of Sciences and Arts. I am indebted to the staff of the Archeographical Department in the Belgrade National Library for opportunities to study the MS itself, while it was awaiting restoration, as well as to read it in microfilm. I am also grateful to His Holiness German, Patriarch of Serbia, for permission to quote passages from the MS in this article.

[5] D. Vuksan, 'Rukopisi manastira Pećke patrijaršije', *Zbornik za istoriju Južne Srbije*, i (1936), 133–89.

[6] V. Mošin, 'Rukopisi Pećke patriaršije', *Starine Kosova i Metohije*, iv–v (1968–71), 5–136.

individually in a fairly good state of preservation, and the text is mostly written in a large, well-formed hand (see Plates 1 (i) and (ii) and Plate 2 (iii)). In the Canticles at the end of the MS (see Plate 2 (iv)) the letters, while basically unchanged in form, are more cramped and square and are written less evenly. This may signal the work of a different scribe, though it could simply be the result of haste toward the end of the work. The intervention of a later scribe is, however, visible in the thorough and minute correction to which the whole MS has been sub-jected. Some attempt has been made to imitate the original handwrit-ing, but several peculiarities indicate that the corrector was not the man who wrote the MS. On fol. 38^r, line 4, the tail of the ǫ slants to the right, rather than slightly to the left as in the other examples of this letter; on fol. 113^v, line 12, the corrector has used a quite different form of з from the з which begins the next line; on fol. 153^r, lines 10 and 13, the words мнѡжїцєю and дѣлашє, written over partial or complete erasures, employ a wide є foreign to the practice of the original scribe, who used only the narrow є and ѥ. The best illustration of the corrector's hand is to be seen on fol. 192^r, lines 7–8, 9–10, 12, 14, and 16: the right-hand tilt of the tail of the ǫ and the straight, right-slanting tail of the з are well in evidence, even if in a couple of places (lines 8 and 10) the з with a curved tail is imitated; the wide є occurs at the end of line 9; and the central bow of the м in lines 8, 12, and 16 dips more sharply below the line than it does in the original hand.

Fortunately it is often possible to discern not only that a correction has been made, but also how long the original word or phrase was and where it included letters with ascenders and descenders, e.g. in the places already mentioned on fols. 38^r, 153^r, and 192^r. Sometimes, indeed, where words have simply been erased, they can still be read, e.g. on fol. 192^r, line 8 има твоѥ , line 9 сѣ҃нѥ. Corrections are on the whole easier to detect in the MS itself than in microfilm or photograph; scanning under ultra-violet or infra-red light might perhaps elucidate places where the original reading is obscure and reveal some extra corrections.

The purpose of these corrections was to make the text conform to a particular version of the Church Slavonic Psalter which has been found in MSS from the mid fourteenth century onward and is thought to have originated on Mt. Athos. The Athonite redaction of the Psalter has been the special object of research by I. Bujukliev[7] and E. V. Češko.[8] Using variant readings from a fifteenth-century psalter which the scribe Ioann, a priest on Mt. Sinai, said he had copied from two psalters of the

[7] I. Bujukliev, 'Kăm văprosa za săštestvuvaneto na nova redakcija na slavjanskija prevod na psaltira', *Chiljada i sto godini slavjanska pismenost 863–1963. Sbornik v čest na Kiril i Metodij* (Sofia, 1963), 171–7.

[8] E. V. Češko, 'Vtoroe južnoslavjanskoe vlijanie v redakcii psaltyrnogo teksta na Rusi (XIV–XV vv.)', *Palaeobulgarica*, v (1981), no. 4, pp. 79–85.

Athonite redaction, Česko has been able to compile a list of diagnostics for identifying the Athonite version of the Church Slavonic Psalter. Her findings confirm Bujukliev's suggestion that the Šopov Psalter (Cyril and Methodius National Library No. 454)—and its continuation (identified by O. A. Knjazevskaja) the Karadimov Psalter (Cyril and Methodius National Library No. 1138)—contain the fourteenth-century corrected version of the Psalter. She also shows that other psalter MSS, such as the Tomič Psalter, belong to the Athonite redaction and may indeed represent it in an earlier and purer form than does Ioann's copy.[9]

Comparison of the corrections in Peć 68 with Česko's diagnostic variant readings from the Athonite redaction reveals almost complete coincidence. The tables of variant readings in the present article are intended in the first place to demonstrate that the corrected text of Peć 68 is the Athonite one. As Ioann's MS is later in date and in any case is not available *in extenso*, I have drawn on my own copy of variant readings from the Karadimov Psalter[10] (hereafter abbreviated as *Kar*) to represent the Athonite redaction; but as I have not had the opportunity to check my notes against the MS, I have supplemented them from two published MSS, the Kiev Psalter[11] (= *K*), which in Česko's view follows the Athonite redaction from Ps. 30,[12] and the Munich Psalter[13] (= *M*), which contains basically the same version.

The second purpose of the tabulated material is to show the relationships between the two versions of the psalter text in Peć 86, particularly the original one as far as it can be established, and versions which were in use before the Athonite revision. The tables contain variant readings from four MSS of the so-called[14] 'archaic' redaction, viz. the eleventh-century Glagolitic *Psalterium Sinaiticum*[15] (= *S*), the thirteenth-century Pogodin (= *P*) and Bologna (= *B*) Psalters, and the early twelfth-century Tolstoj Psalter (= *T*).[16] Jagić's edition of *P* and *B* includes variant readings from the Sofia and Bucharest Psalters, but I have not tabulated these, since the MSS are roughly contemporary with Peć 68

---

[9] E. V. Česko, 'Redakcija i osobennosti perevoda Psaltyri Tomiča', *Starobălgarska literatura*, xiv (1983), 37–58, especially 52.

[10] I am grateful to the Bulgarian Academy of Sciences, and to Mr J. Burnip, for the opportunity to study this MS in detail during a two-month visit to Bulgaria in 1982.

[11] T. V. Jurova (ed.), *Kievskaja psaltir' 1397 goda* (M., 1978).

[12] E. V. Česko, 'Ob afonskoj redakcii slavjanskogo perevoda Psaltyri v ee otnošenii k drugim redakcijam', in *Jazyk i pismennost' srednebolgarskogo perioda* (M., 1982), 60–92.

[13] S. Dufrenne, Sv. Radojičić, R. Stichel, and I. Ševčenko, *Der serbische Psalter*, i–ii (Wiesbaden, 1978–83).

[14] By Česko, op. cit. (n. 8), *passim*.

[15] Quoted from S. Sever'janov, *Sinajskaja psaltyr'* (Pgr., 1922). See also M. Altbauer, *Psalterium Sinaiticum* (Skopje, 1971).

[16] Quoted from V. Jagić, *Psalterium Bononiense* (Vienna–Berlin–Spb., 1907). Jagić prints the texts of *P* and *B in extenso* and gives readings in which *T* differs from *B* in an appendix. See also I. Dujčev, *Bolonski psaltir* (Sofia, 1968).

and show signs of a late and contaminated stage in the textual tradition. As Karačorova[17] points out, the Bucharest Psalter clearly incorporates elements from the Athonite redaction. The Sofia Psalter in the main follows the 'archaic' redaction, but it contains a scattering of readings more typical of what is sometimes called the 'Russian' redaction. Their presence in the Sofia Psalter is open to more than one interpretation: they may simply be readings indiscriminately current in the pre-Athonite tradition, or they may have originated in the 'Russian' redaction and spread into MSS such as the Sofia Psalter by some process of contamination.

The textual tradition which Pogorelov[18] tentatively isolated and labelled conventionally as 'Russian' is here represented by two MSS: the late thirteenth-century Simonovskaja Psalter published by Archimandrite Amfilochij[19] ($=A$) and MS Sinai 6[20] ($=S6$), regarded as belonging to the 'Russian' redaction both by Lunt[21] and by Tóth.[22] The Byčkov Psalter, published by the latter, is a fragment of the same eleventh-century codex.

In order to facilitate comparison with Česko's findings, which are based primariy on Pss. 18–58, and to keep within the space available to me here, I have concentrated on Pss. 34 (where *Kar* begins) to 58. I have excluded most orthographical corrections, although the corrector clearly attached importance to them, witness his habit of changing илк to ісрлк, e.g. on fol. 38ʳ, line 2, and fol. 153ʳ, lines 7 and 10. I have also left out of consideration his frequent addition and deletion of the conjunction и, his switches between definite and indefinite adjectival endings, his practice of changing the accusative plural masculine pronoun ѥ to ихк, and the full range of places where сии has been altered to сиꙗ (Pss. 41.5, 43.18, and 48.2 as well as the tabulated 49.21 and 22). All other alterations which I have been able to detect are cited, either in the tables or in the accompanying comments, and are followed by the original readings when these can be deciphered or inferred with reasonable confidence. Where several MSS share essentially the same reading, I quote from the first MS listed. Places where the Sofia Psalter coincides with *S6* and *A* against the four MSS of the 'archaic' redaction are marked with an asterisk.

Table I reproduces Česko's diagnostic readings for the Athonite

---

[17] Op. cit. (n. 3), 38.

[18] Developing a broad distinction drawn by V. I. Sreznevskij, *Drevnij slavjanskij perevod psaltyri* (Spb., 1877), *passim*.

[19] Archimandrit Amfilochij, *Drevle-slavjanskaja Psaltir' Simonovskaja do 1280 goda*, 2 ed., i–iv (M., 1880–1).

[20] M. Altbauer and H. G. Lunt, *An Early Slavonic Psalter from Rus'*, i (Cambridge, Mass., 1978).

[21] H. G. Lunt, 'The Byčkov Psalter', *Slovo*, xxv–xxvi (1976), 255–61.

[22] I. H. Tóth [I. Ch. Tot], 'Byčkovskaja psaltyr' XI v.', *Acta Universitatis Szegedensis de Jozsef Attila nominatae, Dissertationes slavicae*, viii (1972), 71–114.

redaction and demonstrates that this was the source for the corrected version of Peć 68. In only two instances, Ps. 57.6 and Ps. 58.6, has the text of Peć 68 not been altered to agree with *Kar*, *M*, and *K*, and in only one, Ps. 56.7, is the result of alteration at variance with those MSS. However, in a number of places (Pss. 35.13, 37.7, 39.12, 48.18, 49.17, 55.8, and 58.4) the Athonite reading in Peć 68 is original, not the result of correction, and in three of these (Pss. 35.13, 39.12, 49.17) it is also attested in one or both of the MSS from the 'Russian' redaction. This observation does not invalidate the use of these variants as diagnostic for the Athonite redaction, but it serves as a reminder that in this type of tradition isolated readings are not reliable, unambiguous indications of textual affiliation and that MSS can only be assigned to one or other redaction on the basis of a collective preponderance of characteristic variants. In Ps. 36.27 the original reading seems to me to be вѣккȣ. This may be a misinterpretation, since the letter ȣ is characteristic of the corrections, not of the original text. On the other hand, the same reading is found in the Sofia Psalter.

Table II is intended to supplement Table I. It contains the other corrected readings in Peć 68 which agree with the Athonite redaction (as reflected in two or all of *Kar*, *M*, and *K*) against all the six pre-Athonite MSS considered here. As shown in the studies of Bujukliev and Češko, it emerges that the Athonite revision of the text was radical and comprehensive, ranging from the adoption of distinct Greek readings and new translations of Greek words to details of grammatical and derivational forms. The innovations tabulated here may provisionally be regarded as diagnostic between the Athonite and preceding versions, at any rate until such time as they are found in thirteenth-century or earlier MSS.

Table III presents a more complex picture. It lists the places where the Athonite redaction coincides with at least one, though not all representatives of the pre-Athonite tradition, but where no clear correlation with either the 'archaic' or the 'Russian' redaction can be seen. The large number of such instances demonstrates how much diversity there was within the early psalter tradition and how difficult it is to establish secure groupings among the MSS which represent it. At first glance there seems to be no pattern of correspondences between either the Athonite corrections or the original text in Peć 68 and the pre-Athonite MSS. Indeed, in a few instances (Pss. 38.12, 47.15, 51.10, 54.3) the corrected version of Peć 68 itself does not clearly agree with *Kar*, *M*, and *K*. However, a count of the coincidences between the two sets of readings in Peć 68 and each individual early MS reveals an interesting complementary distribution: the Athonite readings of Peć 68 are most often identical with the readings of *S* (approximately ×47, with a few extra doubtful cases where *S* is defective) and least often with those of *A*.

Conversely, the original readings of Peć 68, where they can be discerned, coincide most often with A ($\times$43) and least often with S ($\times$27). The other pre-Athonite MSS display less clear-cut relationships to the old and new texts of Peć 68, as all their coincidences number between 33 and 41.

Similarity between S, probably the oldest extant Church Slavonic Psalter, and the Athonite redaction bears out Češko's view[23] that the Athonite revision was an archaizing one. It is perhaps curious that the readings of P coincide with the Athonite ones slightly more often ($\times$39) than do those of the earlier MSS $S6$ ($\times$35) and T ($\times$33), though the numerical differences are hardly large enough to be significant. More remarkable is the link indicated between the original text of Peć 68 and the Russian MS A. It is possible to glean supporting evidence for this connection and for some common ground between Peć 68 and $S6$ from Tables I and II. In a number of the places listed in these Tables the pre-Athonite MSS are not unanimous in their readings. If one compares the variants from each one of these MSS in turn with the original readings in Peć 68, a striking pattern of correspondences emerges. In Table I, out of 9 relevant instances, 6 show coincidence between Peć 68 and A, and 6 (not all the same ones) between Peć 68 and $S6$, whereas there are only 3 coincidences each with T and S, and only 2 each with P and B. In Table II, out of 25 clear cases where the pre-Athonite tradition is split, 19–20 show coincidence between Peć 68 and A and 18–19 between Peć 68 and S (though it must be added that in four instances the Sofia Psalter shares the common reading of A and $S6$). P, B, and T all share 13 readings (not always the same ones) with Peć 68 in Table II, while S only shares 8.

Further light is cast by Tables IV, V, and VI on the relationships between the two versions in Peć 68 and the 'archaic' and 'Russian' redactions. Table IV consists of the places where the Athonite corrections in Peć 68 coincide with 'archaic' readings in the pre-Athonite tradition, presumably as a result of continuity between the two redactions. It is striking that all the original readings in Peć 68 here are the same as those in $S6$ and A, the representatives of the 'Russian' tradition (but one of these readings is shared with the Sofia Psalter).

In Table V readings from Peć 68 are listed which are attested in $S6$ and A but not in the four MSS of the 'archaic' redaction (though 11 out of 34 do occur in the Sofia Psalter) and which have presumably been left unaltered either by oversight or, in the majority of cases, because they coincided with the Athonite redaction. Many of them are minor morphological variants, secondary sigmatic aorists and third persons dual in -ᴛᴀ, which come as no surprise in an early fourteenth-century

---

[23] Expressed in conversation.

MS. It is, however, noteworthy that they were established in the 'Russian' redaction, as represented by *S6*, by the end of the eleventh century.

Table VI, on the other hand, sets out the rather small number of places where the Athonite reading is the same as the 'Russian' one of *S6* and *A* while the original text of Peć 68 reflects more or less clearly the 'archaic' redaction. Though few, these instances are important because they suggest a possible link between the 'Russian' redaction and the Athonite one, which would then be the product of a very complicated process of conflation and revision.

Equally, some of the distinctive 'archaic' readings, here and in earlier tables (Table II, Pss. 34.17 and 57.6; Table III, Pss. 39.5, 39.9, 44.3, 44.15, and 52.2), in the original version of Peć 68 make a straightforward affiliation to the 'Russian' redaction untenable. It would in fact be possible, if space allowed, to counter Table V by compiling a list of unaltered readings from Peć 68 which are shared with the 'archaic' redaction and not found in the 'Russian' one, such as the following:

Ps. 42.3 вь села твоꙗ *P B T S*; *Kar* въ сѣни твоѧ *S6 A*
 M K Peć 68

Ps. 46.10 въꙁнѣсꙗ сѧ *P B S*   въꙁдвигошасѧ *S6 A*
 въꙁнесошасѧ *T*; *Kar M K*
 прѣвьꙁнесошесе *Peć 68*

Ps. 48. 17 не вои сѧ *P B T S*; *Kar K* не оубою сѧ *S6 A*
 не оувон се *M Peć 68*

A further problem is raised by original readings of Peć 68 which are not attested in any of the six pre-Athonite MSS used here. One appears in Table I (Ps. 48.18 оумирдиетъ); the others which were thought worth correcting are assembled in Table VII. Some of them, of course, may have been due simply to scribal error, but others were doubtless current within the pre-Athonite tradition and parallels to them might be found if one were to examine a wide enough range of MSS. For example, five of the original readings here (Pss. 38.5, 48.9, 52.4, 52.7, and 57.3) appear in the Serbian Psalter MS Sinai 8.[24] Table VII also contains a few places where the corrected reading in Peć 68 is not clearly supported by the three Athonite MSS, *Kar*, *M*, and *K*. These are in Pss. 37.9, 37.21, 39.11, and 49.8. Presumably they

---

[24] M. Altbauer, *Der älteste serbische Psalter* (Slavistische Forschungen, 23) (Cologne–Vienna, 1978). Although this MS has been ascribed to the thirteenth century, I have excluded it from the tabulated comparisons here, partly because it is defective at several relevant places, but mainly because I suspect that its mixture of 'archaic' and 'Russian' readings may be the result of conflation, as can be detected in Ps. 67.34:

на нбо нбние нбоу *S8* на нбо нбною *Peć 68, S6 A*; *Kar M K*
 на нбо нбоу *P B T* (*S* missing)

indicate the difficulty of observing uniform practice in the days before printing.

The textual information and comparisons given here are of necessity limited and the resulting picture incomplete and perhaps in some points distorted. Nevertheless, it is possible on this basis, if not to draw firm conclusions, at least to suggest directions for further investigation.

Firstly, the textual antecedents of the Athonite redaction need more study. It clearly represented a wholesale revision of the Psalter text and introduced a range of characteristic innovatory translations, but it also seems to have involved selection among pre-existing variant readings. The basis on which this selection was made is as yet a matter for speculation, but some of the material presented here, particularly in Tables IV and VI, suggests that both the 'archaic' and the 'Russian' redactions were used in compiling the Athonite version of the text.

Secondly, the problem of conflation, to which Alekseev has drawn attention in his study of the Church Slavonic Gospel text,[25] must be given serious consideration in textual analysis of the Psalter. It is immediately relevant to the original version of Peć 68. The conflicting patterns of coincidence with the 'archaic' and 'Russian' redactions, described above, in themselves suggest that textual traditions have been merged here. Strong supporting evidence can be found in Canticle 7, v. 46, where underlying the Athonite correction can be seen an original reading which pleonastically combines elements from the 'archaic' and the 'Russian' versions:

i. сѣрою и смолю ⟨......⟩   нафʼѳоѭ и смолоѭ *Kar M K*
ii. сѣрою и нафʼѳою пеклом   сѣрою пекломь *A (S6 missing)*
                               нафтоѭ и пеклом' *P B (T S* missing)[26]

It would appear that the man who wrote the original version of Peć 68 was working from two texts, one similar to *A*, the other to *P* and *B*. For the most part, when their readings diverged, he chose one or the other; what motivated his choice is an interesting but probably insoluble question. At this point in the Song of the Three Children, however, he embarked on copying the 'Russian' version, then changed in mid course to the 'archaic' one, and so produced an imperfect blend of the two.

If this interpretation is right, it casts light on the processes by which the text of the Psalter developed in the pre-Athonite period. A need

---

[25] A. A. Alekseev, 'Opyt tekstologičeskogo analiza slavjanskogo Evangelija', *Palaeobulgarica*, x (1986), no. 3, pp. 8–19.
[26] But cf. I. C. Tarnanides, *The Slavonic Manuscripts Discovered in 1975 at St. Catherine's Monastery on Mount Sinai* (Thessaloniki, 1988), 275.

was apparently felt, even before the Athonite redaction was compiled, to do away with obvious textual discrepancy between MSS. The original version of Peć 68, no less than the corrected one, claims our attention as an example of deliberate revision, a conscious attempt to resolve the conflicting textual traditions of the early Church Slavonic Psalter.

Table I

Ps. v.		Peć 68	Athonite redaction	Pre-Athonite redactions
35.10	i.	о тєбє ⟨·⟩ (sic)	ѿ тєбє *Kar M*	ѿ тєбє єстъ *P B T S S6 A*
	ii.	оу тєбє ѥ	ѿ тѡбє єстъ *K*	оу тєбє єстъ *P B T S S6 A*
35.10	i.	жнвотȣ	жнвотоу *Kar M K*	жнвотоу *P B T A*
	ii.	жнвота		жнвота *S S6*
35.13		падоше	падоша *Kar M K*	падоша *S6 A* падѫ *P T* падѫтъ *B S*
36.27	i.	въ вѣкы вѣка	въ вѣкы вѣка *Kar M K*	въ вѣкъ вѣка *S6 A*
	ii.	въ вѣкы вѣкȣ		въ вѣкъ вѣкоу *P B T S*
37.7	i.	с’мѥкнх’сє	смѧкохсѧ *Kar* смѥкнхсє *M K*	смѥкохъсѧ *B T S6 A* смѧх’сѧ *P S*
37.11	ii.	смѫтѥсє	смѧтнсѧ *Kar M K*	смѧтесѧ *P B T S S6 A*
39.5	i.	въ соуѥ тнаа	въ соуѥт’наа *Kar M K*	въ соуѥта *P B T S S6 A*
	ii.	въ соуѥ		
39.12		выноу ꙁастоупннста	вынѫ ꙁастѫпннста *Kar M K*	вынѫ ꙁастѫпннста *S6 A* вынѫ ꙁастѫпннсте *P T S* прнсно ꙁастѫпнсте *B*
39.14	i.	на помоцъ мою вънꙛмн	въ помоцъ мѡж вънꙛмн *Kar K*	на помоцъ моа прнꙁрн *P B T S S6 A*
	ii.	на помоцъ мою прнꙁрн	на помоцъ мою вънꙛмн *M*	
41.10	i.	нѥгда стоуꙗжѥ мн врагъ	ѥга стѫжꙉетꙗмн врагъ *Kar M K*	ѿ пєчалн вра моѥго *P B T S S6 A*
	ii.	ѿ пєчалн врага моѥго		
45.7	i.	смѫтншєсє	смѧтншесѧ *Kar M K*	съмѧсѧшѧсѧ *S* смѧшашѧсѧ *P*
	ii.	смєтошєсє		съмѧтошѧсѧ *B T S6 A*

48.18	i. оучнндаіе⟨..⟩	зинндаж *Kar M K*	оучнндаж *P B T S S6 A*	
48.18	ii. оучнндаіетъ	въсѣ *Kar M K*	въсего *P B T S S6 A*	
48.18	i. в'сѧ	слава его *Kar M K*	слава домоу его *P B T S S6 A*	
	ii. слд ⟨.....⟩ иего			
	слд домоу иего			
49.17	ѿвръже	ѿвръже *Kar M K*	ѿвръже *A* їзвръже *P B S6* въівръже *S* възвръже *T*	
49.22	i. сни	сіа *Kar M K*	сн *P T S* вси *B S6 A*	
	ii. сни			
54.5	i. смѧтесе (*sic*)	смѧтнса *Kar M K*	смѧтеса *P B T S S6 A*	
	ii. смѣтесе			
54.8	i. оуд'воріх'се въ поустыню	въдворіх'сѧ въ поустынн *Kar*	въдвориѫ'сѧ въ поустынн *P B T S; М*	
	ii. въд'воріх'се въ поустыню	въдворнѫ'ьсѧ въ поустынн *Kar*	въдворнѫ'ьсѧ въ поустыню *S6 A; K*	
55.8	спсешн нѫ	спсеши нѫ *Kar M K*	спсеши іа *P B T S S6 A*	
56.7	i. синѣтнше	слакоша *Kar*	сълакоша *S6* слаша *P B T S*	
	ii. сннѣрнише	синѣрннше *M K*	сълѣѣнша *A*	
56.10	i. ⟨..⟩поѫ	поѫ *Kar M K*	въспоѫ *P B T S S6 A*	
	ii. въспоѫ			
57.6	оуслышнтъ	слышнтъ *Kar M K*	въслышитъ *P B T S S6* слышитъ *A*	
58.4	безаконнне	безаконіе *Kar M K*	безаконенніеже *B T S6 A* безаконеннеже *P S*	
58.6	i. не ⟨.⟩ѹщедрн	не ѹщедрн *Kar M K*	не помлоун *P B T S S6 A*	
	ii. не помлоун			
58.6	творещнхъ	д'клажщнхъ *Kar M K*	творѧщнн *P B T S S6 A*	

Table II

Ps. v.	Peć 68	Athonite redaction	Pre-Athonite redactions
34.4	i. посрамлⷮ҇се посрамлꙗютꙿсе	посрамлѧтʾсѧ *Kar M K*	посрамлѧютʾсѧ *P B T S S6 A*
34.7	i. тоунѥ ii. тоунѥ iii. ? (reading with ꙋ)	тоунѥ *Kar M* вьсоуе *K*	дшютъ *P T S* спѧтн *B* безоума *S6 A**
34.8	i. аꙋⷮ҇ⷡ҇ꙋ ii. аꙋꙁⷡ҇	ловитвꙑ *Kar M K*	лѣстъ *P B T S S6 A*
34.8	i. ꙷбьнметъ нѥ ii. ꙷбьнметъ нѥ ?	ꙷбьнметъ его *Kar M* ꙷбьꙑдетъ его *K*	ꙷбьнметъ і *S S6 A* ꙷбьꙑдетъ ꙗ *P B T*
34.8	i. выпадетъⷮ҇ⷡⷨⷣ ii. выпадꙋтъ ?	выпадетʾсе *Kar M K*	въпадетъ *S S6 A* въпадѫтъ *P B T*
34.12	i. въꙁаꙗющѥ ii. въꙁдадꙋꙋ	въꙁⷣдаꙗщен *Kar M K*	въꙁдадꙗꙁ *P B T S S6 A*
34.16	i. нскꙋснше ii. моуⷱ҇ꙋнше	нскоусние *Kar M K*	мѫⷱꙑша *P B T S S6 A*
34.17	i. злодⷭ҇нства ⷯ̃ н ii. злобꙑ нꙗⷯ	злодⷭ҇нст҇ва нꙗⷯ *Kar M K*	злобы нꙗⷯ *P B S S6 A* ꙁꙿлобнⷮ҇ьнꙿⷯ *T*
34.17	i. нноⷱ҇редꙋꙋю (*sic*) ii. нноⷱ҇редоꙋю	еднноⷱ҇рад᾿нѫꙗ *Kar M K*	нноⷱꙑадꙗꙁ *P B T S* ѥдннорⷱ҇адоꙋю *S6 A*
34.19	i. мⷨ᷍нⷯ᷍⟨᷍⟩н⟨᷍⟩ ii. мнѣ	мн *Kar M K*	мнѣ *B T S6 A* мꙗ *S* мене *P*
34.19	i. тоунѥ ii. безоⷣ҇ꙋⷣ҇ма	тоунⷯ *Kar M* вьсоуе *K*	дшютъ *P T S* спѧтн *B* безоума *S6 A**
34.25	i. нн ѕрекоутъ ii. нн ѕрекоутъ	нн да рекꙗⷯ *Kar M K*	нн рекѫтъ *P B T S S6 A*

34.26	i.	посрамѥ⟨...⟩т'сѧ	посрамлѧютсѧ K M	посрамлѣѭтсѧ P B T S S6 A; Kar
	ii.	посрамлѣнют'сѧ		
34.27	i.	и да рекѫтъ	и да рекѫтъ Kar M K	и глѧтъ P B S S6 A
	ii.	и глѥтъ		глющє T
34.28	i.	хвалѣ твоеи	хвалѣ твоеи Kar M K	хвалѧ твоѭ P T S6 A
	ii.	хвалоу твою		въ хвалѧ твоѭ B S
35.2	i.	нѣ бо	нѣ Kar M K	нѣстъ бо P B T S S6 A
	ii.	нѣ бо		
35.3	i.	ѕѣсти	ѕѣсти Kar M K	вѣльсти P B T S S6 A
	ii.	вѣльсти		
35.5	i.	прѣкста в'сѣкомоу поути неблг҃оу	прѣста в'сѣкомоу пѫти неблг҃оу Kar M K	ста на всѣхъ пѫтехъ неблаг҃ыхъ P ста на всѣкомь пѫти неблѫдѣ B T S
	ii.	прѣста на всѣкомь поути неблѫдѣ		прѣста на всѣкомь поути неблѫдѣ S6 A
35.13	i.	дѣлаѭщеи	дѣлаѭщеи Kar M K	творѧщеи P B T S S6 A
	ii.	творѧщиин		
36.9	i.	наслѣдѧтъ землю	наслѣдѧтъ землѭ Kar M K	обладаѭтъ земѭ P B T S S6 A
	ii.	обладаютъ земинѥ		
36.20	i.	ицез⟨.⟩оше	ицезоша Kar M K	ицезѭ P B T S
	ii.	ицезноутъ		ицезноутъ S6 A*
36.37	i.	правтоу	правотъ Kar M K	правоты P B T S
	ii.	правдоу		правдоу S6 A*
36.38	i.	бездакон⟨......⟩ницн	бездаконницн Kar M K	законопрѣстѫлиницн P B T S S6 A
	ii.	законопрѣстоупинцин		
37.9	i.	з҃ѣла	доѕѣла Kar M K	ѕѣло P B T S S6 A
	ii.	з҃ѣло		
37.12	i.	искрьн⟨.⟩ны	искрьнии Kar M K	и ближнкы P T S6 without н: B A
	ii.	и ближнікы		

Table II (cont.)

Ps. v.		Peć 68	Athonite redaction	Pre-Athonite redactions
37.17	i.	⟨ ⟩да когдӓ	да не когдӓ *Kar M K*	ѥда когда *P B T S* нѥгда къгда *S6 A*
	ii.	нѥда когдӓ		
37.21	i.	въздобⷣлга	въз блага *Kar M K*	въ добⷣрⷣа *P B T S S6 A*
	ii.	въздобⷣрⷣа		
38.2	i.	въста⟨..⟩ти грькш'номоу	въстати грькш'номоу *Kar M K*	въстанеть грькшнпкъ *P B T S6 A*
	ii.	въстанеть грькш'нпкъ		
38.6, 8	i.	състась мон, съставь мон	съставь мон ×2 *Kar M K*	упостась моа ×2 *P B T S S6 A*
	ii.	упостась моа ×2		
39.7	i.	всесьженнїа	всесьжежнїа *Kar M K*	въсесьжⷣгаемыⷯ *B S* ѡлокавтоматы *P T S6 A*
	ii.	ѡлокавтомат-?		
39.11	i.	прав'дъ твою	прав'дъ твою *Kar M K*	правⷣы твоѥж *P B T S S6 A*
	ii.	правⷣы твоюѥ		
40.13	i.	незлобїѥ	незлобиѥ *M K*	незлобѫ *P B T S S6 A; Kar*
	ii.	незлобоу		
41.2	i.	желанⷮеть	желанⷣеть *Kar M K*	жѧданⷣеть *P B T S S6 A*
	ii.	желанⷣеть		
41.6	i.	прнскⷣбⷪна	прнскрⷣⷪ'на *Kar M K*	печална *P B T S S6 A*
	ii.	печалⷪна		
41.7	i.	къ мнⷩѣ самомⷧ (*sic*)	въ м'нⷩѣ самомⷮ *Kar M K*	къ мнⷩѣ самомоу *P B T S S6 A*
	ii.	къ мнⷩѣ самомоу		
42.2	i.	дрьжава	дрьжава *Kar M K*	крⷣѣпкость *P B T S S6 A*
	ii.	крⷣѣпкость		
43.10	i.	посрамнлаⷩ ѥсн наⷮ	посрамнлⷩ ѥсн наⷮ *Kar M K*	посрамн ны *P B T S S6 A*
	ii.	посрⷣамн ны		

43.14	i. положилъ iеси на ҃ ii. положилъ ны iеси	положилъ еси насъ *Kar M K*	положжна ны еси *P B T S S6 A*
43.17	i. понаю҃щаго ii. поносещаго	понашажщаго *Kar M K* поносещаго *M*	поносѧщаго *P B S S6 A* поношенаго *T* извѣкстъ *P B T S S6 A*
43.22	i. свѣкстъ ii. извѣкстъ	съвѣкстъ *Kar M K*	
43.27	i. избави на ҃ ii. избави ны	избави на ҃ *Kar M K*	избави ны *P B T S S6 A*
44.4	i. шроужие⟨.⟩ свое ⟨...⟩ ii. шроужнем свонмь	шроужіе свое *Kar K* шроужние твое *M*	шроужнемь твонмъ *B P T S S6 A*
44.6	i. цревь ҃ ii. ?	цѣевъ *Kar M K*	цѣъ *P B T S* цѫ̃ *S6 A*
44.9	i. синр'на ii. издинр'на	синр'на *Kar M K*	зминрона *P B T S S6* издиорона *A*
44.10	i. цѣн ҃ ii. ?	цѣн *Kar M K*	цѣѫ *P T S S6 A* цѫрн *B*
44.12	i. въжелеть ii. въсхощеть	въжелеке *Kar* въжелекетъ *M K*	въсхощеть *P B T S S6 A*
44.13	i. люк⟨.⟩цнн ii. любн ?	людьстїн *Kar M K*	люднѣ *P B T S A* люди ? *S6*
44.14	i. въноутрь ii. въноутрьждоу	въньтрь *Kar M K*	въньтрьжьдѣ *P* въньтрьждоу *B T S S6 A*
44.15	i. въсакдъ ке ii. по нен ?	въсакдъ еж *Kar M K*	по нен *P B T S S6 A*
46.10	i. дръжавни ii. крѣпцн	дръжав'нни *Kar M K*	крѣп'цнн *P B T S S6 A*
47.6	i. слѧтишее ii. слѧтошее	слѧтишѫсѧ *Kar M K*	смасаса *P S* сѫлѫтошѧсѧ *B T S6 A*

Table II (cont.)

Ps. v.		Peć 68	Athonite redaction	Pre-Athonite redactions
49.7	i.	свѣ́ктела́ствоую	засвѣ́ктела́ствоуж *Kar M K*	свѣдѣ́ктествоуж *P B T S S6 A*
	ii.	свѣ́ктела́ствоую		
49.7	i.	бъ ⟨.....⟩ бъ ткои	бъ бъ ткои *M* гъ бъ ткои *Kar*	ꙗко бъ бъ ткои *P T S S6*
	ii.	ꙗко бъ бъ ткои	бъ бъ *K*	ꙗко бъ ткои *B A*
49.12	i.	не ѳекоу	не ѳекж *Kar M K*	не поѵѣклъ *P B T S S6 A*
	ii.	не повѣклѣ		
49.18	i.	татѣ	татѣ *Kar K* татꙑ *M*	татѣ *P B T S S6 A*
	ii.	татѣ		
49.21	i.	синꙗ⟨.⟩ ствоорилꙑ	сиꙗ сѣтвоорилꙗ еси *Kar M K*	си еси ствоорилꙗ *P B T S S6 A*
	ii.	сии еси ствоорилꙗ		
49.22	i.	⟨.⟩да кога	да некогда *Kar M K*	еда когда *P B T S A*
	ii.	еда кога		иегда кѣгда *S6*
50.6	i.	⟨.⟩лоуаве	лжкавое *Kar M K*	злое *P B T S S6 A*
	ii.	злое		
50.19	i.	срⷣце скроушено и смѣрено	срⷣце скроушено и смѣрено *Kar M K*	срⷣца скроушена и смѣрена *P B T S S6 A*
	ii.	срⷣца скроушена и смѣрена		
51.11	i.	исповѣклꙗ⟨.⟩ се	исповѣклꙗꙁ сѧ тевѣ *Kar M K*	исповѣклꙗтисѧ *P B T S6 A*
	ii.	исповѣклꙗтисе		
52.6	i.	ѵⷧкоугоⷣ´нико	ѵⷧкоугоⷣ´никоⷨ *Kar M K*	ѵⷧкоугоⷣникѣ *P B T S6 A*
	ii.	ѵⷧкоугоⷣ´никѣ		ѵⷧкоугоⷣꙑникоу *S*
54.3, 5	i.	с´мꙋтиⷯ´се смѣтеее (*sic*)	смꙗтнꙋ´сѧ смꙗктнисѧ *Kar M K*	смꙗсѣсѧ *P S* смꙗтоꙋксѧ *B T S6 A*
	ii.	с´мⷮоⷯ´се смѣтеее		смꙗтесѧ *P B T S S6 A*
54.9	i.	⟨...⟩ѡ мⷶ⟨.⟩ло⟨...⟩дшіа	ѡ малоⷣшіа *Kar M K*	ѿ прѣкнемаганна *P B T S A*
	ii.	ѡ прѣкнемаганна		ѿ прѣкнемаганнꙗ (*sic*) *S6*

Ref		Reading 1	Reading 2	Reading 3
54.13	i.	⟨..⟩бннмь ѕбо	бннмь ѕбо *Kar M K*	бннм *P B T* оүбо бнцѣ *S*
	ii.	оүбо бнцѣ	бнцѣ оүбо *M*	оүбо бнцѣ *S6 A*
54.13	i.	⟨....⟩ бнцѣ	бнни *Kar* бнцѣ *M K*	оүбо бнни *P* бннм оүбо *S* оүбо бнцѣ *B*
	ii.	оүбо бнцѣ	бнцѣ (retouched) *S6*	оүбо бнцѣ *T A*
54.14	i.	зна⟨..⟩ѥлн мон	знаѥмын мон *Kar M K*	знанне моѥ *P B T S S6 A*
	ii.	знанне моѥ		
54.16	i.	да прндеть же	да прндеть же *Kar K*	да прндеть *P B S S6 A; M*
	ii.	да прндеть		н прндеть *T*
54.22	i.	ѥлѣа	ѥлѣа *Kar M K*	шлѣа *P B T S S6 A*
	ii.	шлка		
55.6	i.	словесь мон гнѡшнадꙋссе (*sic*)	словесь монѵь гнѡшнадꙗсѧ *Kar M K*	словеса мога мрьзкꙗхь нлнь *P B T S6 A*
	ii.	словеса мога мрьзкꙗѵ нлнь		
55.13	ii.	вь мнѣ бѣ млтвы	вь мнѣ бѣ млтвы *Kar M K*	вь мнѣ сѫть бѣ шбѣкты *P B T S S6 A* (without бѣ *S6*)
	i.	вь м'нѣ ⟨.....⟩ бѣ млтвы		
56.8	i.	вспою н пою	вьспою н пою *Kar M K*	пою н вьспою *P B T S S6 A*
	ii.	н пою вспою ?		
57.5	i.	аспнда глоүѵн затыкане⟨..⟩н	аспнда глоүѵын затнкахн *Kar K*	аспнды глоүхы затыкахцнн *P B T S*
	ii.	аспнда глоүѵа затыкаюцн- ?		аспнда глоүха затыкаюцн *S6 A; M*
57.6	i.	шбавлоюцнѵь	шбаважцнн *Kar M K*	шбавлꙗцаго *P B T S S6 A*
	ii.	шбавлоюцаго		
57.6	i.	шбавлѣмь шбаваѥт'се ш прѣлюѕда	шбавлѣмь шбаваѥтьсѧ ш прѣлюжда *Kar K*	шбавлѣма ш шбавлоюцаго ш прѣлюѕда *A*
	ii.	ш прѣлюоүда шбаваннка шбавлѣма	шбавлѣма шбаваѥт'се ш прѣлюоүда *M*	⟨ѡ⟩бавлѣма обаюцнсѧ отъ прѣмꙗѕда *S6* штъ прѣлюжда шбаваньннка шбавлѣма *B P T S*
57.10	i.	разоүмкѣтн	разоүмкѣтн *M K*	разоүмкѣтъ *P S* разоүмкѣте *B T S6 A*
	ii.	разоүмн- ?		разоүмкѣшѧ *Kar*

Table II (cont.)

Ps. v.	Peć 68	Athonite redaction	Pre-Athonite redactions
58.6	i. посєтн всє⟨...⟩ ѥзыкы ii. посѣтн всєхь ѥзыкь	посѣтнтн вьсѧ ѩзыкы *Kar M* посєтн⟨тн erased⟩ всѧ ѩзыкы *K*	посѣтн вєкхъ ѩзыкъ *P B S S6 A*; посєтнтн ...? *T*
58.12	i. ⟨.⟩да кога	да нєкога *Kar M K*	єда кѫгда *P B* єгда когда *S S6 A*; *T* missing
58.12	єда кога i. нѕло⟨.⟩жн н ii. раздроүшн ѥ	ннѕложн нѫь *Kar M K*	раздроүшн ѩ *P B S S6 A*; *T* missing

Table III

Ps. v.	Peć 68		Pre-Athonite = Athonite redaction	Pre-Athonite versions
34.8	i.	прндетъ ємȣ	прндетъ ємȣ S T S6 A; Kar M K	прндетъ нмъ P B
	ii.	прндетъ нмъ		
34.8	i.	сѣкѣстъ	сѣвѣстъ S S6? (retouched) A; Kar M K	сѣвѣдаѧтъ P B T
34.8	ii.	свѣк⟨ᵀ...⟩	съкрꙑ S S6 A; Kar M K	скрꙑша P B T
	i.	скрн⟨...⟩		
	ii.	скрнше		
34.24	i.	по прав²д⁴к твонн	по правд⁴к твоєн P S A; Kar M	по прабѣд⁴к моєн B T S6; K
	ii.	по прав²д⁴к моєн		
34.26	i.	н ⟨...⟩ сраанъ	н сдаанъ P; M K	н въ сꙗдаанъ B T S S6 A; Kar
	ii.	н въ сраанъ		
35.4	i.	оȣблѫжнтъ⟨.⟩	оȣблѫжнтъ P S S6; Kar M K	оȣблѫжнтъ і B T A
	ii.	оȣблѫжнтъ н		
35.7	i.	прав²да твоа	правда твоа P T B S S6; Kar M K	правдꙑ твоꙗ A
	ii.	прав²дꙑ твоє		
35.13	i.	могȣтъ	могѫтъ B T S; Kar K	могѫ P могоша S6 A; M
	ii.	могоше		
36.1	i.	⟨..hole⟩двннн⟨.....⟩лнъ	лѫкавьннꙗнъ P B T; Kar M K	лѫкавьноȣѭщннмъ S S6 A
	ii.	лоȣкавноȣющннмъ		
36.6	i.	соȣд²ꙑȣ твоє	сѫд²ꙑ⫽ твоѭ B T S S6 A; Kar M K	сѫд²ꙑ твоꙗ P
	ii.	соȣд²ꙑ твоє (sic)		
36.14	i.	лоȣкꙑ⟨.⟩ свон	лѫкъ свон B S S6 A; Kar M K	лѫкꙑ своꙗ
	ii.	лоȣкꙑ своє		
36.14	i.	ннца⟨...⟩	ннцта B T S6; Kar M K	ннцааго P S A
	ii.	ннцааго		

Table III (cont.)

Ps. v.		Peć 68	Pre-Athonite = Athonite redaction	Pre-Athonite versions
36.19	i.	въ дни глада	въ дни глада M K въ дни глада T A	въ дени глада S S6; Kar
				въ дьнь гладоу P B
	ii.	въ дни глада ᷉к		
36.21	i.	гръши'нын	гръшиннкъ P T S; Kar K	гръши'нъ B S6 A; M
	ii.	гръши'нын		
36.23	i.	поуты	пать B T S; Kar M	пати P S6 A; K
	ii.	поуты⟨ ⟩		
36.25	i.	быхъ	быхъ B T S S6; Kar M	бѣхъ P A; K
	ii.	бѣхъ		
37.12	i.	ѿ дале ᷉	ѿтъ дале T; Kar M K	дале P B S S6 A
	ii.	дале ᷉		
37.13	i.	гладоу	гладж S; Kar K	глаша P B T S6 A; M
	ii.	гладше		
37.14	i.	ѿвръздае	ѿтвръздаж B T S S6; Kar M K	ѿвръздахъ P ѿвьодоухъ A
	ii.	ѿвръздаъ		
37.17	i.	велеркуевадоу	велеркуедоу S6; Kar K	вельречевашe P B T S A; M
	ii.	велеркуевадше		
37.22	i.	нн ѿстоупн	не ѿстжпн P B T S A; Kar M ̇К	нн ѿстоупн S6
	ii.	нн ѿстоупн		
38.4	i.	раз'горксе	радгорнтсе P B T S6; Kar K	ра⟨жеж⟩еттсм S радгорксе A
	ii.		въдгорнт'се M	
38.7	i.	скрі сънбдаетъ	скрываетъ B S; Kar M K	сънбдаетъ P T S6 A
	ii.	сбнбаетъ		

Ref		Lemma	Reading A	Reading B
38.12	i.	въ ѡблъченӥ ⟨.⟩	въ ѡблъченӥн P; Kar M K	въ ѡблъченъюъ B T S S6 A
	ii.	въ ѡблъченӥни		
38.13	i.	⟨...⟩ ѥсмь	ѥсмь азъ A S; Kar M K (ѥсмь erased)	азъ ѥсмь P B T S6
	ii.	азъ ѥсмь		
39.5	i.	ненстовъ' лѥ	ненстовѥнна P S; Kar M K	ненставанна B ненстовьна T
	ii.	ненстовьна		гнѣвъы S6 A
39.9	i.	чрѣва моѥго	чрѣва моѥго S6; Kar M K	срца моѥго P B T S
	ii.	срьдца моѥго		оутробы моѥа A
39.18	i.	прнѥт'	прнѥт P B S S6 A; Kar M	прнѥт T; K
	ii.	прнѥт'		
40.7	i.	въ ⟨.⟩ хожаше	н въсхождаше P B T S6 A; Kar M K	ї въсхождаше S
	ii.	въсхожаше		
40.13	i.	оутвръдн ме	оутвръднлъ мѧ ѥсї S; Kar M K	оутвръдн мѧ P B T S6 A
	ii.	оутвръдн ме		
40.14	i.	боудеть ⟨.⟩ боудеть	бѫдеть бѫдеть P B S S6; Kar M K	боудеть н боудеть A бѫдеть T
	ii.	боудеть н боудеть		
41.2	i.	нѫже ѡбрадоумь	ıмьже ѡбрадомь S; Kar M K	такоже P B T S6 A
	ii.	такоже		
41.5	i.	до домоу	до домоу S6; M K	домоу B P T S A; Kar
	ii.	домоу		
43.5	i.	спсенна нѧковла	спсенна нѧковлѧ P B S A; Kar M	спсеннѥ нѧковлѥ S6 T; K
	ii.	спсеннѥ нѧковлѥ		
43.7	i.	спсе	спсеть B T S S6 A; Kar M K	спсе P
	ii.	спсе		
43.8	i.	ненавндѧщен нѧ	ненавндѧщѧ нѧсъ B T S; Kar M K	ненавндѧщѧ ны P S6 A
	ii.	ненавндѧщен ны		
43.14	i.	поношеннѥ	поношенне S6; Kar M K	поношенно P B A въ поношенье T
	ii.	поношенно		поношень (sic) S

Table III (cont.)

Ps. v.		Peć 68	Pre-Athonite = Athonite redaction	Pre-Athonite versions
43.22	i.	срⷣца	срⷣца S; Kar K	срⷣцоу P B S6 A; M срⷣце T
	ii.	срⷣцоу		
43.23	i.	заколеннне (sic)	заколеннⷮ P; Kar M K	на заколенне B T S S6 A
	ii.	на заколенне		
44.3	i.	въ оустⷩноу твои (sic)	въ ꙋстноу твоѥⷨ P B T; Kar M K	въ оустьнаⷯ твоиⷯ S6 S A
	ii.	въ оустⷩнаⷯ твои		
44.3	i.	блⷢви	благословиⷮ P B; Kar M	блⷢви T; K блⷢⷪснаⷮ S6 A (with нестъ)
	ii.	блⷢви		блⷢ S
44.6	i.	люⷣе ⟨....⟩	люⷣе S S6 A; M K	люⷣне твои P B T; Kar
	ii.	люⷣне твои		
44.6	i.	въ срⷣци ⟨....⟩	въ срⷣци S T S6 A; Kar M K	въ срⷣциⷯ P въ срⷪцⷩ нⷯ B
	ii.	въ срⷣци нⷯ		
44.8	i.	елеишⷩ	елⷦенⷦ A; Kar M K	олⷦнаⷦ P B T S масолⷨ S6
	ii.	?		
44.9	i.	стак²тн	стак²ти S6 A*; Kar M K	стакⷮтⷮ P S станкта B стак²та T
	ii.	стак²т-?		
44.10	i.	шⷣⷦна	одⷦна P B; Kar M K (by correction)	одⷦна S T S6 A
	ii.	шⷣⷦна		
44.14	i.	рⷦсны	рⷦсны B (by correction); M K	трⷦсны P T S S6 A; Kar
	ii.	трⷦсны		
44.14	i.	шⷣⷦна	шⷣⷦна P; Kar M	шⷣⷦна B T S S6 A; K
	ii.	шⷣⷦна		

44.15	i. нскрьннее	нскрьнаѧ єѧ *B T; Kar M K*	нскрьнаѧ *P* нскрьнаѧ єı *S*
	ii. нскрьннее		блнжьнаѧ єı *S6 A*
44.18	i. поменоу ⟨..⟩	поманоу *A; Kar M K*	поманѫтъ *P B T S S6*
	ii. поменоуть		
45.4	i. смѫтншеесе	смѫтншаСѧ *P; Kar K*	съмѧсѧ сѧ *S*
	ii. сметошее		съмѧтошѫ сѧ *B T S6 A; M*
46.8	i. поите ⟨....⟩ разоумı'но	поите разоумıн *P S S6; Kar M K*	поите и разоумıьно *B T*
	ii. поите ıемоу разоумı'но		поите ıемоу разоумıьно *A*
47.2	i. гъ ⟨....⟩	гъ *P S S6 A; Kar M K*	гъ нашъ *B T*
	ii. гъ нашь		
47.9	i. в' вѣккы ⟨⟩	въ вѣккы *B T S A; Kar K*	въ вѣккы *P S6; M*
	ii. в' вѣккы		
47.12	i. соудѣк твоиць ⟨....⟩	соудѣк ради твоиць *S6 T A; Kar K*	сѫдьбъ твоиць ради *P B S; M*
	ii. соудѣк твоиць ради		
47.15	i. в' вѣккы вѣкка	въ вѣккъ вѣкка *P B; Kar M K*	въ вѣкъı вѣкка *S* въ вѣкъ вѣккоу *T A*
	ii. в' вѣккы вѣккоу		въ вѣкъı вѣккоу *B T S6*
48.6	i. шбндаи	шбидетъ' *M P S A; Kar M K*	шбиде мѧ *B T S6*
	ii. шбндаи		
48.9	i. в' вѣккъı	въ вѣккъ *S6; Kar M K*	въ вѣкъ *P B T S A*
	ii. в' вѣккъ		
48.16	i. пои⟨.⟩м⟨.⟩ıет'	приιемлеть *S6; M K*	приιемлеть' *P B T S; Kar*
	ii. приıемлıет'		приιать *A*
49.1	i. ѿ въстокъ	ѿ въстоукъ *P B S A; Kar M*	отъ въстока *S6 T; K*
	ii. ѿ въстока		
49.1	i. до западьь	до запада *P B S A; Kar M K*	до запада *S6 T*
	ii. до запада		
49.12	i. нплинн	испльнение *P S S6 A; Kar M K*	кнци *B T*
	ii. конци		

Table III (cont.)

Ps. v.	Peć 68	Pre-Athonite = Athonite redaction	Pre-Athonite versions
49.14	i. бѣн ii. бѹ	бѣн B T A; Kar M K	бѹ P S S6
49.19	i. льщенига ii. льщение	льщениа P T S A; Kar M K	льщение B S6
49.20	i. на сна ii. на снь	на сна P B T S; Kar M K	на сынь S6 A
50.3, 5	i. беꙁаконие мое ×2 ii. беꙁаконига мога ×2	беꙁаконие мое ×2 B T; Kar M K беꙁаконение мое v. 5 P S	беꙁаконига мога ×2 S6 A беꙁаконена мога v. 3 P S
50.9	i. ꙋсополь ii. ꙁ сополь	ꙋсополь P B; M нешполь Kar нєсофомь K	осополь S T A ꙋгѡфꙑмь S6
51.10	i. в̾ вѣкꙑ вѣкꙋ	въ вѣкъ вѣка P S; Kar M K	въ вѣкꙑ вѣкꙋ S6 въ вѣкъ вѣкꙋ A T
	ii. в̾ вѣкꙑ вѣкꙋ		въ вѣка вѣкъ B
52.2	i. въ беꙁаконии 〈……〉	въ беꙁаконенꙑ S въ беꙁаконнцъ Kar M K	въ беꙁаконенйцъ своихъ P въ беꙁаконницъ своихъ B T въ начинаннихъ своихъ S6 A
	ii. въ беꙁаконии своихъ		
52.6	i. ꙋсꙋтрашесе ii. ꙋбѡташесе	ꙋстрашишьсе P A; Kar M K	ꙋбѡташишьсе B T S6 бѡкшишасм S
53.6	i. помагает̾ мнѣ ii. помагает̾ ми	помагеть мнѣ S6; Kar M K	помагаеть ми P B T S A
53.6	i. ꙁастꙋп'ннкъ 〈..〉 ii. ꙁастꙋп'ннкь ѥ	ꙁастꙋпннкъ K Kar M; T	ꙁастѫпннкъ есть P B S S6 A
53.8	i. блго 〈.〉 ii. блго ѥ	блго A; Kar M блгъ K	блго есть P B T S (S6 illegible)

54.3	i.	вьн҄' мн	вьн҄'мн *P B T S6; Kar*	вонъмн *S A; M K*
	ii.	вьн҄' мн		
54.23	i.	печаль твою	печаль твою *P T S S6?; Kar M K*	печаль свою *B A*
	ii.	печаль свою		
54.24	i.	нстлѣннꙗ	нстлѣннꙗ *B T S A; Kar M K*	нстлѣнню *P S6*
	ii.	нстлѣнню		
55.9	i.	прѣ̆ собою	прѣдъ сꙑбою *P S; Kar M K*	прѣдъ тобою *B T A*
	ii.	прѣ̆ тобою		прѣдъ мѣною *S6*
55.14	i.	въсполѧзеннꙗ	въсполѧзнованнꙗ *S6* въсполѧзновеннꙗ *Kar M K*	въсполѧзеннꙗ *P B T S A*
	ii.	въсполѧзеннꙗ ?		
56.4	i.	попнꙁаещнее⟨..⟩ мє	попнꙁаещлꙗ мꙗ *P S6; Kar M K*	попнꙁаѭштнꙗ мꙗ *B T S A*
	ii.	попнꙁаещннꙗ мє		
56.5	i.	нꙁ'бавнаꙗ ѥ	нꙁбавнаꙗ естъ *P B T S S6; Kar M K*	нꙁбавнаꙗ есн *A*
	ii.	нꙁ'бавнаꙗ есн		
58.3	i.	моужь кръвнн	моужь кръвнн *A; Kar M K* мѧжъ кръвьнн *S T* мѧжъ кръвьнн *S6*	мѧжъ кръвьı *B* мѧжа кръвьнн *P*
	ii.	моужа кръвнн		
58.8	i.	оустъхъ	оустънадтъ *T S; Kar M K*	оустъкъ *P B S6 A*
	ii.	оустъкъ		
58.14	i.	не боудѧтъ	не бѫдѫтъ *P S S6; Kar M K*	не бѫдетъ *B A* *T* missing
	ii.	не боудеть		
58.15	i.	ꙗко пъсъ	ꙗко пъсъ *S; Kar M*	ꙗко псꙑ *P B; K* ꙗко пъсı *S6*
	ii.	акı п'сн	акꙑ псн *A; T* missing	

Table IV

Ps. v.	Peć 68	Athonite = 'Archaic' redaction	'Russian' redaction
35.11	i. ⟨ ⟩вѣдоѹщим' ii. свѣдоѹщим'	вѣджщим' *P B T S; Kar M K*	съвѣдоѹщимъ *S6 A*
39.5	i. прїзрѣ ii. прѣзрн ?	прнзрѣ *P B T S; Kar M K*	прѣзьрѣ *S6 A**
39.8	i. въ свїн⟨...⟩цѣ книж'нѣ ii. въ главнзнѣ книж'нѣ	въ свнтцѣ книжнѣмъ *P B T S; Kar M K*	въ главнзнѣ книжьнѣн *S6 A*
39.9	i. ⟨...⟩ створнтн ii. неже створнтн	створнтн *P B T S; Kar M K*	неже сътворнтн *S6 A*
39.11	i. рѣ ii. рекѫ	рѣкѫ *P B T S; Kar M K*	рекоѹъ *S6 A*

40.9	i. ⟨...⟩закон'но ᵖᵒ̃ⷬᵉᷤᵗᵛⁿⁿᵒ	законопⷬⷭѣстѫпно *P B T S; Kar M K*	безаконьно *S6 A*
	ii. безакон'но		
43.12	i. ⟨...⟩снѣды	снѣдн *P B T S; Kar M K*	въ снѣдⷶ *S6 A*
	ii. въ снѣдⷶ		
43.13	i. проⷷдⷶ	проⷷдастⷶ *P B T S; Kar M K*	прⷷдⷶ *S6 A*
	ii. прⷷꙋдⷶ		
48.12	i. в' вѣкъ ⟨.⟩	в' вѣкъ *P B T S; Kar K*	въ вѣкⷶ *S6 A; M*
	ii. в' вѣкы		
50.16	i. ⟨.⟩прав'дⷶ	правдⷶ *P B T S; Kar M K*	ѡ правⷶдⷶ *S6 A*
	ii. ѡ прав'дⷶ		
50.18	i. дадⷶ ⟨...⟩бн⟨.⟩мⷶ ꙗ̃ᵇᵒ	дадⷶ бнлⷶ ꙗбо *P B T S; Kar K*	дадⷶ бⷯъ оубо *S6; M*
	ii. дадⷶ оубо бнⷷ		дадⷶ оубо бⷯъ *A*
54.18	i. ютро ᵗ	ютро *S; M* ꙗтро *P T; Kar K*	zаꙋтра *S6 A*
	ii. zаꙋтра	оутроу *B*	
56.9	i. славо	славо *P B T S; Kar M K*	слава *S6 A*
	ii. слава		

Table V

Ps. v.	Peć 68	'Russian' redaction	'Archaic' redaction
34.11	въсташе	въсташа S6 A; M	въстав'ше P T S; Kar K въставъшиин B
34.21	видѣкта	видѣкта S6 A; Kar M K	видѣсте P B T S
34.27	мнрь	мнрь S6 A*; Kar M K	мнюу P B T S
36.2	скоро	скоро S6 A*; Kar M K	ꙗдро P B T S
36.3	створи	створи S6 A	твори P B T S; Kar K M
36.11	на м'ножтвии	на м'ножьствии S6 A*	на множьствѣ P B T S; Kar M K
36.14	нз'влкоше	нзвлѣкоша S6 A*; Kar M K	нзвлькшѧ P B T S
36.14	напрегоше	напрѧгоша S6 A; Kar M K	налѧша P B S налѧкоша T
36.18	въ вѣккы	въ вѣккы S6 A*; Kar M K	въ вѣкъ P B T S
36.26	въздаиꙗ	въздаиꙗ S6 A; M K	ꙁдаиѧ P B T S; Kar
36.36	мимондохъ	мимондоуъ S6 A; Kar M K	мимонаꙗ P B T S
37.5	прѣвъзндоше	прѣвъзндоша S6 A; Kar M K	прѣвъзыдѫ P B T S
39.6	створилъ нѣси	съ створилъ нѣси S6 A*; Kar M K	ѥси створилъ P B T S
39.13	въз'могоѣ	въздмогоѣ S6 A*; Kar M K	въздмогѫ P B T S
41.12	прискрьбьна	прискрьбьна S6 A; Kar M K	печална P B T S
42.3	наставнета	наставнета S6 A; Kar M K	наставнсте P B T S
42.3	въведоста	въведоста S6 A; Kar M K	въвѣсте P B S въвѣдосте T

43.23	въскѩнихъомъ сє	въскѩнихъомъсѧ S6 A; Kar M K	въскѩнишѧ нъі P B T S
44.5	напрѧзи	напрѧзи S6 A; M K	налѧци P B T S; Kar
44.10	прѣоукрашєна	прѣвкрашєна S6 A*; K (прѣиспъщр'рѣна Kar M)	прѣвкрашєна P оукрашєна B прѣкоуцєна T S прѣкоукрашєна B прѣкоуцєна P T S прѣкрашєна B
44.14	прѣоукрашєна	прѣоукрашєна S6 A*; K (прѣиспъщрѣна Kar M)	прѣкоуцєна P T S прѣкоукрашєна B
47.8	ѳар'синскиє	ѳарсиискъи S6 ѳарєнскъи A (ѳар'синскъѩ Kar M ѳарєнискъиѩ K)	тар'сит'скъі P тарсиск'скъіж B T S
48.12	нарѣкоше	нарѣкоша S6 A; Kar M K	нарѣкша P B T S
48.15	оудолѣють	оудолѣють A; K оудолѣєть S6; Kar ѡдолѣють M	ѕдолѣѭть P B T S
50.6	соудити ти	соудити ти S6 A*; Kar M K	сѣдѧнти сѧ P B T осѫдѧнти сѧ S
52.2	блга	блга S6 A; Kar M K	добра P B T S
54.23	смѧтєнна	смѧтєнна S6 A	мѧвъі P B T S; Kar M K
55.12	оупъвах	оупъвах S6 A*; Kar M K	оупъваж P B T S
56.7	въпадошєсє	въпадошасѧ A (illegible in S6); M K въпадоше Kar	въпадѫ сѧ P B T S
57.8	напрѣжєть	напрѧжєть S6 A; Kar M K	налачєть P B T S
57.8	дон'дєжє	дон'дєжє S6 A; Kar M K	доидєжє P B T S
58.4	нападоше	нападоша S6 A; Kar M K	нападж P B T S
58.5	тєкоѫ	тєкоѫ S6 A*; Kar M K	тєчь P B T S

Table VI

Ps. v.		Peć 68	Athonite = 'Russian' redaction	'Archaic' redaction
44.9	i.	ѡ тѧжестїн	ѿтъ тѧжестїн *S6 A; Kar M K*	ѿт' вароⷩї *P B T S*
	ii.	ѿтъ вароⷩн		
46.7	i.	ⷭ҇цоⷬвї	ⷭ҇цвн *S6 A; Kar M K*.	цⷬою *P B T S*
	ii.	цⷬоу		
46.9	i.	надь ⟨......⟩ юзыкн	надь юзыкы *A S6; Kar M K*	надь вⷭѣхн юзыкы *P B T S*
	ii.	надь вⷭѣхн юзыкн		
47.4	i.	въ тⷮестеⷯ	въ тѧжьстьⷯъ *S6 A; Kar M K*	въ вароⷣⷯъ *P B S*
	ii.	въ вароⷩⷷъ		въ твароⷯъ *T*
48.11	i.	погыбнета	погыбнета *S6 A; Kar M K*	погыбⷧѧтъ *P T* погⷤыбнетⷮ *B S*
	ii.	погⷤыбн?тъ		
48.11	i.	ѡставїта	ѡставнта *S6 A; Kar M K*	ѡставлѧтъ *P B T S*
	ii.	ѡставетъ		
49.18	i.	проⷣлюбодⷣѣ̈мь ⷨ҇ю	проⷣлюбодⷣѣюмь *S6 A*; *Kar M K*	проⷣлюбоⷣⷣн *P B T S*
	ii.	проⷣлюбоⷣⷣн		
54.24	i.	льстн⟨...⟩	льстнн *S6* льстн *A*; *Kar M K*	льстнвⷩъ *P T* льстнвⷩн *B S*
	ii.	льстнвⷩн		

Table VII

Athonite and Pre-Athonite versions

Ps. v.		Peć 68	Athonite and Pre-Athonite versions
34.19	i.	ѹꙗнма ⟨......⟩	ѹꙗнма P B T S S6 A; Kar M K
	ii.	ѹꙗнма свонма	
35.4	i.	ѹстъ	ѹстъ P B T S S6 A; Kar M K
	ii.	ѹсиъ ?	
36.2	i.	нсӥшоѹтъ	нсъшлѫтъ P B T S S6 A; Kar M K
	ii.	нсхноѹтъ	
36.12	i.	нань	нань P B T S A; Kar M K нанє S6
	ii.	занъ	
36.37	i.	чл҃вкꙋ мнꙋ҆нꙋ	чл҃кѹ мнрнѹ P B T S S6 A; Kar M K
	ii.	чл҃вка мнꙋ҆на	
36.40	i.	нзъметъ	нзметъ P B T S S6 A; Kar M K
	ii.	нзбавнтъ	
37.9	i.	ѡнддхъ	ѳнкддхъ P B T S S6 A; Kar M K
	ii.	ѡнкддхъ	
37.21	i.	лн злдд	лнчк злдд P B T S S6 A; Kar K
	ii.	лнчк злдіа	лн злдд M
38.5	i.	ко⟨.⟩ѥ⟨..⟩ѥ	кое естъ P B T S S6 A; Kar M K
	ii.	колнко ѥ	
38.6	i.	вꙗс҆ка сꙋиєтꙗ	вꙗскꙋꙗскдд сѹєтд вꙗсꙗкъ B T S6 A; Kar M K
	ii.	?	вꙗскдд сѹєтд вꙗсꙗкъ P S
39.11	i.	млтн твоѥ⟨.⟩ н нстнны твоѥ⟨⟩	млⷭть твоѭ н нстннѫ твоѭ Kar M K
	ii.	млтн твоѥн н нстнны твоѥн	мⷭлостн твоєн н нстнны твоєꙗ P B T S S6 A
39.15	i.	посрдмнѣтсꙗ	посрдмлѭⷮсѧ P B T S S6? A
	ii.	посрдмет҆сє	посрдмлѫⷮ'сѧ Kar M K

Table VII (cont.)

Ps. v.		Peć 68	Athonite and Pre-Athonite versions
39.17	i.	и реꙗꙁтъ	и реꙁꙗтъ P B T S S6 A; Kar M K
	ii.	и глеть	
43.13	i.	в᾽вьсканцданн⟨ ⟩	въ вьсканцданнⷯъ P T S S6 A; Kar M K
	ii.	в᾽вьсканцданнн	въ вьсклнкновеннꙋⷯъ B
44.18	i.	в᾽ вⷮкⷦъ⟨ ⟩ вⷮкка	въ вⷮкъ вⷮкка P B S; Kar M K
	ii.	в᾽ вⷮккы вⷮккоу	въ вⷮккы вⷮкка T S6 въ вⷮккъ вⷮккоу A
47.11	i.	по нмени твоемъ	по нмени твоемоу P B T S S6 A; Kar M K
	ii.	по нмени твоемь ?	
48.9	i.	⟨...⟩ндбавленнꙗ	ндбавленнꙗ P B T S A; Kar M
	ii.	ꙁа ндбавленне	ндбавленне S6; K
49.5	i.	с᾽берꙋте	съберꙋте P B T S S6; Kar M K
	ii.	с᾽бероутъ	съберетъ A
49.8	i.	всесьꙶженнꙗ же твоꙗ	ꙍлокавтоматы же твоꙗ P B T S6 A; Kar K
	ii.	ꙍлокавтоматы же твоне	вьсесьжагаемаа же твоꙗ S; M
49.21	i.	лнцемь твоннⷧь	лнцемⷮ твоннⷮ P B T S S6 A; Kar M K
	ii.	лнцемь ⟨..?..⟩	
49.23	i.	спⷭенне ᵐᵒᵉ	спⷭенïе мое P B T S S6 A; Kar M K
	ii.	спⷭенне	
50.20	i.	нⷷрдлⷨ᾽скые	нⷷрдлⷨⷮскꙑꙗ S6 A; Kar M нⷷрдлⷨ᾽скꙑ P B T S
	ii.	нⷷрдлⷨовые ?	нⷷрдлⷨовы K
51.7	i.	раꙁроушннт᾽ те ⟨...⟩	бⷮ раꙁдроушнтъ тꙗ P B T S S6 A; Kar M K
	ii.	раꙁроушннт᾽ те бⷮ	
52.4	i.	неключⷨн⟨...⟩	неключⷨнн P B T S S6 A; Kar M K
	ii.	непотрⷮбнн	

52.5	i.	разоумик⟨…⟩ютъ	разоумикѫтъ P B T S S6 A; Kar M K
	ii.	разоумиккаютъ	
52.7	i.	плкне (нїе)	плкненние P B T S S6 A; Kar M K
	ii.	плкнь	
57.2	i.	аще ⟨….⟩ въ истинноу (860)	аще въ истинѫ 860 P B T S6 A; Kar M K ҭще въ рѫкснотѫ S
	ii.	аще оуко въ истинноу	
57.3	i.	въ сѫци ⟨…⟩	въ сѫци P B T S S6 A; Kar M K
	ii.	въ сѫци ⟨.?.⟩	
57.9	i.	па⟨…⟩де шг'нь	паде огнь P B T S S6 A; Kar M K
	ii.	?	

вьстани вьсрѣтеннимон нвнмь

итьн гн бесиллъ бенелнвъ

вьмли и посѣти все нзьикы

не ущеден всѣхъ творещнхъ

безаконин

вьзврате тсе навечрь нвьзаалчют

ико псъ юбидоуть градь

се тн юбещаноть оусты своимли

июроужнн вьоустѣхь нхъ ико

исто слышал

итьи гн посллѣнишнсе нлаь

оуннужниши все нзьикы

дрьжлвоу мою итебѣ схраню

ико тьи бе застоупниисьмен и

снбьмон нмлать иговарнтла

бьмон июнтьмине навраз҃ьмон

исоубни нхъ дмсога злбоуть

ВЕСЕЛИТИСЕ ВЬВЕСЕЛИИ НZЫКА ТВОИ

ХВАЛИТИСЕ СЬДОСТОАНИИМЬ БОНМЬ

СЬГРѢШИХОМЬ СЬ ѠЦЫ НАШИМИ

БЕZАКОНОВАХОМЬ НЕѠПРАВДИХОМ

ѠЦИ НАШИ ВЬ ЕГУПТѢ НЕРАZОУ

МѢШЕ ТИОСЬ ТВОИХЬ

НПОМЕНОУШЕ ОУМНОЖЕННИ

МЛТИ ТВОИЕ

НПРОГНѢВАШЕ ВЬХОДЕЩЕИ ВЬЧРЬ

МНОЕ МОРИЕ

Н СПСЕН ИМЕНИ СВОЕГОРА

НКАZАТЬ ЕМ СИЛОУ СВОЮ

ZАПРѢТИН ЧРЬМНОМОУ МОРЮ ИСЕЧЕ

Н ПРОВЕ Н ПОБѢZНѢ ВЛКОПО ПОУСТЫНИ

Н СПСЕН НZРОУКЫ НЕНАВИДЕЩИѠ

НИZБАВИ ... Ѥ НZРОУКЫ ВРАГЬ

ПОКРН ВОДА СТОУЖАЮЩЕИ ИМЬ

(ii) Peć 68, fol. 113ʳ. Ps. 105, verses 5–11

сыннны ѡкрьтъ трапезы твоѥ

сє таꙛо блгвить сє чл҃вкь боѩисꙛга

блгословить тебь ѿ сн҃ѡна

и оузриши блгаꙗ и҃ероуⷭлⷨ вьсє

дн҃и живота твоѥго

и видиши сн҃ы сн҃овь твоихь

миⷬ бⸯ наⷣ и҃зⷬла   пѣ҇   стⷼе   ρⷯіⷲ

Множию брашесе сьмною ѿ

юности моѥи

да ρⷯетьнаꙗ и҃ρⷵлⸯ множицею

брашесе сьмною ѿ юности моѥи

и бо не прѣдⸯмогоше мене

на хрьбтѣ моѥмⸯ дѣлашеⷮ грѣ

шинⸯцⷵи

о да длⸯжнше безаꙛонни своꙗ

г҃ь праведнⸯ сьсѣчеть выꙗ

грѣшниꙛомⸯ

(iii) Peć 68, fol. 153ʳ. Ps. 127, verses 3–6, Ps. 128, verses 1–4

пещи ꙗко дх҃ъ хладань шоумлеще ⁘
и не прикосноусе нхъ ѿ моудь ѡгньми
ѡскрьбникотоу жи нилъ · тогда ти
трїе ꙗкоєдинѣминоустꙑ по ꙗхоу
и блг҃олꙗхоу, и сла влꙗхоу б҃а вьпе
щигающе ⁘ п҃ѣ т ѣ хмєѡтр̈
и блгⷭ҇нь си гⷭ҇и бе҃ ѿц҃ь нашихъ, прѣпⷮѣ
ти и прѣвьзносимꙑи · вѣ к҃и ⁘
блⷵ҇но имє ... славꙑ твоке сто G
и прѣ пⷮѣ о и прѣ вьзноси кⷨꙑ во ⁘
блⷵ҇нь еси въ цр҃кви ст҃ꙑи славꙑ твоке
прⷮѣ тъ, и прⷮѣ вьзноси кⷨꙑ во вѣ
блⷵ҇нь еси видє и бєзⷣнꙑ сѣдеи на херꙋ
вимⷮѣ, прⷮѣ пⷮѣ тъ и прⷮѣ вьзмоси вⷮѣ
блⷵ҇нь еси на прⷮстоле славꙑ цр҃ствиꙗ
твокего и прⷮѣ пⷮѣ тъ и прⷮѣ вьзмои вⷮѣ

The Arrival of Christianity in Lithuania: Baptism and Survival (1341–1387)

By MICHAŁ GIEDROYĆ

I

IN the course of the thirteenth century the Grand Duchy of Lithuania had annexed the Slav (and Orthodox) territory of Black Rus', and extended its influence over the important region of Polotsk. This Lithuanian expansion into Rus'[1] was one of the two main processes that were to shape the future of the Grand Duchy. The other was the growing confrontation with the Teutonic Order, a confrontation which c.1300 was escalated by the Knights to the level of a full-scale war of attrition.[2]

There is substantial contemporary evidence that during the second half of the thirteenth century the Slavs under Lithuanian rule participated in the military enterprises of the Grand Duchy.[3] The use of Slav resources against the Order during the first half of the fourteenth century (particularly during the reign of Grand Duke Gediminas (Rus. Gedimin, Pol. Giedymin) c.1315—41) is well attested. Ruthenian contingents were deployed in the field and on garrison duties.[4] In the battle on the River Strėva (1348) the army of Grand Duke Algirdas (Rus. Ol'gerd, Pol. Olgierd), a son of Gediminas, included reinforcements from Vladimir, Berest'e (Pol. Brześć), Vitebsk, Smolensk, Polotsk, and probably also from Black Rus' and Pinsk.[5]

Clearly, the level of Ruthenian involvement in the Grand Duchy's

---

[1] In this article the name Rus' refers to areas inhabited by Eastern Slavs.

[2] M. Giedroyć, 'The Arrival of Christianity in Lithuania: Between Rome and Byzantium (1281–1341)', *Oxford Slavonic Papers*, NS XX (1987), 3, 8–12.

[3] For example: in 1252 Tautvilas confronts Grand Duke Mindaugas (reigned c.1238–1263) with the help of, *inter alia*, the forces of Halich-Volyn' (H. Paszkiewicz (ed.), *Regesta Lithuaniae ab origine usque ad Magni Ducatus cum Regno Poloniae unionem*, i (Warsaw, 1930), 48 (no. 244); in 1263 the same Tautvilas attempts to conquer Lithuania with the help of the army of Polotsk (ibid. 86 (no. 428) and H. Paszkiewicz, *Jagiellonowie a Moskwa*, i (Warsaw, 1933), 106 and note 4); later in the same year (1263) Vaišvilkas invades Lithuania at the head of the forces from Pinsk and Novogrudok (Paszkiewicz, *Regesta* (n. 3), 88 (no. 434)); Grand Duke Traidenis (reigned 1269/70–1281/2) also uses Rus'ian troops (evidence compiled in H. Paszkiewicz, *The Origin of Russia* (London, 1954), 222 and note 3). The deduction that Mindaugas himself used auxiliaries from Rus' is inescapable.

[4] For examples, see Paszkiewicz, *Origin* (n. 3), 222 and note 3 (the reign of Grand Duke Vytenis); also ibid. notes 4, 5, 6, and 7.

[5] For examples, see ibid. 222 and notes 1 and 2.

effort on the German fronts rose with the progress of Lithuania's eastern expansion. The striking symmetry (one is tempted to say the correlation) between the escalation of the German pressure from the west[6] and the progress of Lithuanian expansion in the east[7] indicates that the latter amounted to a deliberate Lithuanian response to the Order's aggression. Indeed, the gravity of the German threat to the Grand Duchy's political survival suggests that the transfer of Rus' resources into the Lithuanian–German conflict was the principal motive behind Lithuania's progressive eastern acquisitions. Algirdas came close to articulating this Lithuanian tenet, when in 1371 he reminded Patriarch Philotheos that his realm was waging war on the Order even on behalf of the Muscovites,[8] in other words on behalf of Eastern Slavdom as a whole.[9]

Was this striking pattern of matching the *growing* German pressure with *ever-increasing* eastern expansion merely a succession of *ad hoc* responses (rationalized *ex post facto* by Algirdas in 1371) or was it a deliberate Lithuanian policy conceived as early as the turn of the century? Two features of Lithuania's attitude to Rus' seem to indicate that it was the latter. The first was the early (*c.*1300) transformation of the previously random pattern of predatory exploits into a series of acquisitions based almost entirely on diplomatic persuasion and dynastic match-making.[10] Significantly, this particular change of attitude coincided with the realization that the German war was to become an irreversible and long-term struggle. The second feature was the continuous endeavour by the Lithuanian leadership to create within the confines of its imperial polity conditions more congenial to the Slavs of Rus' than those prevailing under the Tatars. And the cornerstone of this particular policy was the provision of *local* pastoral care for the Orthodox population under Lithuania, in other words the establishment of a Church structure within the Grand Duchy independent of the metropolitans of 'Kiev and All Rus'', residing since *c.*1300 in far-away Suzdalia.[11] In the light of what we have said so far it would thus seem appropriate to speak of a specifically Lithuanian 'policy of dynamic balance'.[12] The question remains: to what extent

[6] H. Łowmiański, 'Agresja Zakonu Krzyżackiego na Litwę w wiekach XIII–XV', *Przegląd Historyczny*, xlv (1954), 338–71. See also Paszkiewicz, *Regesta* (n. 3), *passim* and idem, *Jagiellonowie* (n. 3), *passim* for detailed information on German raids.

[7] M. Giedroyć, 'The Arrival of Christianity in Lithuania: Early Contacts (Thirteenth Century)', *Oxford Slavonic Papers*, NS xviii (1985), 10–20, and Giedroyć, 'Arrival' (n. 2), 29–33.

[8] See last paragraph of Algirdas's letter of 1370/71 to Patriarch Philotheos, in: F. Miklosich and J. Müller (eds.), *Acta Patriarchatus Constantinopolitani MCCCXV–MCCCCII*, i (Vienna, 1860), 580–1 (Russian translation in *Russkaya Istoricheskaya biblioteka*, vi (Spb., 1880), suppl., cols. 135–40).

[9] In 1371 Algirdas controlled the whole of Western Rus' (or Ruthenia), i.e. the territories inhabited by the ancestors of today's Ukrainians and Belorussians (see map on page 39).

[10] See Giedroyć, 'Arrival' (n. 2), 29–33.

[11] Ibid. 14–20.

[12] The symmetry of the 'dynamic balance' is worth noting: the Order drew on reinforcements

was this essentially political tenet matched by a complementary ecclesiastical policy not only towards Constantinople, but also *vis-à-vis* the Papacy?

The negotiations with the Ecumenical Patriarchate for a separate Lithuanian metropolitanate, initiated by the Lithuanian leadership around 1300[13] and doggedly pursued by Algirdas throughout his reign (1345–77), concerned the religious welfare not only of Lithuania's Slav subjects. The conversion of the Lithuanian pagan hinterland to the Eastern rite was also an important element in these negotiations.[14] At the same time, Lithuania's geographic location at the interface of the two main rites, Latin and Eastern, exposed her to advances from the Papacy for Latin baptism. In 1298 Grand Duke Vytenis (Rus. Viten', Pol. Witenes, reigned *c*.1295–*c*.1315) had offered to submit to Roman baptism,[15] but it was almost certainly he who (in collaboration with his brother and successor Gediminas) was instrumental in establishing *c*.1300 the first Orthodox metropolitanate of Lithuania independent of the so far monolithic Church of Rus'. This major concession by the Patriarchate, undoubtedly encouraged by the prospect of converting the pagans of Lithuania to Orthodoxy,[16] did not, however, prevent Gediminas from bringing his subsequent negotiations (1322–4) with Pope John XXII for *Latin* baptism to the point of implementation.[17] Significantly, Avignon's advances were turned down at the eleventh hour, in accordance with the advice of Gediminas's counsellor and confidant, the Dominican friar Nicholas. It seemed that Gediminas, like his predecessor Vytenis,[18] did not as yet wish to commit his pagans to baptism in either rite. The early decades of the fourteenth century thus witnessed what appear to have been first attempts at a 'diplomacy of balance' between the Papacy and the Patriarchate. The manner in which Grand Dukes Algirdas and Jogaila (Rus. Yagailo, Pol. Jagiełło, succeeded in 1377) developed this double ecclesiastical diplomacy, and

from Catholic Europe whilst the Grand Duchy gathered surpluses from Rus'. The latter process was undoubtedly more speculative than the Order's fund-raising and recruitment tied to crusading propaganda.

[13] See Giedroyć, 'Arrival' (n. 2), 14–20.

[14] Ibid. 18–19 and note 120. The view of M. D. Priselkov and M. R. Fasmer, 'Otryvki V. N. Beneshevicha po istorii russkoi tserkvi XIV veka', *Izvestiya Otdeleniya russkogo yazyka i slovesnosti Imperatorskoi Akademii nauk*, xxi (1916), kn. 1, pp. 48–67, is that during negotiations for a separate metropolitanate Gediminas promised to submit Lithuania to Orthodox baptism. This view is reinforced by the fact that in 1354 Algirdas promised to accept Orthodox baptism, as reported by Nicephorus Gregoras (see J. Meyendorff, *Byzantium and the Rise of Russia* (Cambridge, 1981), 146 and note 5, 170 and note 91). On the reliability of Gregoras on Lithuania, see D. Obolensky, 'Byzantium, Kiev and Moscow: a Study in Ecclesiastical Relations', *Dumbarton Oaks Paper XI* (Harvard, 1957), 28–9.

[15] Giedroyć, 'Arrival' (n. 2), 10–12.

[16] See notes 11 and 14 above.

[17] Giedroyć, 'Arrival' (n. 2), 21–8.

[18] Vytenis, whilst maintaining warm relations with the bishop of Polotsk (Giedroyć, 'Arrival' (n. 2), 13 and note 86), negotiated for a Latin baptism (ibid. 10–12).

integrated it into the political tenet of 'dynamic balance', is the main theme of this article.

2

The decade that followed the death of Gediminas (d. 1341) was a difficult, indeed dangerous, time for the Grand Duchy. The pressure from Marienburg (Pol. Malbork) continued to mount and German progress on the Nemunas, helped by the ending of hostilities against Poland (1343),[19] was punctuated by a major crusading invasion of 1345,[20] and then by Lithuania's set-back on the Strėva (1348).[21] The threat from the west was compounded by the internal succession crisis (1341–5) which followed the demise of Gediminas.[22] The fact that Lithuania managed at this critical time to avoid the dangers of 'lateral succession'[23] was a tribute to the quality of the new leadership, the brothers Algirdas and Kęstutis (Rus. Keistut, Pol. Kiejstut, d. 1382), who jointly removed (more or less amicably) the ineffectual Jaunutis (Rus. Evnuty, Pol. Jawnuta) and established in 1345 a finely balanced diarchy, throughout which (until 1377) the new grand duke (Algirdas) enjoyed the support of his brother and *de facto* co-ruler.[24]

In these difficult circumstances Lithuania was not able to exploit in the east the almost simultaneous departure from the scene of Ivan Kalita (d. 1340) and his overlord Khan Uzbek (d. 1341). Fate nevertheless chose to intervene on the side of the beleaguered Grand Duchy. In 1349 German pressure quite suddenly subsided,[25] and it is almost certain that this unilateral cessation of hostilities was the result of the Black Death,[26] which at about that time struck German Prussia (and, incidentally, also Rus′), but affected ethnic Lithuania only marginally. By this means providence chose to shelter the last pagans of Europe.

---

[19] The treaty of Kalisz between Poland and the Teutonic Order secured for Poland Kujawy and Dobrzyń at the price of a (temporary) renunciation of Pomorze and Chełmno. See W. F. Reddaway *et al.* (eds.), *The Cambridge History of Poland*, i (Cambridge, 1950), 168–9, 171. From the perspective of Vilnius the *Drang nach Osten* now became a joint Polish–German venture (ibid. 180).

[20] Paszkiewicz, *Jagiellonowie* (n. 3), 372.

[21] Ibid. 221–2 and note 2, and Paszkiewicz, *Jagiellonowie* (n. 3), 376–7.

[22] The reign of Gediminas's ineffectual successor Jaunutis (Rus. Evnuty, Pol. Jawnuta) lasted from 1341 until 1345 (see Paszkiewicz, *Jagiellonowie* (n. 3), 371–2).

[23] For Gediminas's testament, see ibid. 357–65. For the implication of lateral succession in Rus′, see J. Fennell, *The Crisis of Medieval Russia 1200–1304* (London etc., 1983), *passim*; for Poland, see Reddaway, *The Cambridge History* (n. 19), 50–9, 85–107.

[24] On Lithuanian diarchy in the period 1345–77, see Paszkiewicz, *Jagiellonowie* (n. 3), 373–8 and idem, *Origin* (n. 3), 214 and note 2.

[25] Paszkiewicz, *Jagiellonowie* (n. 3), 374–5 and note 2, and K. Górski, *Zakon krzyżacki a powstanie państwa pruskiego* (Wrocław etc., 1977), 109 (originally published as *L'Ordine teutonico, alle origini dello stato prussiano* (Turin, 1971)).

[26] See P. Ziegler, *The Black Death* (London, 1982), *passim*.

The double impact of the plague—a respite in the west and physical weakening of Suzdalia[27]—undoubtedly encouraged Algirdas and Kęstutis to resume their father's programme of eastern acquisitions. In anticipation of renewed hostilities in the west, threatened by the election in 1352 of the formidable Winrich von Kniprode to the grandmastership of the Teutonic Order, Lithuania returned to the pursuit of 'dynamic balance' by annexing (during the 1350s) Smolensk and Mstislavl'.[28] This delivered into Lithuanian hands the upper reaches of the Dnepr and Dvina. Soon after, Bryansk and Chernigov fell to Algirdas,[29] and with them the upper basin of the Oka. In 1361 the Lithuanians incorporated Kiev into the Grand Duchy,[30] and some two years later administered a sharp defeat to the Tatars at 'Sinie Vody'.[31] Algirdas, thus exploiting the onset of 'great trouble' in the Horde following the murder of Khan Djanibek in 1357,[32] was at the same time sending a message to Eastern Slavdom at large that Lithuania was now ready to challenge the 'Pax Mongolica' in Rus'. This clear message was complementary to the earlier (1358) public announcement of Algirdas's resolve to incorporate into the Grand Duchy the *whole* of Slavonic Rus'.[33] This statement of intent amounted to an open challenge to Moscow. In the idiom of Lithuania's 'dynamic balance', Muscovy was being publicly recognized by Vilnius as a competitor for hegemony over Rus' and, as such, a constraint on Lithuania's fundamental objective: the continuous matching of growing *western* (not just German) pressure with new eastern sources of support.

Algirdas now proceeded with the final preparations for war. The Lithuanian eastern boundary, approximate and fluid though it was, stood nevertheless within 100 miles of Moscow, and provided a forward base from which an intricate system of alliances was now woven around the territory of Grand Prince Dmitry Ivanovich (later to be called 'Donskoi'). Tver' had already been bound to Vilnius by the 1350 alliance,[34] ensuring Lithuanian access to the entire upper basin of the Volga. To the east of Moscow, Nizhnii Novgorod was also bound to Vilnius through a dynastic alliance.[35] Novosil', Karachev, and Zvenigorod followed suite.[36] The map shows how relentlessly the encirclement of Muscovy was being pursued.

[27] R. O. Crummey, *The Formation of Muscovy 1304–1613* (London etc., 1987), 42–3.
[28] Paszkiewicz, *Jagiellonowie* (n. 3), 392–3, 407.
[29] Ibid. 407; idem, *Origin* (n. 3), 216 and note 5.
[30] Paszkiewicz, *Jagiellonowie* (n. 3), 408.
[31] Ibid.
[32] For details on the 'great trouble', see G. Vernadsky, *The Mongols and Russia*, 5 printing (New Haven etc., 1970), 245–63.
[33] In H. von Wartberg's account of negotiations between Algirdas and the envoys of Emperor Charles IV. See T. Hirsch *et al.* (eds.), *Scriptores rerum prussicarum*, ii (Leipzig, 1861–6), 80.
[34] Paszkiewicz, *Jagiellonowie* (n. 3), 385 ff.; also idem, *Origin* (n. 3), 220–1.
[35] Paszkiewicz, *Origin* (n. 3), 221.   [36] Ibid.

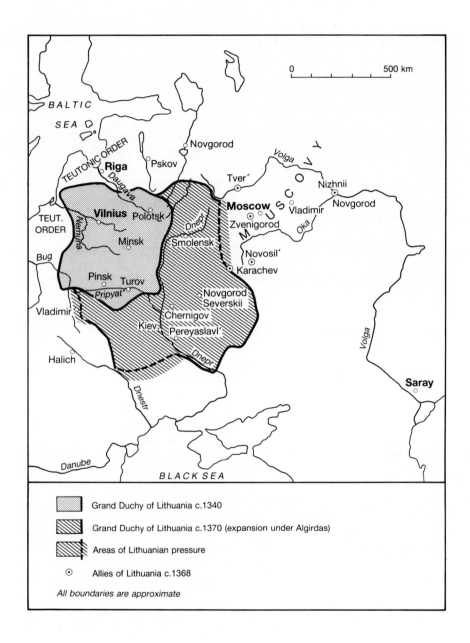

0   500 km

BALTIC
SEA
Novgorod
TEUTONIC ORDER
Riga   Pskov
Daugava   Tver´   Nizhnii
Volga   Novgorod
Vilnius   Polotsk   Moscow   Vladimir
TEUT.   Dnepr   Zvenigorod
ORDER   Neman   Smolensk
Minsk   Novosil´
Bug   Karachev
Pinsk   Turov   Novgorod
Pripyat   Severskii
Vladimir   Chernigov
Kiev   Pereyaslavl´
Halich   Dnepr
Volga
Dnestr
Saray
Danube
BLACK SEA
MUSCOVY
Oka

Grand Duchy of Lithuania c.1340

Grand Duchy of Lithuania c.1370 (expansion under Algirdas)

Areas of Lithuanian pressure

⊙   Allies of Lithuania c.1368

All boundaries are approximate

At the same time steps were being taken in the west to ensure a measure of safety. In 1366 a treaty was negotiated with Poland, purchasing peace at the enormous price of Halich and most of Volyn'.[37] In the following year hostilities on the German fronts were dampened down as far as possible through a separate truce with the Livonian Province.[38] In the summer of 1368 Algirdas was ready for the greatest risk of his career: the concentration of his armed forces on eastern advance positions. His three Suzdalian campaigns (1368, 1370, and 1372),[39] involving two direct assaults on the city of Moscow (1368 and 1370), ended in a stalemate, and in the collapse of the Grand Duchy's ambitious eastern initiative. The two antagonists, in a state of exhaustion, welcomed an opportunity to disengage (resulting in the truce of Lyubutsk in 1372).[40] The Lithuanians now rushed back to shore up the crumbling western defences.

Indeed, Marienburg did not remain passive. Lithuania's hinterland suffered German intrusions during 1369 and again in 1370.[41] The period 1373–6 witnessed a relentless escalation of hostilities.[42] In the spring of 1377, as Algirdas lay dying in Vilnius, the Order's armies stood at the gates of the Lithuanian capital.[43] One may reflect here on one of the more poignant, and generally overlooked, ironies of history: the fact that at this critical time Muscovy should have been helped towards survival, and ultimately towards success, by none other than Winrich von Kniprode and his Teutonic Knights.

Throughout Algirdas's reign Lithuania's diplomacy was not confined to power politics vis-à-vis Marienburg and Cracow in the west and Moscow in the east. Parallel ecclesiastical negotiations with both the Papacy (or its agents) and the Ecumenical Patriarchate became a major and an almost continuous preoccupation of the Lithuanian chancery. In the west, the Grand Duchy engaged in three rounds of negotiations for Latin baptism: in 1349–51, 1357–8, and 1373. During the same period Algirdas mounted a similar number of diplomatic campaigns in Constantinople to secure the Grand Duchy's ecclesiastical independence from the Moscow-dominated metropolitanate of 'Kiev and All Rus'': in 1352–6, 1362–71, and 1375. Two questions must be asked: were these various initiatives interrelated? and, if they were, to what extent did the Lithuanians themselves influence the course of the events in denominational matters? We shall return to these questions presently.

[37] W. Serczyk, Historia Ukrainy (Wrocław etc., 1979), 53–4. Also Meyendorff, Byzantium (n. 14), 61–7 for background.
[38] F. G. von Bunge (ed.), Liv-, Esth- und Curländisches Urkundenbuch, ii (Reval, 1855), cols. 772–3 (no. 1041).
[39] For details, see Paszkiewicz, Jagiellonowie (n. 3), 415–26.   [40] Ibid. 425–6.
[41] For details, see ibid. 420 and notes 2 and 5.
[42] Ibid. 426–7, 432.   [43] Ibid. 432.

3

The first approach during Algirdas's reign offering Roman baptism was made in 1349–51. On 16 September 1349 Pope Clement VI sent to King Casimir of Poland a letter[44] in which he expressed joy at the news (previously reported to the Pontiff by Casimir) that Kęstutis (co-ruler with Grand Duke Algirdas) and his brothers were ready to accept Roman Catholicism ('. . . are hastening to come [. . .] to the truth of the Catholic faith'). Under the same date a similar letter was dispatched by the Curia to the Archbishop of Gniezno,[45] asking him to make arrangements for instruction and baptism of the Lithuanian princes (and, presumably, their subjects). Two days later a third letter signed by the Pope was sent directly to Kęstutis and his brothers,[46] urging them to persevere in their laudable intentions and offering the prospective neophytes royal crowns (note the plural!).[47]

We have no record of any Lithuanian response to these advances. This is hardly surprising in view of the fact that later the same year Casimir, in spite of his missionary initiative, launched an armed incursion into 'Ruthenia' (Halich and Volyn'), over which Poland and Lithuania had been in conflict since *c.*1340. In spite of this set-back, negotiations for baptism were again resumed in 1351 by King Louis of Hungary *in the course* of a military campaign against Lithuania, mounted jointly by Poland and Hungary.[48] The proximity in time of these two initiatives (1349 and 1351) and the fact that the activities of the two allies, Casimir and Louis, were at that time closely synchronized,[49] suggests that from the point of view of Vilnius the events of 1349–51 amounted to a single missionary *démarche*, even though interspersed with armed clashes. The fact that in 1351 Louis rather than Casimir resumed the initiative was the result of the latter's sudden and serious illness just before the beginning of the campaign. Louis consequently took the field in sole charge of the two allied armies, but instead of

---

[44] A. Theiner (ed.), *Vetera monumenta Poloniae et Lithuaniae*, i (Rome, 1860), 525 (no. 691).

[45] Ibid. 526 (no. 692).

[46] Ibid. 526–7 (no. 693).

[47] The fact that the papal letter to the Lithuanian princes mentions by name Kęstutis rather than Algirdas shows that the West was confused by the diarchical arrangements. Kęstutis was the addressee because he was more conspicuous in Lithuania's relations with her western neighbours. The vague offer of royal crowns to the princes further illustrates Avignon's lack of detailed knowledge of administrative arrangements within the Grand Duchy.

[48] For a detailed description and analysis of these events, see R. J. Mažeika, 'The Role of Pagan Lithuania in Roman Catholic and Greek Orthodox Religious Diplomacy in East-Central Europe (1345–1377)' (unpublished Ph.D. thesis, Fordham University, New York, 1987), 110–29.

[49] In spite of antagonism between Poland and Hungary over Halich, to which Hungary made claims, since 1339 Louis was acknowledged as Casimir's heir. The relations between Poland and Hungary were closely co-ordinated by the influential Dowager Queen Elizabeth of Hungary, mother of Louis and sister of Casimir. During Casimir's illness in 1351 Polish lords swore allegiance to Louis as their presumptive sovereign. See Mažeika, 'Role' (n. 48), 112–13.

engaging Kęstutis he entered into negotiations with him.[50] The result was a treaty between Lithuania and Hungary, in which Kęstutis undertook to submit with his brothers and his people to Latin baptism. The Lithuanian leader also promised military assistance to Hungary on condition that Hungary *and Poland* (a commitment on behalf of the incapacitated Casimir!) assisted Lithuania in the recovery of her territories occupied by the Teutonic Order.

Within three days Kęstutis broke the solemn treaty (just sealed by him with an elaborate *pagan* oath)[51] by secretly departing (escaping?) from the Hungarian camp where the negotiations were taking place. Louis's reaction to this was not to resume hostilities, but to withdraw. The outcome of this campaign, however, can hardly merit the description of a bloodless victory for Kęstutis;[52] it was the circumstances that favoured the Grand Duchy. Nevertheless, on the diplomatic front Kęstutis secured for Lithuania a propaganda *coup* by placing on record once again the dangerous implications of the Order's activities on the Baltic.[53]

The second attempt by the West to baptize Lithuanian pagans was on an altogether higher level. On 17 December 1357 King Casimir wrote to Clement's successor, Innocent VI, with the news that once again the Lithuanians—or at least a substantial number of them ('pars eorum non modica')—might be prepared to accept Latin baptism.[54] This intelligence was accompanied by a request that the pope should mobilize ('require and exhort') both Emperor Charles IV and King Louis of Hungary as protectors of 'those neophytes' (presumably 'potential neophytes'). Casimir added in his letter a suggestion that the Catholic converts of Lithuania ('any new churches built in Lithuania') should be placed under the jurisdiction of the Archbishop of Gniezno. The Emperor responded with a golden bull, dated 21 April 1358,[55] inviting 'the prince' (Algirdas) and his brothers to accept baptism and promising in return papal protection against 'other infidels' (but not the Order, the most dangerous adversary of the Grand Duchy).[56] Algirdas responded immediately. He

---

[50] For details, see ibid. 113–14.

[51] See ibid. 115–20 for interesting comments on the extant descriptions of this event.

[52] An incidental advantage to Lithuania was that Kęstutis secured in 1351 the release of his brother Liubartas from Polish captivity.

[53] See Giedroyć, 'Arrival' (n. 2), 21–8 for Gediminas's negotiations with Pope John XXII (1322–4) resulting in major propaganda advantages.

[54] J. Ptaśnik (ed.), *Analecta Vaticana* in *Monumenta Poloniae Vaticana*, iii (Cracow, 1914), 357–8 (no. 375).

[55] H. Grundmann, 'Das Schreiben Kaiser Karls IV an die heidnischen Litauer-Fürsten', *Folia Diplomatica*, i (1971), 89–103. The April bull was the first of two imperial golden bulls on this subject. See J. Karwasińska, 'Złote bulle Karola IV w sprawie chrztu Litwy', *Cultus et cognitio: Studia z dziejów średniowiecznej kultury* (Warsaw, 1976), 233–49.

[56] During the 1357–8 negotiations Emperor Charles IV skilfully manoeuvred the Order

dispatched one of his kinsmen to Nuremberg (where the Emperor was at the time), with a message that he was ready to be converted.[57] Charles now mounted a high level embassy to Lithuania headed by Archbishop Ernst of Prague (and, significantly, including among its members Wolfram von Nellenburg, 'praeceptor' of the Teutonic Order in the Empire).[58] The envoys were briefed to negotiate a truce between Marienburg and Vilnius and to arrange for one of Algirdas's brothers to travel to Bohemia to conclude the arrangements for baptism. The Emperor then moved to Wrocław (Ger. Breslau) to await the arrival of the Lithuanian plenipotentiary.

In the meantime the Imperial ambassadors travelled via Prussia to the Grand Duchy, where Algirdas put forward (as a condition of baptism) extravagant territorial demands that were unacceptable to the Order. This amounted to yet another Lithuanian withdrawal. The envoy of the pagan Grand Duke, so eagerly awaited in Wrocław by Charles IV *and* King Casimir (who had travelled to Silesia presumably for that purpose), never came. But the whole of Christendom from Avignon to Constantinople was clearly reminded of Lithuania's struggle with the Order's colonial polity on the Baltic—and also of the *availability* of the last pagans of Europe for the catechumenate. On a practical level, a truce of some two years had been won by the Grand Duchy, a welcome respite after recent (early 1358) and serious German incursions into Samogitia.[59] At the same time Algirdas chose the Imperial negotiating table as an appropriate setting for a public announcement that he intended to incorporate into the Grand Duchy the *whole* of Rus'.[60]

The third western approach offering baptism to be made during Algirdas's reign occurred in 1373. King Casimir having died in 1370,[61] the approach was now a low-key affair, initiated by Ziemowit III, Duke of Mazovia, an immediate neighbour of the prospective converts. There are several letters from Pope Gregory XI on this matter, all dated 23 October 1373.[62] The main missive went directly to Algirdas, Kęstutis, and Liubartas (Rus. Lyubart, Pol. Lubart). The latter was ruler of Volyn'[63] and, incidentally, a convert (Eastern rite). The letter contained a renewed offer of baptism as a means towards avoiding

---

towards a truce with Lithuania. Though not mentioned in the bull, the Order was subsequently involved in the negotiations..

[57] For a good reconstruction of events, see Mažeika, 'Role' (n. 48), 138–46.

[58] See n. 56 above.

[59] See Mažeika, 'Role' (n. 48), 143.

[60] See n. 33 above. For implications, see p. 38 above.

[61] For details and analysis, see Mažeika, 'Role' (n. 48), 166–72.

[62] Theiner, *Vetera Monumenta* (n. 44), 695 (no. 934), 695 (no. 935), and 696 (no. 936).

[63] The chancery of Pope Gregory XI was better informed about Lithuania's precedence than that of Pope Clement VI (see above, n. 47).

further hostilities with the Teutonic Order.[64] It also introduced to the Lithuanian leaders Canon Dobrogost of Cracow (Chancellor of the Duchy of Mazovia) as the person designated by the Pope to conduct the negotiations and, in the event of success, the subsequent catechization of the pagans. Once again, we find no trace in the records of any Lithuanian response to this approach, the last to be made by the Papacy in Algirdas's reign. We shall return later to the question whether any possible advantages to Lithuania were implicit in this *démarche*.

4

Let us now turn to Algirdas's relations with Byzantium. As we have noted, Lithuania returned in the early 1350s to the expansionist eastern policy pioneered in the previous reign. In it ecclesiastical policy had played an integral part, and this particular blend of the secular and the religious was again cultivated with skill by Algirdas. In 1352 he approached the Ecumenical Patriarchate with a request for the appointment of one Theodoret as 'metropolitan of Rus'' in opposition to the ageing Theognostos, metropolitan of 'Kiev and All Rus'', who was committed to the political aspirations of Muscovy.[65] Patriarch Callistos refused to accede, and Theodoret was forced to leave Constantinople empty-handed. Algirdas's response was to ask the Patriarchate of Bulgaria to make him metropolitan. Theodoret travelled to Trnovo, where he was duly appointed. The Ecumenical Patriarchate responded with excommunication.

It may be assumed that the vagueness of Theodoret's title, 'Metropolitan of Rus'', was deliberately devised by Algirdas in order to match Lithuania's expansionist designs.[66] Indeed, Theodoret consistently tried to extend his ecclesiastical jurisdiction beyond the territory actually controlled by Algirdas.[67] In tactical terms, Lithuania's move to detach her Orthodox Slavs from Constantinople in favour of Bulgaria may have been devised in anticipation of the fall of the Cantacuzenos regime, which was opposed to ecclesiastical devolution of Ruthenia within the Grand Duchy (and Poland).[68] In fact, as soon as Emperor

[64] Unlike Emperor Charles IV, Pope Gregory XI was not inhibited in his correspondence to the extent of avoiding all mention of the Teutonic Order (see above, n. 56).

[65] For details, see Meyendorff, *Byzantium* (n. 14), 164–9.

[66] Patriarch Philotheos writes in 1354 about Algirdas's request for the appointment of Theodoret as 'metropolitan of Rus'' (Miklosich and Müller, *Acta* (n. 8), 350). This designation corresponds neither to the title of 'metropolitan of the Lithuanians' (*c.*1300–*c.*1330) nor to the title 'metropolitan of Kiev and All Rus'' still held then by Theognostos.

[67] Theodoret was in control of Kiev and close to being acknowledged by the archbishop of Novgorod. See Meyendorff, *Byzantium* (n. 14), 165, 167.

[68] Ibid. 153 ff.

John VI Cantacuzenos and Patriarch Philotheos were removed (at the end of 1354), Algirdas put forward his final negotiating package. It was difficult to resist, for it included the abandonment of Theodoret in favour of Roman of Tver' (to whom Algirdas was related through his wife Juliana), Lithuania's willingness to return to the jurisdiction of Constantinople, and (most tempting of all) the baptism of Lithuania's pagans in the Eastern rite.[69] This was a major challenge to the incoming successor of Theognostos, Alexis of Moscow, and to the indivisibility of the Church of Rus'.

The new emperor (John V) and the reinstated Patriarch Callistos indeed found this package irresistible. In response to the competitive bribery of Alexis and Roman (1355–6), Byzantium agreed to the division of the Church of Rus' between them.[70] Roman, styled 'metropolitan of the Lithuanians', was given jurisdiction over not only the original Lithuanian province (Novogrudok, Polotsk, and probably Turov),[71] but also the whole of 'Little Rus'' i.e. the bishoprics of Halich, Vladimir, Kholm (Pol. Chełm), Peremyshl' (Pol. Przemyśl), and Lutsk.[72] Like his shadowy predecessor Theodoret, he deliberately overstepped the boundaries of the Grand Duchy, extending his control to Tver', Bryansk, and Kiev; he also assumed, unilaterally (and unlawfully), the title of metropolitan of 'Kiev and All Rus''.[73] In political terms, this was a sign that Algirdas was about to resume his eastward march, pursuing 'dynamic balance' in the face of pressure exerted in the west by the Order and Poland. Indeed, Roman's activities were a mirror-image of the relentless encirclement of Muscovy (see p. 38 above), and the ecclesiastical confusion resulting from the activities of the two competing metropolitans in Rus' continued until the death of Roman in 1362.[74] This event enabled the Patriarchate to restore the unity of the Church of Rus' under Alexis. It was, of course, a serious set-back to Algirdas's ecclesiastical policy, but it no longer had any effect on the momentum of political and military preparations for the assault on Moscow (see pp. 38 and 40 above).

In 1364 Patriarch Callistos was succeeded by the learned Philotheos Kokkinos (this second term of office lasted until 1376).[75] The new patriarch, like his mentor the ex-emperor John Cantacuzenos, was

---

[69] See n. 14 on Algirdas's promise to accept Orthodox baptism.

[70] Meyendorff, *Byzantium* (n. 14), 169–71.

[71] See Giedroyć, 'Arrival' (n. 2), 14–20. Turov (with Pinsk) was annexed by Lithuania between 1328 and 1341 (ibid. 29), and may therefore have been, however fleetingly, a part of the first Lithuanian metropolitanate.

[72] On the emergence of the term 'Little Rus'', see I. Ševčenko, 'Russo-Byzantine Relations after the Eleventh Century', *Proceedings of the XIII International Congress of Byzantine Studies* (Oxford, 1967) (reprinted Nendeln (Lichtenstein), 1978), 100 and note 2.

[73] Miklosich and Müller, *Acta* (n. 8), 427–8.

[74] Meyendorff, *Byzantium* (n. 14), 170–1.

[75] On Patriarch Philotheos, see ibid. 173–99.

committed to the principle of the indivisibility of the Church of Rus'.[76] This he sought to secure, initially at least, by giving his unquestioning support to Metropolitan Alexis.[77] It seems that in this respect Philotheos lacked adequate briefing (a not unexpected state of affairs at the time of the collapse of the Empire and of a deterioration of standards in Byzantine chanceries). Philotheos's advisers failed to grasp the implications of Alexis's total commitment to the political cause of Muscovy. It seems that the Patriarchate was not capable of a policy flexible enough to cover adequately *either* of the two most likely outcomes of the Vilnius–Moscow confrontation, viz. a total victory of one of the antagonists,[78] or a partition of Rus' between them in the event of a stalemate. In the mid-1360s this lack of finesse was, from the point of view of the Patriarchate, a serious shortcoming. One possible reason for the Patriarch's early personal commitment to the cause of Moscow may have been the failure of Algirdas to implement his earlier promise (1354) to accept Orthodoxy. Another may have been the conviction that Lithuania would succumb to Dmitry Ivanovich. The first ought to have been irrelevant to any serious analysis; the second, in the mid-1360s, would certainly have been premature.

The best illustration of the loss of Byzantium's political finesse in handling the matters of Rus' is the *abruptness* with which Philotheos changed his attitude to Alexis in 1371.[79] This change was prompted by a letter from Algirdas to the Patriarch, delivered early in 1371.[80] In it the Grand Duke accused Alexis of being too politicized in favour of Muscovy to the pastoral detriment of Western Rus', and demanded a new metropolitan with jurisdiction not only in the Grand Duchy (now including Smolensk and Kiev) and Little Rus' (most of which was by now in the hands of Catholic Poland), but also in Tver', Nizhnii Novgorod, and Novosil'. This, at the time of repeated attempts to subdue Moscow, was an oblique reiteration of Lithuania's claim to the whole of Rus' *including* Suzdalia, already announced publicly in front of the emperor's envoys in 1358 (see pp. 38 and 43 above). Algirdas's letter to Philotheos concluded with the powerful claim that the Grand Duchy was a shield of Eastern Slavdom in the face of German aggression.[81]

As we have seen, Algirdas's letter was astonishingly effective. It followed a similar ultimatum from King Casimir (1370) saying that unless the metropolitan see in the Polish-held region of Halich were

[76] Ibid. 181.

[77] Ibid. 187–91.

[78] In this scenario only the victory of Muscovy was taken into account.

[79] Miklosich and Müller, *Acta* (n. 8), 320–2 (Russian translation in *Russkaya Istoricheskaya biblioteka*, vi (Spb., 1880), suppl., cols. 155–60).

[80] Ibid. 580–1 (Russian translation, cols. 135–40).

[81] See p. 35 above and nn. 8 and 9.

reinstated, he would be forced to re-baptize the Orthodox of Little Rus'
into the faith of the Latins.[82] Philotheos, under the double impact of
these two forceful—perhaps co-ordinated—initiatives, now realized
that there were grounds for withdrawing his unquestioning support of
Alexis. The Patriarch agreed to the advancement of a bishop to the
metropolitanate of Halich,[83] expressed criticism of Alexis's conduct of
ecclesiastical affairs in Rus', and issued a plea for a reconciliation
between Algirdas and the metropolitan of Kiev and All Rus'.[84] But he
still refused to accede to the Grand Duke's demand for a new metropolitan. At the height of his armed struggle with Dmitry Ivanovich
Algirdas was denied this ultimate ecclesiastical concession.

The Lithuanian–Suzdalian truce of 1372 indicated that in the forsee-
able future Rus' (apart from Little Rus' under Poland) would remain
politically divided between Vilnius and Moscow, but still under the
jurisdiction of a single metropolitan committed to the cause of
Muscovy. Algirdas, frustrated in the east and under intense pressure
from the Order,[85] still found sufficient energy to continue his ecclesiastical diplomacy *vis-à-vis* Byzantium. A new opportunity presented
itself in 1373 with the arrival in the Grand Duchy of Cyprian, a Bulgarian churchman sent to Rus' by Patriarch Philotheos. Cyprian, a
brilliant diplomat,[86] came on the scene burdened with an impossible
brief: to effect a political reconciliation between Vilnius and Moscow.
This was perceived by the ever-hopeful Philotheos (and presumably by
his friend John Cantacuzenos) as a means towards church unity, and
also, perhaps, as a step towards a common front against the Horde.[87]

Cyprian failed in his mission of reconciliation, but he scored a major
personal success. He established with Algirdas a relationship of trust,
which encouraged the Grand Duke to put forward Cyprian as *his* next
candidate for the metropolitanate in opposition to the ageing, and, to
an extent, discredited Alexis. This request was accompanied by a
threat that, if frustrated, Algirdas would be obliged to seek a metropolitan 'from the Latin Church'.[88] Evidently, Casimir's formula,
employed to such a good effect in 1370 did not go unnoticed.
Philotheos gave way and in 1375 advanced Cyprian to the metropolitanate of 'Kiev, Rus', and Lithuania', thus for the second time
detaching Lithuanian Rus' from the metropolitanate of 'Kiev and All

[82] Miklosich and Müller, *Acta* (n. 8), 577–8 (Russian translation in *Russkaya Istoricheskaya biblioteka*, vi (Spb., 1880), suppl., cols. 125–8.
[83] Meyendorff, *Byzantium* (n. 14), 191–3.
[84] See reference in note 79 above.
[85] See notes 42 and 43 above.
[86] For a recent assessment of Metropolitan Cyprian's role in Eastern Europe, see D. Obolensky,
Six Byzantine Portraits (Oxford, 1988), 173–200.
[87] Meyendorff, *Byzantium* (n. 14), 203–4.
[88] See Miklosich and Müller, *Acta* (n. 8), ii (Vienna, 1862), 12–18 and 116–29 (English translations in Meyendorff, *Byzantium* (n. 14), 303–6 and 307–11 respectively).

Rus'' presided over by Alexis.[89] It was a self-confessed act of Byzantine pragmatism (elegantly described by Philotheos himself as 'extreme economy')[90] in the face of confusion and mounting criticism of Alexis for being too biased towards Muscovy and thus unable to exercise proper pastoral care of the Orthodox within the Grand Duchy of Lithuania. This state of affairs persisted beyond 1377, the year in which both Algirdas and his adversary Alexis died.

5

As we have seen, Algirdas's negotiations with the Patriarchate of Constantinople amounted to a succession of initiatives, deployed by the Grand Duchy in support of its political (and military) objectives in Rus'. Lithuania's relations with the Papacy, on the other hand, are more difficult to interpret.[91] The extensive literature on this subject deals mainly with the declared, or implied, tactical motives of those western leaders (King Casimir, King Louis, the Emperor, the grand master of the Order, and so on) who became involved in these negotiations.[92] Such comments as we have on Lithuania's role attempt to offer explanations of Algirdas's reactions and deeds only in terms of the Grand Duchy's intricate and many-sided manoeuvres *of the hour*.[93] To my knowledge no systematic attempt has been made so far at exploring any *interrelation* between the two main diplomatic 'streams': the one directed at the Patriarchate and the other concerning the Papacy. We need an analysis of this interrelation not at the tactical level, but in the context of Lithuania's own strategic objectives. It is my view that this would offer new insights into the fundamental, and so far neglected, question of the extent of Lithuania's *own initiative* in her relations with the West, and create a better understanding of the overall pattern of events.

The diagram on p. 49 illustrates this view. It shows the East–West symmetry of succeeding rounds of negotiations and the apparently deliberate timing of the successive *démarches*, both of which suggest a vital role for the Grand Duchy. This role becomes even clearer if we consider the obvious advantages available to the Grand Duchy at any one step in the sequence as a result of the immediately preceding step. These advantages may be summarized as follows.

[89] For Cyprian's title, see Meyendorff, *Byzantium* (n. 14), 200–1 and note 1.
[90] Ibid.
[91] Lack of Lithuanian sources adds to the difficulties.
[92] For a detailed review, see Mažeika, 'Role' (n. 48), 97–172.
[93] Ibid.

Diagram: The pattern of Lithuania's ecclesiastical diplomacy during the reign of Algirdas (1345–77)

Vis-à-vis the Papacy: *Vis-à-vis* the Patriarchate:

(1) 1349–51: Casimir's initiative and
Louis's negotiations with Kęstutis for Latin baptism;

(2) 1352–6: Algirdas secures a
separate Orthodox metropolitanate;

(3) 1357–8: Algirdas negotiates with
Emperor Charles IV for Latin baptism;

(4) 1358–71: period of Lithuanian-Muscovite
confrontation, backed by pursuit
of ecclesiastical devolution;

(5) 1373: Ziemowit III's approach
to Algirdas for Latin baptism;

(6) 1375: Algirdas secures again a
separate Orthodox metropolitanate.

(1) → (2): the 1349–51 negotiations act as a reminder to Constantinople that Lithuania's pagans are available for baptism in the Latin rite; this strengthens Algirdas's hand *vis-à-vis* the Patriarchate during subsequent negotiations for a separate metropolitanate (1352–6);

(2) → (3): Algirdas's promise to accept Orthodox baptism (1354), though unfulfilled, becomes a powerful incentive in Avignon to provide a counter-offensive; the Curia duly responds by placing the missionary initiative *vis-à-vis* Lithuania in the hands of Emperor Charles IV himself (1357–8);

(3) → (4): Algirdas's conspicuous refusal (1358) to proceed with Latin baptism (accompanied by his public declaration that he wishes to incorporate the whole of Rus') enhances Lithuania's acceptability to Eastern Slavdom ('omnis Russia') as an alternative more congenial than 'Pax Mongolica';

(4) → (5): the Patriarchate's refusal to appoint a metropolitan of Lithuania's choice in opposition to Alexis (1371) and the collapse of Algirdas's bid to subdue Muscovy (1372) become an encouragement to Ziemowit III of Mazovia to proceed with the launching of yet another offer by the Papacy of Latin baptism (1373);

(5) → (6): Ziemowit's initiative is used by Algirdas as an additional incentive vis-à-vis the Patriarchate to secure the appointment of Cyprian as metropolitan of 'Kiev, Rus', and Lithuania' (1375).[94]

The apparent consistency of purpose in these interrelations seems to contradict the traditional view that Lithuania was a merely passive recipient of the three advances from the West. Indeed, it suggests that the Lithuanian leadership exercised as much initiative in the West as it so clearly did in the East (even though there is a lack of sources actually attesting this). There are two further arguments in support of this particular view. The first concerns the nature of the Roman Church. Its powerful proselytizing urge was an integral part of Latin Christendom of the period. The Mendicant Orders were a channel for this urge, whose least palatable variant was the crusading ideology practised by the Teutonic Order. Contemplating the last major missionary prize, the conversion of the pagan Lithuanians, the West stood ever ready to respond to any signals from Vilnius that Lithuania might be prepared to consider entering the orbit of Catholicism. Algirdas understood this attitude of readiness very well. Ever since the middle of the thirteenth century the Grand Duchy had engaged in negotiations for Latin baptism, whenever it suited Lithuania's purpose;[95] but they were always aborted. In this light, the claim in the papal letters that in all three instances (1349, 1357, and 1373) the Curia was responding to Lithuania's readiness to submit to baptism, may indeed be taken at face value and interpreted as confirmation that in each instance Algirdas and his advisers deliberately encouraged the ever-ready West. The fact that throughout Algirdas's reign the Grand Duchy had sound and immutable strategic reasons ('dynamic balance') to encourage (at the right moment) such negotiations (see diagram on p. 49) is the

[94] Mažeika, Role (n. 48), 171, acknowledges the likelihood of this particular interrelation.

[95] On negotiations in 1251, see Giedroyć, 'Arrival' (n. 7), 20–6; on negotiations in 1282, see idem, 'Arrival' (n. 2), 1–6; on negotiations in 1298, see ibid. 10–12; on negotiations in 1322–4, see ibid. 21–8.

second argument in support of the view that Vilnius was no passive recipient of Catholic advances.

I venture to conclude, therefore, that any analysis of either of the two diplomatic 'streams' *in isolation*, even though yielding useful insights, does not fully explain Lithuania's role in these matters, precisely because the two streams were deliberately made interdependent by the Lithuanians themselves. In the final analysis, a full understanding of these two interlocked diplomacies becomes possible only in the context of Lithuania's strategic tenet of 'dynamic balance'. This balance was sought with single-mindedness and continuity of purpose. The political and military plans for expansion in Rus′ were deliberately complemented by a matching ecclesiastical policy in Constantinople, and the latter in turn was reinforced, at appropriate moments, with a series of initiatives *vis-à-vis* the Papacy in order to make negotiations with the Patriarchate as effective as possible.[96] This interpretation need not deny that the Lithuanians fully appreciated the various tactical advantages available from the West. These were pursued, and secured whenever possible.[97] But tactics—and the Lithuanians were past-masters in tactics—never obscured the Grand Duchy's main purpose: the gathering of eastern surpluses for the German war, the cornerstone of the realm's ability to survive.

The pattern of the events under discussion also illustrates how clearly the Lithuanian leadership was aware of the bargaining value of baptism. This particular asset was repeatedly used by Algirdas, but never surrendered. It is probable that the Grand Duchy came close to embracing Christianity in its Eastern form at the time of the Suzdalian campaigns of 1368–72. The subjugation of Muscovy might have justified conversion and entry into the Eastern *Oikouméne*. Nevertheless, the failure of Algirdas's plans was interpreted in Vilnius as a signal for return to the denominational *status quo ante*. On his death-bed Algirdas was handing over to his successor Jogaila the principal bargaining advantage that Lithuania possessed—the baptism of her pagans—still more or less intact. For the time being the Grand Duchy was to continue with its even-handed religious toleration, a toleration enforced severely,[98] but matched in matters spiritual by pragmatism,

[96] It may be noted that the Curia's passivity as regards Central and Eastern Europe and its lack of detailed knowledge of the complex affairs of that area were probably helpful to Algirdas in the sense that they allowed him freedom to choose the timing of the successive rounds of negotiations for Latin baptism.

[97] For example, the truce of four years secured by Gediminas in the wake of the 1322–4 negotiations (see Giedroyć, 'Arrival' (n. 2), 28) and the two year respite won by Algirdas in 1358 (see Mažeika, 'Role' (n. 48), 163–5).

[98] Gediminas had two Franciscan missionaries executed because they disregarded the Lithuanian principle of toleration. See Giedroyć, 'Arrival' (n. 2), 32. During the reign of Algirdas three Lithuanian converts to Orthodoxy suffered death for not dissimilar reasons. For detailed

which never discouraged—and often encouraged—an openness to Christian influences from without.[99]

6

We have observed that the Lithuanian pursuit of 'dynamic balance' finally encountered an insurmountable external constraint: the challenge of Muscovy. Grand Duke Jogaila succeeded in 1377 to a situation which amounted to the most serious crisis that the Grand Duchy had ever faced. And this called for a fundamental reappraisal of political *grandes lignes*.

After Algirdas's three Suzdalian campaigns (1368–72) Dmitry Ivanovich was not capable of any serious counter-offensive, or even of a tactical retaliation, against the Lithuanian hinterland. He was now totally absorbed by the imminent confrontation with the Horde. In September 1380 the grand prince of Vladimir and Moscow faced the Tatars in an open battle and defeated Mamai at Kulikovo Pole. This was to be the turning-point on the road towards liberation from the Mongol overlordship. But the long struggle was only beginning. In the spring of 1381 Mamai himself was defeated and deposed by Khan Tokhtamysh, a protégé of Tamerlane. In 1382 the new ruler of the Horde mounted a retaliatory campaign against Dmitry, culminating in the total destruction of Moscow.[100] From the point of view of Vilnius this was a welcome relief, in view of Lithuania's rapidly deteriorating situation both on the German flank and internally.

Marienburg's military superiority was now overwhelming. At the same time there occurred in the wake of Jogaila's accession a serious collapse of discipline within Lithuania's numerous ruling family. In the east two of Jogaila's half-brothers submitted to Moscow,[101] and in the

discussion, see Mažeika, 'Role' (n. 48), 60–78. The enforcement of toleration was indeed even-handed and symmetrical.

[99] For the period prior to 1341, see Giedroyć, 'Arrival' (n. 7), *passim*, and idem, 'Arrival' (n. 2), *passim*. During the reign of Algirdas and subsequently many members of the Lithuanian dynasty either embraced Orthodoxy, or were under its influence. See T. Wasilewski, 'Prawosławne imiona Jagiełły i Witolda', *Analecta Cracoviensia*, xix (1987), 105–16. Peter Philarghi of Candia, an Oxford man (and in 1409–10 the Pisan Pope Alexander V) was present at the court of Algirdas, probably acting as tutor to Jogaila and his cousins. See A. Przeździecki (ed.), *Joannis Dlugossii Opera Omnia*, xii (Cracow, 1876), 592–3, and F. Ehrle, SJ, *Der Sentenzenkommentar Peters von Candia* (Münster, 1925), 8–9; also S. M. Kuczyński, *Król Jagiełło, ok. 1351–1434* (Warsaw, 1985), 20 and 156 note 35.

[100] For details of events in 1380–2, see G. Vernadsky, *Mongols* (n. 32), 258–67. During the 1380 campaign Mamai and Jogaila were allies. However, the Grand Duke did not engage his army at Kulikovo Pole which suggests that the alliance with Mamai was treated by Jogaila as a tactical device.

[101] See Paszkiewicz, *Origin* (n. 3), 234. Vladimir of Kiev (another of Jogaila's half-brothers) at that time collaborated with Andrew of Polotsk, one of the defectors.

south several of his kinsmen elected to pay homage to Louis, King of Hungary and, since 1370, King of Poland.[102] Marienburg now adopted a skilful diplomatic campaign aimed at exploiting this internal disarray. In 1379–80 the Order entered into separate and secret negotiations with both Grand Duke Jogaila and his uncle Kęstutis, which soon destroyed such initial trust as there had been between the young sovereign and his formidable uncle. The outcome amounted to civil war, which in the autumn of 1382 led to the death of Kęstutis in Jogaila's captivity.[103] When Vytautas (Rus. Vitovt, Pol. Witold), the gifted, if impetuous, son of Kęstutis went over to Marienburg in search of assistance,[104] the Order's diplomatic triumph seemed complete, and its final victory imminent.

At this, the darkest hour of Jogaila's reign, the Grand Duke and his advisers displayed a striking capacity for what today might be called 'crisis management'. While Poland and Hungary were facing their own difficulties following the death of Louis in 1382, Jogaila negotiated with his main adversary, the Teutonic Order, a treaty amounting to submission (October 1382).[105] We have evidence that the Grand Duke had no intention of fulfilling the extravagant—some may say suicidal—terms.[106] Instead, he was securing a fleeting respite, during which the search for and weighing-up of options for survival could be carried out.[107]

The most obvious option was to seek a long-term accommodation with the main adversary, the Order.[108] This possibility had been understood by both parties since the time of Mindaugas, and it offered now, as it did then, undeniable economic advantages to Lithuania. However, in political terms it amounted to nothing short of the surrender of the Grand Duchy's political identity. In the face of an unavoidable threat from the Order, Lithuania had no choice but to begin a serious search for a suitable ally. A potential partner had to meet at least three requirements: he had to be in conflict with the Order (actually or potentially); to be geographically adjacent; and to be compatible—not overbearing, yet strong enough to offer joint superiority over Marienburg. These criteria were sufficient for an early disqualification (for different sets of reasons) of the Empire, Bohemia, Hungary, and the Horde. There remained a short-list of Muscovy and Poland. The

---

[102] Ibid. 233–4.

[103] See Paszkiewicz, *Jagiellonowie* (n. 3), 438–46, and Kuczyński, *Król Jagiełło* (n. 99), 33–45.

[104] Paszkiewicz, *Origin* (n. 3), 234 and note 6.

[105] For further details, see Kuczyński, *Król Jagiełło* (n. 99), 48.

[106] J. Ochmański, *Historia Litwy*, 2 ed. (Wrocław etc., 1982), 71, and Kuczyński, *Król Jagiełło* (n. 99), 48–9.

[107] In July 1384 Vytautas was persuaded to rejoin Jogaila. See note 104.

[108] On the German option, see M. Giedroyć, 'Lithuanian Options prior to Krėva (1385)', in: P. Rabikauskas (ed.), *La cristianizzazione della Lituania. Colloquio internazionale di storia ecclesiastica* (Rome, forthcoming).

choice between them now depended to a large extent on the fourth, and most important criterion: the capacity to provide immediate military assistance.

The pro-Suzdalian sympathies in the Grand Duchy gathered around two focuses within the ruling house. One centred on Jogaila's Orthodox half-brothers,[109] the other on Jogaila's remarkable mother, Juliana of Tver', herself a devout Orthodox Christian. In each case motives were different, but one may presume that Juliana, encouraged perhaps by Metropolitan Cyprian,[110] would have tried to use pro-Suzdalian sympathies to mend the rift between her son the Grand Duke and his half-brothers. In 1384 an agreement between the Grand Duchy and the Great Principality of Vladimir and Moscow was actually concluded by Juliana (acting for her son) and Dmitry Ivanovich.[111] The alliance was conditional on Jogaila's marriage to one of Dmitry's daughters, and on the acceptance by the Lithuanian pagans of Orthodox baptism.[112]

Jogaila's assessment of Moscow's suitability as an ally would have involved a number of considerations. The long-term perspective in the east (assuming the survival of the Grand Duchy and the ultimate decline of the Tatar influence) amounted to either a renewed struggle between Vilnius and Moscow for control of all Rus', or to a territorial partition of Eastern Slavdom between them. In *either* case Orthodox baptism would have been seen by the Lithuanian leadership as an advantage, bringing with it a reassurance both to Lithuania's Slav subjects and to the patriarch of Constantinople. On the other hand, the short-term (and most vital) objective of the alliance—immediate help for the German war—must have appeared doubtful to Vilnius. In 1382 Tokhtamysh reimposed his will on Moscow. In 1384 large indemnities

[109] Three of Jogaila's half-brothers, Andrew of Polotsk, Dmitry of Bryansk, and Vladimir of Kiev (all Orthodox) gravitated towards Muscovy (see note 101). These sentiments were probably shared by the remaining two Orthodox half-brothers Konstantin and Fedor.

[110] Meyendorff, *Byzantium* (n. 14), 242.

[111] L. V. Cherepnin, *Russkie feodal'nye arkhivy XIV–XV vekov*, part 1 (M.-L., 1948), 50–1, 207–8. The relevant entries in the 'Opis' arkhiva Posol'skogo prikaza 1626' in the Tsentral'nyi gosudarstvennyi arkhiv drevnikh aktov, Moscow (fols. 3–6ᵛ) have a discrepancy in dating, but Cherepnin, Paszkiewicz, and others agree that the correct date is 1384. Recently T. Wasilewski, 'Prawosławne imiona' (n. 99), 112–15, argued that the treaty must have been concluded in late 1381 or early 1382, because (i) Vytautas did not participate in these negotiations; (ii) Jogaila's temporary exile in Vitebsk (1381–2) would have encouraged him to seek Dmitry's protection; and (iii) Jogaila's professed *intention* to marry Dmitry's daughter in 1384 is implausible. I find these arguments difficult to accept because (i) until July 1384 Vytautas was in Marienburg; (ii) Jogaila's supposed desire to seek Dmitry's protection in 1381/2 is incompatible with his consistent endeavours to regain the grand-ducal office; and (iii) there is little doubt that Jogaila did not intend to implement the treaty with Dmitry (see pp. 55 and 56 below). I am of the opinion that the signing of the treaty in 1384 is entirely compatible with the political aims of the Lithuanian state at that time and with Jogaila's personal aspirations.

[112] The wording of the entry in the 'Opis' arkhiva Posol'skogo prikaza 1626' (see n. 111) indicates that the condition of Orthodox baptism did not apply exclusively to Jogaila.

and tributes were again exacted by the Horde from Suzdalia, and soon there also emerged a clear prospect of a conflict between Tokhtamysh and Tamerlane, into which Suzdalian manpower would have been drawn. In these circumstances the chances of Moscow's participation in the Lithuanian–German conflict would have been small.[113] And, in the event of a renewed Muscovite challenge to the Tatars, they would have been even more remote. It is not surprising, then, that—even though the alliance with Moscow was actually concluded—Jogaila delayed its implementation. This proved a prudent course, because soon afterwards an opportunity emerged in the west, far more promising than the alliance with Dmitry.

This new opportunity was, of course, the plan for a close partnership, or union, with Poland.[114] The treaty of Koszyce anticipated in 1374 that the Polish throne would go to one of the daughters of Louis of Hungary. In the late 1370s this became a virtual certainty. In the summer of 1384 the ten-year-old Jadwiga, the youngest daughter of Louis, arrived in Cracow and succeeded in October to the Polish crown. From then on events began to move with extraordinary speed. In January 1385 a Lithuanian embassy arrived in the Polish capital and it was then that the plan emerged for a Lithuanian–Polish union.

The principal terms of the plan were as follows: Jogaila would marry Jadwiga (as soon as the law allowed, i.e. in early 1386) and he would then be crowned king of Poland after submitting to baptism in the Latin rite. In return, the Grand Duke would unite for ever ('perpetuo applicare') his realm with the Kingdom of Poland. Latin baptism of the ethnic Lithuanian pagan population would then be administered. Clearly, this plan was far more than a mere option for an alliance.[115]

In August 1385 the Polish and Hungarian envoys arrived in Kréva, where they met Jogaila, Vytautas, and three brothers of the Grand Duke. The result was the famous document[116] stating Jogaila's undertakings in the event of his marriage to Jadwiga.

---

[113] See Vernadsky, *Mongols* (n. 32), 268, 269 ff.

[114] For discussion of Poland's suitability as Lithuania's partner, see Giedroyć, 'Lithuanian Options' (n. 108), *passim*.

[115] For an analysis of the advantages and disadvantages of the Polish liaison, see ibid. The circumstances provided the Grand Duchy with ample opportunities to retain a large measure of independence within the new political structure. Subsequently these opportunities were fully exploited.

[116] The authenticity of the Kréva document has recently been questioned on the grounds that its existence in the archives of the Cracow Chapter was never mentioned until 1837. See J. Dainauskas, 'Kriavo Akto Autentiškumas', *Lituanistikos Instituto 1975 Metu Suvažiavimo Darbai* (Chicago, 1976), 51–71 (Polish translation: 'Autentyczność Aktu Krewskiego', *Lituano-Slavica Poznaniensia. Studia Historica*, ii (Poznań, 1987), 125–42). The lack of references to the Kréva document in sources is, of course, an insufficient reason for its classification as a forgery. The document is contemporary to the events in question and all circumstantial evidence clearly supports its authenticity.

7

The question remains: why was the alliance with Dmitry actually concluded in spite of Moscow's inability to fulfil the most fundamental condition—the provision of immediate help? The answer suggests itself in the context of Lithuania's consistent diplomacy of balance between East and West. It will be remembered that feelers were put out by Vilnius in Cracow (and in Hungary) as early as 1379,[117] i.e. at the time when female succession to the throne of Cracow was virtually certain. Contacts with Poland would also have been maintained through the Catholic kinsmen of Jogaila who held Podoliya as a Polish fief.[118] These were indications of an early Lithuanian initiative. That the Polish option was cultivated seriously and thoroughly is further confirmed by the speed (January 1385 to February 1386) with which the usually cautious Jogaila was able to conclude and implement the discussions which had been going on since 1379.

It was entirely in keeping with the established Lithuanian practice to deploy in the east a parallel initiative, aimed at generating tactical support for the Polish venture.[119] Poland's pro-Lithuanian faction will have been urged on by what seemed like a serious alternative, while it was clear that immediate advantages, stemming from the mere *promise* of Orthodox baptism, would be secured on the eastern flank. I venture to suggest that the 1384 agreement with Moscow can be satisfactorily explained only in those terms. It is difficult to escape the impression that, unless Dmitry's motives were strictly religious, he was outmanoeuvred by the seasoned Vilnius politicians. Lithuania, even though totally incapable of assisting Moscow against the Tatars, was gaining tactical advantages by declaring its willingness to accept Orthodoxy—a move which, from the political point of view of Moscow, was actually counterproductive.[120]

The fulfilment of this, the last and the most accomplished in the long series of Lithuania's two-sided diplomatic enterprises, came in early 1386. On 15 February Jogaila was baptized in Cracow under the name of Władysław, three days later he was married to the twelve-year-old Jadwiga, and on 4 March he was crowned king of Poland. In the following year the pagan population of Aukštaitija was baptized *en masse* in the Latin rite.[121] The ultimate fate of the new Polish–

---

[117] See Paszkiewicz, *Origin* (n. 3), 238–9.

[118] Ibid.

[119] In this instance Jogaila, unlike Algirdas, used a diplomatic manoeuvre in the east in support of a chosen venture in the west.

[120] An officially pagan Lithuania would have been a preferable adversary in the struggle for hegemony over Rus´ to one sympathetic (or committed) to the Eastern rite.

[121] Only Aukštaitija (the more powerful politically of the two major regions of ethnic Lithuania) was submitted in 1387 to Latin baptism, because Žemaitija (Lat. Samogitia), the other region, was

Lithuanian venture now depended, above all else, on the satisfactory accommodation of the interests of the Ruthenian Slavs, the ancestors of today's Ukrainians and Belorussians, who found themselves placed between the *political* Lithuanian–Muscovite boundary in the east and the new *denominational* boundary jointly created in the west by the Poles and the ethnic Lithuanians.

at that time in the hands of the Teutonic Order. Baptism of Samogitia was eventually carried out in 1417 under the joint auspices of King Władysław Jagiełło (Lith. Jogaila) of Poland and Grand Duke Vytautas. For details, see P. Rabikauskas, 'La cristianizzazione della Samogizia (1413–1417)' in: idem, *La cristianizzazione* (n. 108).

Biography in Eighteenth-Century Russia

By W. GARETH JONES

As late as 1835, memoirs were still considered by Belinsky to be 'among the most unusual phenomena' in the literary world of his age.[1] Biographical writings had certainly not emerged as a separate literary category in the eighteenth century, even though it was a time when minds were acutely attuned to the recognition of genre. The absence of biography as a distinct genre is reflected in the *Svodnyi katalog russkoi knigi grazhdanskoi pechati XVIII veka* (1963–7) where 'biography' does not feature as a heading in the comprehensive and detailed 'systematic index'.[2] As biographies grew in popularity in the nineteenth century, however, manuscript memoirs of the previous century were rediscovered and published. In his three pioneering essays, reviewing eighteenth-century memoirs, in the *Sovremennik* of 1855, P. P. Pekarsky was interested above all in the curiosities of their language and expression and their recital of factual detail.[3] It was the factual nature of these biographies that long remained the centre of attention. When N. D. Chechulin inaugurated a series of lectures on eighteenth-century Russian memoirs at the University of St Petersburg in 1891, he said that they were of particular value and could be considered to have been written 'with frankness and simplicity', since they had not been intended for publication in their day; their authors, declared Chechulin, 'doubtless wrote as they thought'.[4] For him autobiographies excelled belles-lettres in their sincerity.[5] In the twentieth century, however, the focus of more sceptical critics has shifted from the facts in biography first to the psychology of its authors and then to the texts themselves as free-standing literary forms.[6] This new critical awareness informs G. G. Elizavetina's recent article which examines the way in which Russian eighteenth-century classicism nurtured the genres of biography.[7] Yet, if genre is understood as a systemized

[1] V. G. Belinsky, *Polnoe sobranie sochinenii*, i (M., 1953), 159.
[2] *Svodnyi katalog russkoi knigi grazhdanskoi pechati XVIII veka 1725–1800* (M.-L., 1963–7), v. 127–37.
[3] P. P. Pekarsky, 'Russkie memuary XVIII veka', *Sovremennik*, 1855 no. 4, pp. 53–90; no. 5, pp. 29–62; no. 8, pp. 63–120.
[4] N. Chechulin, *Memuary, ikh znachenie i mesto v ryadu istoricheskikh istochnikov* (Spb., 1891), 8.
[5] Ibid. 10.
[6] William C. Spengemann, *The Forms of Autobiography* (New Haven–London, 1980), 187–9.

[See p. 59 for n. 7]

signal from an author to his readers, Elizavetina's analysis suffers from the drawback of being based on works which, though considered to be among the most interesting examples of their kind, were not available to the reading public of their day. For example, the autobiography of Ya. P. Shakhovskoy (1705–77), which dates from the 1770s, was not published fully until 1830, although extracts had appeared in *Vestnik Evropy* in 1808;[8] that of V. A. Nashchokin (1707–60) was not published until 1842;[9] and M. V. Danilov's autobiography, written in 1771, also remained unpublished until 1842.[10] Fonvizin and Bolotov were other significant figures whose memoirs remained unpublished in their time.

   The aim of this article is not to examine the eighteenth-century manuscript memoirs which were published a generation or more later in response to the growing appetite for biography, but rather to consider only those biographical works which were printed in the eighteenth century and thus definitely intended for the public arena. However, the public were not helped to recognize biography as a distinct category of literature by the use of a generic label. A search for the relevant titles in the *Svodniy katalog* reveals that, so novel was the act of describing the course of an individual life, that no single generic term such as *biografiya* was available. The nearest thing to a specific word (though it occurs in a title only once) is *zhizniopisanie* (a calque of the English word *biography*) which in 1790 headed the translation of the *Memoirs of the Life of William Pitt Earl of Chatham*. Otherwise, French *mémoires* was often conventionally translated as *zapiski*, as Belinsky explained.[11] The traditional hagiographic term *zhitie* continued to be employed, although in a new sense, for the biography of a private person, but *zhizn'* was the most common indicator of such a work throughout the century. This lack of one conventional generic label reflects the difficulty of finding an exact definition for biography at this time: at one extreme it may be a bald chronicle of events witnessed and at the other a self-analysis of intimate, fleeting emotions, thoughts, and reflections. However, what all biographical compositions have in common is that the life of a single, private person is the centre of attention for the writer, whether he is writing his own or another's life. It is also necessary to note that, although much criticism has in recent years been directed at demarcating autobiography from biography,[12] the

---

[7] G. G. Elizavetina, 'Stanovlenie zhanrov avtobiografii i memuarov', in: *Russkii i zapadno-evropeiskii klassitsizm: proza* (M., 1982), 235–63.

[8] *Zapiski kn. Yakova Petrovicha Shakhovskogo, pisannye im samim* (M., 1830).

[9] *Zapiski Vasiliya Aleksandrovicha Nashchokina* (Spb., 1842).

[10] *Zapiski Artillerii maiora Mikhaila Vasil'evicha Danilova, napisannye im samim v 1771 godu* (M., 1842).

[11] Belinsky, loc. cit. (n. 1).

[12] James Olney, 'Autobiography and the Cultural Moment: A Thematic, Historical, and Bibliographical Introduction', in: idem (ed.), *Autobiography: Essays Theoretical and Critical* (Princeton, 1980), 20.

distinction between them did not exist in the eighteenth century: the titles of autobiographies, such as *Zhizn' Davyda Gumma, opisannaya im samim* (1781), kept the readers' attention focused on the course of the subject's life with the locution 'written by himself' merely added to indicate the author.

The emergence of biography in Russia in the eighteenth century was another instance of how the development of her secular literature, though guided by European example, lagged behind that of her Western neighbours. Russia's experience fits well into Georges Gusdorf's argument that secular biography (to be distinguished, of course, from hagiography) is peculiar to modern European civilization, dependent on post-Renaissance individualism. The Petrine reforms had put an end to the sense, prevalent throughout most of human history, that 'there is no new thing under the sun', as Ecclesiastes had put it, and that, consequently, describing individual lives had no purpose, since 'the individual does not oppose himself to all others, he does not feel himself to exist outside others, and still less against others, but very much with others in an interdependent existence that asserts its rhythms everywhere in the community'.[13] Men had to have a sense of historical change, and dissolution, before they felt the need to fix their own image, and before each wondered at the mystery of his own individual destiny; 'the historic personage now appears, and biography, taking its place alongside monuments, inscriptions, statues, is one manifestation of his desire to endure in men's memory. Famous men—heroes and princes—acquire a sort of literary and pedagogical immortality in those exemplary "Lives" written for the edification of future centuries.'[14] While Gusdorf dates this development to the seventeenth century, Russia had to wait a little longer for the conditions to be ripe for biography.

The same cultural lag may account for the fact that those Russian eighteenth-century memoir-writers, who only generations later were discovered by the common reader, did not seek publication during their own lifetime. They were most often writing for themselves, their works being seen as something akin to private diaries or confessions, or else for their immediate family, friends, and descendants. Nevertheless it has to be recognized that they constituted a vital stage in the development of modern biographical writing which Wayne Shumaker in his *English Autobiography: Its Emergence, Materials and Form* noted as occurring in the seventeenth century in the case of England.[15] Men and women were bringing order into their own conscious experience, but

---

[13] Georges Gusdorf, 'Conditions and Limits of Autobiography', ibid. 29.

[14] Ibid. 31.

[15] Wayne Shumaker, *English Autobiography: Its Emergence, Materials and Form* (Berkeley–Los Angeles, 1954), 28.

were analysing it for their own purpose. The purpose could be the chronicling of the recent past in order to make sense of the cultural revolution that had taken place at the turn of the century. Andrey Artamonovich Matveev gave a justification for his memoirs (published in 1841) that anticipated Tvardovsky's editorial in the fortieth-anniversary issue of *Novyi mir* in 1965, which stressed the conscious role of that journal in telling of the experience of Stalinism through biography and autobiography: 'it [the Stalinist period] was stifling man's vital memory of events which had been really experienced and of the significance and role in them of individuals whose names were unmentionable. It is not only we but the generations to come after us who will have cause to regret it.'[16] Matveev wrote: 'Therefore this author not for his own vanity and not for idle praise, but for the general memory of all, endeavoured to undertake this little work, in order that forever in the Russian state intelligent and interested readers, profiting from their instruction, would keep this alive in their memory for their own future information and for the knowledge of their own sons from generation to generation.'[17] The authors themselves in the early years of the century were painfully aware of the risky novelty of memoir writing and Boris I. Kurakin (1676–1727) prefaced his *zapiski* with the defensive observation that such compositions had long been accepted by European nations. 'Therefore I have not done this on my own behalf but, knowing the custom of all persons, from high, middling and most lowly rank who describe their life, so did I follow it.'[18]

Many were to follow the Western example, first of all in writing lives primarily for themselves, and then for others through publication. In parallel with an expanding book-trade throughout Europe there was growth in the demand for biographies, and it is clear that in Russia too the publication of biographies kept in step with the number of books printed, so that there was a decided increase in the last two decades of the eighteenth century.

Was the increase in printed biographies in Russia merely a mechanical reflection of the increasing ratio of such works in European publishing? Or did Russian writers, publishers, and readers feel a need for such publications? If it could be said that by about 1800 European biographers seemed to be writing confidently in a tradition instead of feeling their way into a new literary genre,[19] was the same true for Russia? Had the new European insights into the 'writing of lives' become established in Russia by 1800?

[16] A. Tvardovsky, 'Po sluchayu yubileya', *Novyi mir*, 1965 no. 1, p. 7.

[17] 'Zapiski Andreya Artamonovicha, grafa Matveeva', in: *Zapiski russkikh lyudei*, ed. I. P. Sakharov (Spb., 1841), 2.

[18] 'Zhizn' knyazya Borisa Kurakina', in: *Arkhiv knyazya F. A. Kurakina*, ed. M. I. Semevsky, i (Spb., 1890), 244.   [19] Shumaker, op. cit. (n. 15), 5.

Legitimacy had been given to the writing of lives by linking modern biography to a classical background.[20] Although the classical tradition was limited in eighteenth-century Russia, it supplied a foundation for biography, most obviously in the unmatched popularity of Marcus Aurelius, whose works were published in 1740, 1760, 1775, 1786, 1789, 1797, and 1798. Marcus Aurelius was a writer of antiquity who had expressed the modern concept that each individual life may influence the history of mankind and is therefore of interest to everyone who lives a life. He had contemplated his own personal experience and, as a stoic, had preached indifference to the blows of fate, and the acceptance of the good and evil co-existing in the world. Along with Epictetus (whose Ἐγχειρίδιον was published in Russian translation in 1759), Marcus Aurelius gave the prestige of antiquity to the Pietist introspection that was so prevalent in Germany and among English dissenters. That Protestant attitude to the importance of self and of an individual Christian life had been transferred to Russia, particularly by Masonic groups, and was reflected in the popularity and influence of John Mason's *Self Knowledge* (translated into Russian from the German in 1783) with its dutiful references to Marcus Aurelius and Epictetus. Alexander Pope's *Essay on Man* was another influential work which may have affected the development of biographical writing for he too 'called upon one to be attentive to a man's inner world, and taught that a man should know himself'.[21] These works, while not biographies themselves, nevertheless prepared the mental atmosphere for the understanding of a written life.

Marcus Aurelius was not only important as an ancient who had demonstrated his awareness of the importance of the individual's separate personality and his autonomous life in the general community; he was also appealing as an exemplary 'enthroned philosopher', a truly humane and enlightened sovereign. This exemplary depiction of a historical figure was supported by other classical works such as the *Lives* of Plutarch and Suetonius, and Julius Caesar's *Gallic Wars*. Not only the ancient classics may have been influential in this way but also such acknowledged European classics as the memoirs of Sully and Cardinal de Retz.

In the list of eighteenth-century Russian biographies it is the exemplary lives of monarchs, statesmen, and soldiers that are most apparent. An interesting use of an ancient exemplar to bolster a modern equivalent is seen in the coupling of Marcus Aurelius with Charles XII of Sweden in a 1758 translation by I. S. Barkov of

---

[20] Elizavetina, op. cit. (n. 7), 242. An early example of a classical model was the translation of Quintus Curtius' *History of Alexander the Great* in 1709, which was republished in Moscow in 1711 and 1717, and in Petersburg in 1722 and 1724; see *Svodnyi katalog* (n. 2), ii. 108.

[21] Elizavetina, op. cit. (n. 7), 257.

miscellaneous pieces by the two monarchs, published in 1786. Peter the Great was the subject for by far the largest number of biographies, followed by Frederick the Great. Other monarchs were Elizabeth I of England, Charles XII, Maria Theresa, and Louis XVI (in 1793). Statesmen were represented by N. I. Panin (three editions of Fonvizin's *Life* were published), William Pitt, and Benjamin Franklin (an autobiography); soldiers by Loudon, Suvorov, Lefort, Minin, and Patrick Gordon.

Most of these biographies were published during the reign of Catherine the Great, and although it cannot be said that they resulted from any imperial directive on publishing, they nevertheless supported Catherine and her policies. In one instance a biographical work seemed to relate directly to current politics. This was a translation of Coyer's life of Jan Sobieski, whose second volume appeared in 1773, the year after the First Partition of Poland. It is possible that a reminder of Jan Sobieski's agreement that Kiev should remain permanently Russian was thought opportune at a time when justification was sought for imperial claims on Polish territories. Generally, however, it was the concept of the enlightened sovereign that was sustained by biographies of the great. The books in praise of Peter the Great would reinforce the idea of him as the historic personage who had created the legacy bequeathed to Catherine as surely as the statue of the Bronze Horseman. Novikov's *Painter* provides good evidence for the purpose of these exemplary biographies in adding to Catherine's prestige. The second part of the journal begins with a eulogy to Catherine flanked by an extract from *Matinées royales*, a work supposedly composed by Frederick the Great; it is a juxtaposition which encouraged readers to compare the two enlightened monarchs with each other.[22] A short item in the *Painter*, part I, no. 23, following a long letter from Frederick to Catherine in praise of her *Nakaz*, brings many of the biographical subjects together in a letter from the Prussian Ambassador in St Petersburg, Count von Solms, to N. I. Panin:

I hasten to acquaint your Excellency with a letter which the King my sovereign sent in reply to a letter dispatched by her Imperial Majesty concerning the Instruction on the composition of a New Code of Laws in Russia, commanding me to present it through you to her Imperial Majesty and furthermore he adds in his own hand in the letter sent to me.

'I have read with reverence the composition of the Empress and did not wish to tell her everything that I thought of it, since she might suspect me of flattery, but I can tell you without troubling her humility, that this work is one of courageous and strong power and worthy of a great person. History tells us that Semiramis commanded an army, that Queen Elizabeth was considered skilful in politics, that the Empress Queen [Maria Theresa] showed much firmness on her accession to the throne but not one

---

[22] *Satiricheskie zhurnaly N. I. Novikova*, ed. P. N. Berkov (M.-L., 1951), 380–1.

woman has yet been a law-giver. This glory has been given to the Russian Empress who is of course worthy of it.

signed: Frederick'[23]

Panin, too, figures in this item, and Fonvizin's *Life of Count Nikita Ivanovich Panin*, although it has been viewed as a document emphasizing Panin's policy disagreements with Catherine,[24] would have been read as the biography of one of the empress's chief and most loyal ministers. The same general support for Catherine could be drawn from Novikov's preface to his publication in 1776 of *The History of the Innocent Incarceration of the Blizhnii Boyar Artemon Sergeevich Matveev* in whom Novikov saw the true patriot and ideal citizen who, while imprisoned under tyranny, would have flourished under an enlightened sovereign. It was with pride that he stated in the preface that the exemplary biography had been brought to his attention by Catherine herself and that the copy used in the edition was the one received from her Imperial Majesty's personal library.[25]

Sovereigns and statesmen were the preferred subjects under Catherine, and soldiers, such as Suvorov and Lefort, did not make their appearance until her reign had ended. These military men, however, were still presented as exemplary figures, and their biographies were not read in order to gain insights into their professional life. Indeed one type of biography that was now flourishing in Western Europe but remained absent from Russia was the special professional biography where occupational settings were exploited to entertain, not family or friends, but an audience of curious citizens. Crime, of course, may be a profession, and it is true that a criminal, Ivan Osipov, nicknamed Van'ka Kain, enjoyed particular popularity with his often reprinted memoirs, but Kain's appeal was not that of a professional man; rather he was the Russian singleton in the established European mode of sensational, 'rogue' biography modestly represented in Russia by the notorious lives of characters such as Cartouche, John Norcross, and William Dodd. These 'true lives' merged with sensational fiction, and the mysterious Kain even became the subject for romance.[26]

It was only the profession of writer that established an enduring appeal. Even in this case at first the purpose was propagandistic. A striking example of the use of a writer's biography to foster the

---

[23] Ibid. 360–1.

[24] Walter Gleason (ed.), *The Political and Legal Writings of Denis Fonvizin* (Ann Arbor, 1985), 19.

[25] I. V. Malyshev and L. B. Svetlov (eds.), *N. I. Novikov i ego sovremenniki: Izbrannye sochineniya* (M.-L., 1961), 329–32.

[26] For Matvey Komarov's reworking of Kain's biography, see *Svodnyi katalog* (n. 2), ii. nos. 3058–63, and suppl. 144 'O Van'ke Kaine slavnom vore i moshenike kratkaya povest''. The relationship between the 'biography' and the fictional variants is discussed by I. R. Titunik, 'Matvej Komarov's *Van'ka Kain* and Eighteenth-Century Russian Prose Fiction', *Slavic and East European Journal*, xviii (1974), 354–5.

international standing of Russian culture in mid-century was the publication in Holland in 1749 and in Paris the following year of *Satyres de Monsieur le Prince Cantemire avec l'histoire de sa vie* at the behest of the Ministry of Foreign Affairs with the collaboration of the St Petersburg Academy of Sciences.[27] The calculation that Kantemir's biography would evoke immediate interest and admiration in the West was confirmed by a favourable review in the April 1750 issue of the Paris journal *Mémoires pour l'histoire des sciences et des beaux arts*.[28] As yet such biographies were not expected to elicit domestic enthusiasm, and even in 1762 the sanctioning of Kantemir's satires for publication was an event important enough in itself to overshadow the appended sketch of his life. The first significant promotion of the writer as an honoured public figure came ten years later with Novikov's *Essay at an Historical Dictionary of Russian Writers*, remarkable not only for its contents but also for the fact that it had been preceded in 1772 by fewer than a score of biographies, and that all, save one (I. S. Barkov's *Life* of Kantemir in 1762), had been translations. Indeed, in his preface Novikov explained that translation was now not a one-way affair and that translations from Russian authors were an indicator of the growing international prestige of Catherinian Russia. Russian writers were now influential and exemplary figures, like their counterparts elsewhere in Europe, for 'all European nations have endeavoured to preserve the memories of their writers'.[29] The short biographical entries in Novikov's *Essay* hardly went beyond this 'preservation of memory'. Typically an entry merely stated a writer's rank and position and listed his works. But Kantemir, as might be expected, was addressed at length. Only occasionally was the personality of a writer characterized, as, for example, in the case of Lomonosov: 'He had a merry disposition, was a man of few and witty words and liked to employ barbed witticisms in his conversation; he was true to his fatherland and friends, a patron to those exercising in the literary arts and their encourager; in social intercourse he was in the main kind, and generous to those seeking his favour, but at the same time was hot-tempered and irascible.'[30] It was also made plain that Lomonosov was the equal of the exemplary great men of classical literature in verse quotations from Sumarokov:

> He is the Malsherbes of our lands, the equal of Pindar[31]

and from Popovsky:

> What Cicero had, and what Vergil had in Rome
> He alone had in his understanding.[32]

[27] N. A. Kopanev, 'O pervykh izdaniyakh satir A. Kantemira', in: *XVIII vek*, xv. *Russkaya literatura XVIII veka v ee svyazyakh s iskusstvom i naukoi* (L., 1986), 164.

[28] Ibid. 151.

[29] *N. I. Novikov: Izbrannye sochineniya*, ed. G. P. Makogonenko (M.-L., 1951), 277.

[30] Ibid. 322.   [31] Ibid. 323   [32] Ibid. 323.

Although Novikov's 'biographies' were mainly an avowed attempt to assert Russia's national prestige, the consideration of individual writers was an indication of the growing eighteenth-century interest in knowing the personality of the writer to which Guasco's biographical sketch of Kantemir had responded and exploited. Short biographies, therefore, began to be attached to writers' works. In 1778, for example, Novikov's little essay on Lomonosov was used as a preface for Damaskin's collected edition of the poet's work. Such a limited perspective did not seek to illuminate the source of a writer's ideas and the occasion for the genesis of each of his works, yet this is what the biographical sketches of authors increasingly endeavoured to do. It is significant that in 1784 Novikov's sketch was superseded as a preface to Lomonosov's collected works by Verevkin's *Life* which allowed that the products of a personality had a relationship to that individual personality; this would not be a list of positions and works but a biography 'compiled on the basis of notes by J. J. Stählin, archival material of the Zaikonospasskii monastery and a questionnaire of persons who had known Lomonosov'.[33]

Between these two editions of Lomonosov, there had appeared in 1781, just four years after its original publication in 1777, *The Life of David Hume, Esq.: Written by Himself*, which has been recognized as one of the first 'literary' lives which would be imitated in increasing numbers in subsequent years. Hume, in fact, according to Shumaker, was 'the first English author of note to feel the propriety of describing his writing career'.[34] It would not be true to say that the translation of Hume led in Russia to a stream of literary biographies illuminating an author's work, although there was *Zhizn' slavneishego g. Vol'tera s priobshcheniem k nei poemy Estestvennyi zakon, ego zhe sochineniya* in 1787, and Cramer's *Obraz dobrodeteli blagonraviya, ili Zhizn' i svoistva Gellerta* in 1789. Nevertheless, it has often been recognized that the translation of a work into Russian was often a sign of approbation, a recognition of that work's significance. It could have been the novelty, or even impropriety, of Hume's *Life*, that had been responsible for its swift translation.

Until 1781 biography had concerned itself with prominent men with exemplary lives. In 1781 the Russian reader met two famous men of letters through their autobiographies—Hume and Rousseau—yet their writing of their own lives was in both cases unconventional. In the case of Rousseau's supposedly tell-all *Confessions* the manner of writing was startling. Fonvizin was one Russian struck by Rousseau's method of baring 'without the slightest pretence his whole soul, the extent of its vileness at certain moments, how these moments drew him into the

---

[33] *Svodnyi katalog* (n. 2), ii. 166.
[34] Shumaker, op. cit. (n. 15), 25.

worst of crimes, how he returned to virtue.'[35] 'The book which he has written', wrote Fonvizin, 'is nothing more than the confession of all his deeds and thoughts', and it is indicative of the influence of the work on Fonvizin that towards the end of his life he entitled his own unfinished confessional autobiography *Chistoserdechnoe priznanie v delakh moikh i pomyshleniyakh.*[36] The Russian reader did not see Fonvizin's 'confession' in print, but he was introduced to the mood of intimacy in Rousseau's *Confessions* by Radishchev's anonymous publication of *The Life of Fedor Vasil'evich Ushakov.*

The series of anecdotes of Peter the Great, which had little connection with his official acts, shifted the focus on his life from Peter's statecraft and military campaigns, from Peter as an institution to Peter the private man. These anecdotes were an example of the consolidation in the eighteenth century of the view that there should be a natural, general interest in the private character and actions of prominent men in society. Such interest in the lives of famous writers was also becoming acceptable. However, it was still a novel development to consider that the private reflections of any insignificant person could be of interest. The appearance of the *Life of Ushakov* created a stir in the Russian Academy, where the establishment considered the portrayal of an obscure personage disturbing—or at least that is what we gather from Dashkova's memoirs.[37] Her brother, Count A. R. Vorontsov, thought that writing the life of a nonentity was unnecessary 'since Ushakov did not do or say anything remarkable'.[38] It was a view still shared as late as 1911 by Sir Sidney Lee, then editor of the *Dictionary of National Biography*, namely that 'the life of a nonentity or a mediocrity, however skilfully contrived, conflicts with primary biographic principles'.[39] For Dashkova herself—armed, it must be said, with hindsight—the depiction of an obscure life was abhorrent and dangerous. As I have shown, the dominant subjects of biography under Catherine were figures which bolstered her image. Dashkova may well have sensed the way in which such an obscure life usurped the significance of those exemplary lives of enlightened monarchs. The conclusion that she drew from the 'silly brochure' was that 'a man who had only existed to eat, drink, and sleep could only find a panegyrist in one thirsting to spread his thoughts in print, and that this writer's itch might someday induce Radishchev to write something more reprehensible.'[40]

Radishchev for his part was clear-sighted in his aims in writing the

---

[35] *Russkaya literatura XVIII veka*, ed. G. P. Makogonenko (L., 1970), 344.

[36] Ibid. 373.

[37] Ekaterina Dashkova, *Zapiski 1743–1810*, ed. G. N. Moiseeva and Yu. V. Stennik (L., 1985), 171.

[38] Ibid. 171.

[39] Quoted by Shumaker, op. cit. (n. 15), 62.

[40] Dashkova, loc. cit. (n. 37).

eulogy of his obscure friend. His formative education in Leipzig had evidently introduced him to the new perspectives on biography emerging in the West. Firstly he set out to disarm anticipated criticism of his approach: the *Life of Ushakov* was written for his own pleasure, he insisted, and he cared little if readers were bored by a narrative without any memorable deeds. He assaults the prevailing notion that 'great men' alone are worthy of being commemorated in biographies, anticipating the Tolstoyan distaste for great historical figures, whether good or evil. Indeed, Marcus Aurelius is provocatively mentioned in the same breath as Nero, as illustrations of the mighty.[41] The choosing of his obscure friend is a deliberate supplanting of the great and a reproach to the brokers of power. 'Oh you directors of minds and rulers of the will of nations, how often are you short-sighted and myopic, how many times do you overlook an opportunity for the common good, stifling the ferment exalting the hearts of youth.'[42] With this in mind Radishchev declares that, in the case of his deceased friend, 'I will endeavour to seek out in his deeds what is attractive, not for those who search for brilliant exploits in narratives and who read with equal appetite Quintus Curtius and Cervantes, but for those whose hearts are open to the affection of youth.'[43]

Indeed, what was highlighted in the *Life* was not any brilliant exploit, but apparently insignificant events which had great consequences for the individual's life—in Radishchev's own words 'an event insignificant in itself but having a great effect on our attitude to our chief.'[44] This dire happening was the serving of a supper, by Major-General Bokum who was in charge of the group of students sent to Leipzig, of bread, butter, and hunks of cold meat, which was a severe culture shock to the young Russians who were used to soup and pasties. In Russia this concentration on the apparently inconsequential was a new procedure in biography. Fonvizin too had described in his confessional autobiography how the gaudy backs of a deck of playing cards, seen when he was a child, had made a deeper and more lasting impression on him than Raphael's masterpieces.[45] This awareness of the potency of the trivial had, of course, been fostered by the domestic fictional biographies of popular novelists such as Richardson. Yury Lotman in his explication of *Eugene Onegin* suggests how Pushkin in his line 'I Dunya razlivaet chai' recalls the tea-drinking of Richardson's Clarissa and showed his appreciation of how important these trivial domesticities had become.[46] It was not only the triviality in itself that

[41] A. N. Radishchev, *Polnoe sobranie sochinenii* (M.-L., 1938), i. 178.
[42] Ibid. 173.
[43] Ibid. 178.
[44] Ibid. 162.
[45] Makogonenko, *Russkaya literatura* (n. 35), 375.
[46] Yu. M. Lotman, *Roman A. S. Pushkina 'Evgenii Onegin': Kommentarii* (L., 1980), 10.

was of interest but the way in which it could engender great consequences. Fonvizin's childish weakness for gaudy cards eventually led to contrition, confession to his aunt, and a moral conviction that honesty was the best policy; Ushakov's un-Russian supper led to his depression and death. That this was a new awareness of the meaning of an individual's life is evident if one contrasts the *Life of Ushakov* with Novikov's biographical sketches which, with their statement of rank, character assessment, and list of works, were frozen snapshots. Hume, Rousseau, Radishchev, and Fonvizin showed the flux of mental states, the development of a personality, and its effect on the works created by that personality.

This new awareness crystallized from the changing consciousness of the age. The curiosity of the individual about himself has been seen as linked with the Copernican Revolution,[47] and the reason for the emergence of an interest in life histories has been found in the substitution of inductive thought habits for deductive.[48] It may well be suggested that the spread of the Newtonian world-view affected biography. Modern science revealed the ability to relate cause and effect, and Newton's second law F=ma, which may be viewed as a prescription for predicting the future, led the French eighteenth-century mathematician Pierre Simon de Laplace to claim that, given the position and velocity of every particle in the universe, he could predict the future for the rest of time.[49] The application of such an intoxicating idea to human behaviour led to the philosophical conclusion that man's behaviour was predetermined. But it was predetermined not by great exploits but by the trivial bits of behaviour that seemed to correspond to the physicists' particles of matter. This suggestion is only tentative, of course, since it is not possible to trace the direct effect of philosophical ideas on literature. It is, however, not wholly fanciful to recognize a Newtonian clock in the one that prompted Tristram Shandy to recall the fateful words at his conception, 'Pray my dear . . . have you not forgot to wind up the clock'.[50] The philosophical import of that incident was recalled in his memoirs by Vinsky who, from his later standpoint (1811), had a clearer view of the use and significance of trivialities in biography: 'The witty Shandy from one unguarded and untimely question: "is the clock wound up" draws the deepest philosophizing about conception, birth, and the consequences thereof for a man's whole life.'[51]

---

[47] Gusdorf, op. cit. (n. 13), 31.

[48] Shumaker, op. cit. (n. 15), 29.

[49] James P. Crutchfield, J. Doyne Farmer, Norman H. Packard, and Robert S. Shaw, 'Chaos', *Scientific American*, 1986 no. 6, p. 38.

[50] Lawrence Sterne, *The Life and Opinions of Tristram Shandy, Gentleman*, ed. Graham Petrie (Harmondsworth, 1967), 35.

[51] *Moe vremya: zapiski G. S. Vinskogo*, ed. P. E. Shchegolev (Spb., 1914), 4.

While it is true that Radishchev's *Life of Ushakov* prompted no imitators among biographers in his day, his perspective on the significance of the trivialities of obscure lives flourished in the fictional biographies which far surpassed the non-fictional lives in number and did not suffer the disdain evinced by this one attempt at biography in the new mode.

Yet this single example, although unique in Russia, was one more in a line of European works which had demonstrated to the reading public that writers could do with real lives what novelists like Richardson had done with fictitious ones. From one point of view it is possible to say that by 1800 Russian biography had assimilated the main characteristics of biography as it had developed throughout the rest of Europe. The exemplars of classical antiquity were available to the Russian reader, as were more recent key-works such as Hume's *Life* and Rousseau's *Confessions*. Pietistic introspection was encouraged by such works as Mason's *Self-Knowledge*, and practised in the journals. The lives of the great were commemorated. And the lives of writers had become important: if initially their lives were merely chronicled as exemplars, later the courses of those lives were shown to have a relevance to the author's writings.

Yet even if the main features were apparent, it cannot be said that a firm tradition of modern biographical writing had been established. Biographies brought to press by the end of the eighteenth century in Russia were meagre in number, more often than not translated and, if original, were slim in size. The dominant purpose of published biography in Catherine's reign was to extol the enlightened, and sometimes female, sovereign and thereby reinforce the appeal of the Empress's image. These biographies were the literary counterpart to the sculpture of the equestrian Peter bearing the legend *Petro Primo Catherina Secunda*. For the time being, intimate, obscure biographies, such as Ushakov's, were as disdained as poor Evgeny in Pushkin's *Bronze Horseman*. Their day was yet to come.

BIBLIOGRAPHY OF BIOGRAPHICAL WORKS AND BOOKS CONTAINING BIOGRAPHIES (1740–1800)

The bibliography is chronological by year of publication, with the subjects of the biography listed alphabetically within each year. The subject is given first, followed by a transliteration of the short Russian title. The name of the original author is provided, and an indication is given of the language from which translations were made. Reference is made to the relevant entry in the *Svodnyi katalog* (*SK*) by volume and item number.

The bibliography is followed by an alphabetical list of the subjects of the biographies with references to the year of publication.

1740

EUGÈNE, François of Savoy, Prince. *Opisanie zhitiya i del printsa Evgeniya gertsoga Savoiskogo*. From German. *SK*, ii, 4936.

MARCUS AURELIUS. *Zhitie i dela Marka Avreliya Antonina*. From German, J. A. Hofman. *SK*, i, 45, 46.

1748

ROMAN GENERALS. *Korneliya Nepota Zhitiya slavnykh generalov*. From Latin. *SK*, ii, 3138.

1750

ALEXANDER THE GREAT. *Istoriya o Aleksandre Velikom*. From Latin, Quintus Curtius. *SK*, ii, 3386.

1759

EPICTETUS. *Epikteta stoicheskogo filosofa Enkhiridion i Apoffegmy* (pp. 1–54, 'Zhitie Epikti-tovo'). From Greek, *SK*, iii, 8650.

1760

BACON, Francis. *Zhitie kantslera Frantsiska Bakona*. Via French from English, David Mallet. *SK*, ii, 4022.

DON CARLOS. *Istoriya o gishpanskom printse, Don Karlose syne gishpanskogo korolya Filippa II*. From French, C. V. de Saint-Réal. *SK*, iii, 6427.

MARCUS AURELIUS. *Zhitie i dela Marka Avreliya Antonina* (2nd ed.). *SK*, i, 47.

1762

DON CARLOS. *Istoriya o ishpanskom printse, done Karlose syne ishpanskogo korolya Filippa II*. From French, C. V. de Saint-Réal. *SK*, iii, 6428.

KANTEMIR, A. D. *Satiry i drugie stikhotvorcheskie sochineniya knyazya Antiokha Kantemira, s istoricheskimi primechaniyami i s kratkim opisaniem ego zhizni*. *SK*, ii, 2788.

NADIR SHAH. *Istoriya ò persidskom shakhe Takhmas Kuly-khane*. From French, André de Claustre. *SK*, ii, 2939.

1763

HORACE. *Kvinta Goratsiya Flakka Satiry ili Besedy s primechaniyami, s latinskogo yazyka pre-lozhennye rossiiskimi stikhami Akademii nauk perevodchikom Ivanom Barkovym* (pp. 9–10, 'Zhitie Kvinta Goratsiya Flakka'). *SK*, i, 1560.

1765

LIVES OF ANCIENTS. *Zhitie slavnykh v drevnosti muzhei*. Via French, Plutarch. *SK*, ii, 5397.

1767

ALEXANDER THE GREAT. *Istoriya o Aleksandre Velikom* (2nd ed.). From Latin, Quintus Curtius. *SK*, ii, 3387.

EPICTETUS. *Epikteta stoicheskogo filosofa Enkhiridion i Apoffegmy* (2nd ed.) (pp. 1–54, 'Zhitie Epiktitovo'). From Greek. *SK*, iii, 8651.

THEODOSIUS THE GREAT. *Istoriya o imperatore Feodosii Velikom*. From French, F. Esprit. *SK*, iii, 7802.

1768

CICERO. *Zhizn' Marka Tulliya Tsitserona*. From German. *SK*, i, 2258.

1770

EUGÈNE, François of Savoy, Prince. *Opisanie zhitiya i del printsa Evgeniya gertsoga Savoiskogo*. From German. *SK*, ii, 4937.

SOBIESKI, Jan. *Opisanie zhizni Ioanna Sobeskogo, korolya pol'skogo*. From French, G. F. Coyer. *SK*, ii, 3017.

SULLY, Maximilien de Béthune, Duc de. *Zapiski Maksimiliana Betyuna gertsoga Syulli*. From French. *SK*, iii, 7097.

1771

CARTOUCHE. *Podlinnoe opisanie zhizni frantsuzskogo moshennika Kartusha*. Via German from French. *SK*, ii, 5437.

PETER I. *Sokrashchennoe opisanie zhizni Petra Velikogo*. From French, P. A. Alletz. *SK*, i, 99.

1772

PETER I. *Zhitie Petra Velikogo*. Via Greek from Italian, Antonio Catiforo. *SK*, ii, 2878.

PETER I. *Zhitie i slavnye dela gosudarya imperatora Petra Velikogo*. Z. Orfelin. *SK*, ii, 5027.

PETER I. *Istoriya imp. Petra Velikogo*. Feofan Prokopovich. *SK*, iii, 7734.

RUSSIAN AUTHORS. *Opyt istoricheskogo slovarya o rossiiskikh pisatelyakh*. N. I. Novikov. *SK*, ii, 4668.

1774

EPAMINONDAS. *Istoriya o Epaminonde, fivskom polkovodtse*. From French, Séran de la Tour. *SK*, iii, 6444.

JULIUS CAESAR. *Zapiski o pokhodakh ego v Galliyu* (pp. iii–xii, 'Kratkaya zhizn' Kaiya Yuliya Kesarya'). From Latin. *SK*, iii, 8090.

OVID. *Dve iroidy, ili Dva pis'ma drevnikh iroin', sochinennye Publiem Ovidiem Nasonom, s priobshcheniem avtorovoi zhizni*. From Latin. *SK*, ii, 4830.

PETER I. *Zhitie i slavnye dela Petra Velikogo*. Z. Orfelin. *SK*, ii, 5028.

ROMAN EMPERORS. *Zhizni dvenadtsati pervykh tsesarei rimskikh*. From Latin, Suetonius. *SK*, iii, 6333.

1775

MARCUS AURELIUS. *Zhitie i dela Marka Avreliya Antonina* (3rd ed.). *SK*, i, 48.

OVID. *Prevrashcheniya* (pp. 5–11, 'Kratkoe opisanie zhizni Publiya Ovidiya Nasona, vybrannoe iz raznykh pisatelei'). From Latin. *SK*, ii, 4835.

TREDIAKOVSKY, V. K. *Deidamiya tragediya* (pp. 5–14, 'Kratkoe opisanie zhizni i uchenykh trudov, sochinitelya sei tragedii'). *SK*, iii, 7346.

ROMAN EMPERORS. *Shest' pisatelei Istorii o Avgustakh*. From Latin. *SK*, iii, 8251.

1776

MATVEEV, A. S. *Istoriya o nevinnom zatochenii blizhnego boyarina Artemona Sergievicha Matveeva*. N. I. Novikov. *SK*, i, 2709.

ROMAN EMPERORS. *Zhizni dvenadtsati pervykh tsesarei rimskikh*. From Latin, Suetonius. *SK*, iii, 6333.

1777

CHARLES XII. *Istoriya ili opisanie zhizni Karla XII korolya shvedskogo*. From German. *SK*, i, 2700.

KAIN, Van'ka (Osipov, Ivan). *Zhizn' i pokhozhdeniya rossiiskogo Kartusha, imenuemogo Kaina . . . Pisannaya im samim*. *SK*, i, 2246, 2247.

1778

LOMONOSOV, M. V. *Sobranie raznykh sochinenii* (vol. 1, 'Zhizn' M. V. Lomonosova'). *SK*, ii, 3732.

1779

CARTOUCHE. *Obstoyatel'nye i vernye istorii dvukh moshennikov: pervogo . . . Van'ki Kaina. . . . Vtorogo frantsuzskogo moshennika Kartusha i ego sotovarishchei*. Matvey Komarov. [This contains Komarov's fictionalized life of Kain together with the version of Cartouche's biography published in 1771 q.v.]. *SK*, ii, 3060.

1780

ALBERONI, G., Cardinal. *Zhizn' i primechaniya dostoinye dela kardinala Alberoniya byvshego pri gishpanskom dvore pervym ministrom*. *SK*, i, 2252.

CONFUCIUS. *Opisanie zhizni Konfutsiya*. From Latin. *SK*, ii, 4935.

MONTAGU, Edward Wortley. *Izvestiya o Eduarde Vortlee Montag*. From English (?), anon. *SK*, i, 2451.

1781

HUME, David. *Zhizn' Davyda Gumma, opisannaya im samim*. Via French from English. *SK*, iii, 8708.

ROUSSEAU, J. J. *Vypiska iz uvedomleniya o poslednem vremeni zhizni Zhan Zhaka Russo*. From French, A. G. Le Bègue de Presle. *SK*, ii, 3490.

THEODORE I, King of Corsica. *Istoriya o Feodore I korole korsikanskom*. From French. *SK*, i, 2724.

1782

ELIZABETH I. *Istoriya Elisavety korolevy aglinskoi*. From French, G. Leti. *SK*, ii, 3667.

KAIN, Van'ka (Osipov, Ivan). *Istoriya slavnogo vora, razboinika i byvshego moskovskogo syshchika Van'ki Kaina . . . pisannaya im samim*. *SK*, i, 2727.

SCANDERBEG, King of Albania. *Sokrashchennoe opisanie zhizni i del Skanderbega*. From French, Belin de Monterzi. *SK*, i, 460.

1783

ABELARD AND HÉLOISE. *Sobranie pisem Abel'yarda i Eloizy, s prisovokupleniem opisaniya zhizni sikh neshchastnykh lyubovnikov*. From French. *SK*, i, 1.

GAY, John. *Basni gospodina Ge* (vol. i, pp. iii–xviii, 'Zhitie Ioanna Ge'). From English via French. *SK*, i, 1279.

ST GREGORY OF NAZIANZUS. *Zhitie sv. Grigoriya Nazianzina pisannoe im samim*. *SK*, i, 1632.

1784

DODD, William. *Razmyshleniya aglinskogo presvitera Dodda v temnitse* (pp. vi–xvii, 'Kratkoe opisanie Doddovoi zhizni'). From English. *SK*, i, 1946.

LOMONOSOV, M. V. *Polnoe sobranie sochinenii Mikhaila Vasilevicha Lomonosova, s priobshcheniem zhizni sochinitelya*. *SK*, ii, 3733.

NIKON, Patriarch. *Zhitie svyateishego patriarkha Nikona*. I. K. Shusherin. *SK*, iii, 8517.

ORTHODOX SAINTS. *Opyt istoricheskogo slovarya o vsekh v istinnoi pravoslavnoi greko-rossiiskoi vere svyatoyu neporochnoyu zhizniyu proslavivshikhsya svyatykh muzhakh*. S. P. Sokovnin. *SK*, iii, 6665.

1785

BAUR, F. V. *Izobrazhenie zhizni pokoinogo generala inzhenera i kavalera Fedora Vilimovicha Boura*. From German. *SK*, i, 2459.

JESUS CHRIST. *Sokrashchenie istoricheskoe zhizni Iisusa Khrista*. From French. *SK*, iii, 6684.

KAIN, Van'ka (Osipov, Ivan). *Istoriya slavnogo vora, razboinika i byvshego moskovskogo syshchika Van'ki Kaina*. *SK*, i, 2728.

MATVEEV, A. S. *Istoriya o nevinnom zatochenii blizhnego boyarina Artemona Sergievicha Matveeva* (2nd ed.). N. I. Novikov. *SK*, i, 2710.

ROMAN GENERALS. *Korneliya Nepota Zhitiya slavnykh generalov*. From Latin. *SK*, ii, 3138.

1786

CHARLES XII AND MARCUS AURELIUS. *Sluchivshiesya vo vremena imp. Marka Avreliya rimskogo i Karolusa 12 shvedskogo*. From Latin and Swedish. *SK*, ii, 5165.

COOK, James. *Poslednee puteshestvie okolo sveta kapitana Kuka . . . s priobshcheniem kratkogo opisaniya ego zhizni*. From German, H. Zimmermann. *SK*, iii, 8103.

KAIN, Van'ka (Osipov, Ivan). *Zhizn' i pokhozhdeniya rossiiskogo Kartusha, imenuemogo Kaina*. *SK*, i, 2248.

PANIN, N. I. *Zhizn' grafa Nikity Ivanovicha Panina* (2nd ed.). D. I. Fonvizin. *SK*, iii, 7847.

PETER I. *Lyubopytnye i dostopamyatnye skazaniya o imperatore Petre Velikom*. From German, J. von Stählin. *SK*, iii, 8472.

PETER I. *Podlinnye anekdoty Petra Velikogo*. From German, J. von Stählin. *SK*, iii, 8490.

VOLTAIRE, F. M. A. de. *Zhizn' slavneishego g. Vol'tera*. From French. *SK*, i, 2261.

1787

ALEXANDER THE GREAT. *Istoriya o Aleksandre Velikom* (2nd ed.). From Latin, Quintus Curtius. *SK*, ii, 3388.

ST AUGUSTINE. *Ispovedaniya*. From Latin. *SK*, i, 17.

PANIN, N. I. *Zhizn' grafa Nikity Ivanovicha Panina*. D. I. Fonvizin. *SK*, iii, 7848.

PETER I. *Sobranie raznykh zapisok i sochinenii, sluzhashchikh k dostavleniyu polnogo svedeniya o zhizni i deyaniyakh gosudarya imp. Petra Velikogo*. F. O. Tumansky. *SK*, iii, 7403.

PETER I. *Lyubopytnye i dostopamyatnye skazaniya o imperatore Petre Velikom*. From German, J. von Stählin. *SK*, iii, 8473.

PETER I. *Podlinnye anekdoty Petra Velikogo* (2nd ed.). From German, J. von Stählin. *SK*, iii, 8491, 8492.

VOLTAIRE, F. M. A. de. *Zhizn' slavneishego g. Vol'tera*. From French. *SK*, i, 2262.

1788

CARTOUCHE. *Obstoyatel'nye i vernye istorii dvukh moshennikov: pervogo . . . Van'ki Kaina . . .; vtorogo frantsuzskogo moshennika Kartusha i ego sotovarishchei*. Matvey Komarov. [This contains Komarov's fictionalized life of Kain together with the version of Cartouche's biography published in 1771 q.v.]. *SK*, ii, 3061.

COOK, James. *Poslednee puteshestvie okolo sveta kapitana Kuka s obstoyatel'stvami o ego zhizni i smerti*. From German, H. Zimmermann. *SK*, iii, 8104.

FREDERICK II. *Zhizn' i deyaniya Fridrikha Velikogo*. From German, J. A. H. Guibert. *SK*, i, 1430.

L'HOSPITAL, Michel de. *Zhizn' Mikhaila del-Opitalya, kantslera frantsuzskogo*. From French, J. S. Lévesque de Pouilly. *SK*, ii, 3519.

KAIN, Van'ka (Osipov, Ivan). *Istoriya slavnogo vora, razboinika i byvshego moskovskogo syshchika Van'ki Kaina*. *SK*, i, 2729.

PETER I. *Kratkoe opisanie zhizni i slavnykh del Petra Velikogo*. From French, P. A. Alletz. *SK*, i, 98.

PETER I. *Deyaniya Petra Velikogo*. I. I. Golikov. *SK*, i, 1487.

PETER I. *Zhitie Petra Velikogo* (2nd ed.). Via Greek from Italian, Antonio Catiforo. *SK*, ii, 2879.

PETER I. *Kratkoe opisanie slavnykh i dostopamyatnykh del imp. Petra Velikogo*. P. N. Krekshin. *SK*, ii, 3296.

PETER I. *Skazanie o rozhdenii, o vospitanii i narechenii na vserossiiskii prestol ego tsarskogo presvetlogo velichestva gosudarya Petra Pervogo*. P. N. Krekshin. *SK*, ii, 3299.

PETER I. *Polnoe opisanie deyanii e.v. gosudarya imp. Petra Velikogo*. F. O. Tumansky. *SK*, iii, 7402.

PETER I. *Istoriya imp. Petra Velikogo* (2nd ed.). Feofan Prokopovich. *SK*, iii, 7735.

PETER I. *Anekdoty o imperatore Petre Velikom*. From German, J. von Stählin. *SK*, iii, 8464.

SCANDERBEG, King of Albania. *Istoriya o Kastriotte Albanskom*. From French, S. Zanović. *SK*, i, 2319.

ANCIENT PHILOSOPHERS. *Kratkoe opisanie zhiznei drevnykh filosofov*. From French, Fénelon. *SK*, iii, 7700.

1789

ALEXANDER NEVSKY. *Sozertsaniye slavnyya zhizni svyatogo blagovernogo velikogo knyazya Aleksandra Yaroslavicha Nevskogo*. F. O. Tumansky. *SK*, iii, 7404.

CHARLES, Duke of Burgundy. *Sokrashchenie zhizni i deyanii Karla gertsoga Burgundskogo*. From Latin, J. Sleidan. *SK*, iii, 6543.

CHARLES XII. *Izvestiya, sluzhashchiya k istorii Karla XII*. From French, W. Theyls. *SK*, iii, 7171.

CHARLES XII. *Razsuzhdeniya Friderika II, korolya prusskogo, o svoistve i voinskikh darovaniyakh Karla XII, posleduemye lyubopytnymi anekdotami gosudarstvovaniya i osobennoi zhizni velikogo sego monarkha*. From French. *SK*, iii, 7920.

DODD, William. *Razmyshleniya Dodda i setovaniya ego v temnitse* (2nd ed.) (pp. x–xxii, 'Kratkoe opisanie Doddovoi zhizni'). From English (?). *SK*, i, 1947.

FREDERICK II. *Izobrazhenie velikogo Friderika korolya prusskogo*. From French, S. F. Bourdais. *SK*, i, 778.

GELLERT, C. E. *Zhizn' i svoistva Gellerta*. Via French from German, J. A. Cramer. *SK*, ii, 3209.

HENRI IV. *Istoriya korolya Genrikha Velikogo*. From French, H. de Beaumont de Péréfixe. *SK*, ii, 5197.

HENRI IV. *Dukh Genrika IV*. From French, L. L. Prault. *SK*, ii, 5688.

MARCUS AURELIUS. *Zhitie i dela Marka Avreliya Antonina* (4th ed.). *SK*, i, 49.

MARIA THERESA. *Zhizn' imperatritsy avstriiskoi Marii Terezii*. *SK*, i, 2256.

PETER I. *Kratkoe opisanie slavnykh i dostopamyatnykh del imp. Petra Velikogo* (2nd ed.). P. N. Krekshin. *SK*, ii, 3297.

PETER I. *Podlinnye anekdoty Petra Velikogo* (3rd ed.). From German, J. von Stählin. *SK*, iii, 8493.

PHOCION. *Istoriya Fokiona afineiskogo generala*. From French. *SK*, i, 2731.

SOLON. *Zhizn' afinskogo zakonodatelya Solona*. From French. *SK*, i, 2240.

USHAKOV, F. V. *Zhitie Fedora Vasil'evicha Ushakova*. A. N. Radishchev. *SK*, iii, 5798.

1790

CONFUCIUS. *Zhitie Kung-Tseea ili Konfutsiusa*. From French, J. M. Amiot. *SK*, i, 135.

COOK, James. *Podrobnoe i dostovernoe opisanie zhizni i vsekh puteshestvii slavneishego aglinskogo morekhodtsa kapitana Kuka*. Via French from English, Andrew Kippis. *SK*, ii, 2915.

JOSEPH II. *Lyubopytnye skazaniya o Iosife Vtorom imperatore rimskom*. From German. *SK*, ii, 3865.

NADIR SHAH. *Istoriya o persidskom shakhe Takhmas Kuly-khane* (new ed.). From French, André de Claustre. *SK*, ii, 2940.

PITT, William. *Zhizniopisanie slavnogo anglinskogo ministra Villiama Pitta, grafa Chetamskogo*. From English. *SK*, i and Suppl., 2238.

1791

MARIA THERESA. *Istoriya gosudarstvovaniya Marii Terezii*. From French, Fromageot. *SK*, iii, 7925.

VOLTAIRE, F. M. A. de. *Polnoe sobranie . . . sochinenii g. Voltera . . . s prisovokupleniem zhizni sego znamenitogo pisatelya*. From French. *SK*, i, 1086.

1792

COOK, James. *Puteshestvie okolo sveta kapitana Kuka i zhizn' ego*. From German, H. Zimmermann. *SK*, iii, 8105.

JOSEPH II. *Nachertanie zhizni Iosifa II imperatora rimskogo*. From German. *SK*, ii, 4515.

KAIN, Van'ka (Osipov, Ivan). *Istoriya slavnogo vora, razboinika i byvshego moskovskogo syshchika Van'ki Kaina*. *SK*, i, 2730.

MOHAMMED. *Obstoyatel'noe i podrobnoe opisanie zhizni lzheproroka Magomeda*. From English, H. Prideaux. *SK*, ii, 5642.

NERO. *Zhizn' i uzhasnye deyaniya rimskogo imperatora Nerona*. From French. *SK*, i, 2254.

PANIN, N. I. *Zhizn' grafa Nikity Ivanovicha Panina* (new ed.). D. I. Fonvizin. *SK*, iii, 7849.

RABENER, G. W. *Sobranie sochinenii* (part 1, 'Zhizn' i svoistva sochinitelya'). From German. *SK*, iii, 5781.

1793

ALEXANDER THE GREAT. *Istoriya o Aleksandre Velikom* (3rd ed.). From Latin, Quintus Curtius. *SK*, ii, 3389.

CARTOUCHE. *Obstoyatel'nye i vernye istorii dvukh moshennikov: pervogo*... *Van'ki Kaina*...; *vtorogo frantsuzskogo moshennika Kartusha i ego sotovarishchei*. Matvey Komarov. [This contains Komarov's fictionalized life of Kain together with the version of Cartouche's biography published in 1771 q.v.]. *SK*, ii, 3061.

FREDERICK II. *Poslednii god zhizni Fridrikha II*. From German, E. W. von Hertzberg. *SK*, i, 1406.

LOUDON, E. G. *Zhizn' avstriiskogo generalissimusa barona Laudona*. Via French from German, J. Pezzl. *SK*, ii, 5298.

LOUIS XVI. *Zhizn' i stradanie Lyudovika XVI, korolya frantsuzskogo*. From French, G. de Limon. *SK*, ii, 3690.

PETER I. *Podlinnye anekdoty Petra Velikogo* (4th ed.). From German, J. von Stählin. *SK*, iii, 8494, 8495.

RUSSIAN SOVEREIGNS. *Istoricheskii slovar' rossiiskikh gosudarei*. I. V. Nekhachin. *SK*, ii, 4591.

1794

CARTOUCHE. *Obstoyatel'nye i vernye istorii dvukh moshennikov: pervogo*... *Van'ki Kaina*...; *vtorogo frantsuzskogo moshennika Kartusha i ego sotovarishchei*. Matvey Komarov. [This contains Komarov's fictionalized life of Kain together with the version of Cartouche's biography published in 1771 q.v.]. *SK*, ii, 3062, 3063.

BUFFON, G. L. L., Comte de. *Zhizn' Byuffona*. From French. *SK*, i, 2242.

LOMONOSOV, M. V. *Polnoe sobranie sochinenii Mikhaila Vasil'evicha Lomonosova, s priobshcheniem zhizni sochinitelya* (2nd ed.). *SK*, ii, 3734.

PETER I. *Kratkoe opisanie slavnykh i dostopamyatnykh del imp. Petra Velikogo* (3rd ed.). P. N. Krekshin. *SK*, ii, 3298.

RETZ, Cardinal de. *Zapiski kardinala de Rettsa*. From French. *SK*, iii, 5942.

STUART, Charles Edward. *Zhizn' i strannye priklyucheniya umershego v 1788 godu Karla Eduarda, pretendenta Velikobritanskoi, Frantsuzskoi i Irlandskoi korony*. From German. *SK*, i, 2253.

TIKHON, Bishop of Voronezh. *Kratkoe opisanie zhizni preosvyashchennogo Tikhona pervogo episkopa Voronezhskogo i Eletskogo*. Timofey (Sambikin). *SK*, iii, 7213.

ROMAN EMPERORS. *Zhizni i deyaniya dvenadtsati pervykh tsesarei rimskikh*. From Latin, Suetonius. *SK*, iii, 6334, 6335.

1795

BULGAKOV, F. M. *Kratkoe istoricheskoe nachertanie zhizni leibgvardii podporutchika Feodora Mikhailovicha Bulgakova*. Yuvenalii (I. G. Voeikov). *SK*, iii, 8686.

DODD, William. *Razmyshleniya Dodda i setovaniya ego v temnitse* (3rd ed.) (pp. x–xii, 'Zhizn' Dodda'). From English (?). *SK*, i, 1948.

ELIZABETH I. *Istoriya Elisavety, korolevy aglinskoi*... *s pribavleniem Istinnogo kharaktera seya korolevy i ee favoritov*. From French, G. Leti and supplement 'Istinnyi kharakter' via French from English, Robert Naunton. *SK*, ii, 3668.

PETER I. *Skazanie o rozhdenii, o vospitanii i narechenii na vserossiiskii prestol ego tsarskogo presvetlogo velichestva gosudarya Petra Pervogo* (2nd ed.). P. N. Krekshin. *SK*, ii, 3300.

PETER I. *Yadro istorii gosudarya Petra Velikogo*. I. V. Nekhachin. *SK*, ii, 4596.

TRENCK, F. von der. *Zapiski barona F. Trenka, im samim pisannye*. From German. *SK*, iii, 7361.

1796

BULGAKOV, F. M. *Kratkoe istoricheskoe nachertanie zhizni leibgvardii podporutchika Feodora Mikhailovicha Bulgakova* (2nd ed.). Yuvenalii (I. G. Voeikov). *SK*, iii, 8687.

DIMITRY, Metropolitan of Rostov. *Zhitie . . . Dimitriya mitropolita Rostovskogo*. *SK*, i, 2265.

MONTAGU, Edward Wortley. *Podlinnaya istoriya slavnogo Eduarda Uortli Montegyu*. From English. *SK*, ii, 5436.

NORCROSS, J. *Udivitel'naya zhizn' i trittsatiletnee zaklyuchenie Iogana Norkrossa*. From German, C. P. Rothe. *SK*, iii, 6085.

OVID. *Izbranneishie pechal'nye elegii* (pp. 12–18, 'Kratkoe nachertanie zhizni sochinitelevoi'). From Latin. *SK*, ii, 4831.

PETER I. *Dopolnenie k Deyaniyam Petra Velikogo*, vol. 17 '. . . soderzhashchee anekdoty, kasayushchiesya do sego velikogo gosudarya'. I. I. Golikov. *SK*, i, 1488.

TIKHON, Bishop of Voronezh. *Polnoe opisanie zhizni preosvyashchennogo Tikhona*. E. A. Bolkhovitinov. *SK*, i, 2101.

1797

MENSHIKOV, A. D. *Sokrashchennoe opisanie zhizni knyazya Aleksandra Danilovicha Men'shchikova*. *SK*, iii, 6687.

ROUSSEAU, J. J. *Ispovedanie Zhan Zhaka Russo*. From French. *SK*, iii, 6217.

1798

AGRICOLA. *Zhizn' Yuliya Agrikoly*. From Latin, Tacitus. *SK*, iii, 7165.

CHARLES XII AND PETER I. *Dukh Petra Velikogo imperatora vserossiiskogo i sopernika ego Karla XII, korolya shvedskogo*. O. P. Belyaev. *SK*, i, 485.

MARCUS AURELIUS. *Zhitie i dela Marka Avreliya Antonina* (5th ed.). *SK*, i, 50.

PETER I. *Anekdoty, kasayushchiesya do gosudarya imp. Petra Velikogo* (2nd ed.). I. I. Golikov. *SK*, i, 1486.

TIKHON, Bishop of Voronezh. *Kratkoe opisanie zhizni preosvyashchennogo Tikhona pervogo episkopa Voronezhskogo i Eletskogo*. Timofey (Sambikin). *SK*, iii, 7214.

1799

FRANKLIN, Benjamin. *Otryvok iz zapisok Franklinovykh s prisovokupleniem Kratkogo opisaniya ego zhizni*. Via French. *SK*, iii, 7886.

LEFORT, F. *Zhitie Frantsa Yakovlevicha Leforta*. I. I. Vinogradov. *SK*, i, 984.

LEFORT, F. AND MININ, Koz'ma. *Zhitie Frantsa Yakovlevicha Leforta rossiiskogo generala i Opisanie zhizni nizhegorodskogo kuptsa Koz'my Minina*. I. I. Vinogradov. *SK*, i, 985.

MILTON, John. *Zhizn' Ioanna Mil'tona*. Via French from English, S. Johnson. *SK*, suppl. 492.

MININ, Koz'ma. *Opisanie zhizni i bezsmertnogo podviga slavnogo muzha nizhegorodskogo kuptsa Koz'my Minina*. N. S. Il'insky. *SK*, i, 2496.

PETER I. *Dopolneniya k Kratkomu opisaniyu zhizni velikogo gosudarya*. I. I. Golikov. *SK*, i, 1489.

SUVOROV, Alexander. *Zhizn' i voennye deyaniya generalissimusa knyazya Italiiskogo grafa Suvorova Rymnikskogo*. From German, J. F. Anthing. *SK*, i, 191.

TIKHON, Bishop of Voronezh. *Kratkoe opisanie zhizni preosvyashchennogo Tikhona . . . episkopa Voronezhskogo i Eletskogo*. Timofey (Sambikin). *SK*, iii, 7214.

1800

ALEXANDER THE GREAT. *Istoriya o Aleksandre Velikom* (4th ed.). From Latin, Quintus Curtius. *SK*, ii, 3390.

LEFORT, F. AND GORDON, Patrick. *Istoricheskoe izobrazhenie zhizni i vsekh del slavnogo zhenevtsa, Frantsa Yakovlevicha (Frantsiska Iyakova) Leforta . . . i sosluzhebnika ego . . . znamenitogo shotlandtsa . . . generala anshefa Patrika Gordona, izvestnogo u nas pod imenem Petra Ivanovicha Gordona*. I. I. Golikova. *SK*, i, 1490.

SUVOROV, A. V. *Zhizn' i voennye deyaniya generalissimusa, knyazya Italiiskogo grafa Aleksandra Vasil'evicha Suvorova Rymnikskogo*. From German via French, J. F. Anthing. *SK*, i, 192.

TIKHON, Bishop of Voronezh. *Kratkoe opisanie zhizni preosvyashchennogo Tikhona . . . episkopa Voronezhskogo i Eletskogo*. Timofey (Sambikin). *SK*, iii, 7216.

INDEX OF BIOGRAPHIES
(references are to years)

Gordon, Patrick (1635–99), 1800
Gregory, Saint, of Nazianzus (329–89), 1783

Héloise (1101–64), 1783
Henri IV, King of France (1553–1610), 1789 (2)
Horace (65–8 BC), 1763
l'Hospital, Michel de (1505–73), 1788
Hume, David (1711–76), 1781

Jesus Christ, 1785
Joseph II, Holy Roman Emperor (1741–90), 1790, 1792

Kain, Van'ka (Osipov, Ivan) (b. 1718), 1777 (2), 1782, 1785, 1786, 1788, 1789, 1792
Kantemir, Antiokh Dmitrievich (1708–44), 1762

Lefort, François Jacob (1653–99), 1799 (2), 1800
Lomonosov, Mikhail Vasil'evich (1711–65), 1778, 1784, 1794
Loudon, Ernst Gideon, Freiherr von (1717–90), 1793
Louis XVI, King of France (1754–93), 1793

Marcus Aurelius Antoninus (121–80), 1740, 1760, 1775, 1786, 1789, 1798
Maria Theresa (1717–80), 1789, 1791

Matveev, Artamon Sergeevich (1625–82), 1776, 1785
Menshikov, Aleksandr Danilovich (1673–1729), 1797
Milton, John (1608–74), 1799
Minin, Koz'ma (d. 1616), 1799 (2)
Mohammed (c.570–632), 1792
Montagu, Edward Wortley (1713–76), 1780, 1796

Nadir Shah (1688–1747), 1762, 1790
Nero (AD 37–68), 1792
Nikon, Patriarch (1605–81), 1784
Norcross, John (1688–1758), 1796

Osipov, Ivan, see Kain, Van'ka
Ovid (43 BC–c.AD 18), 1774, 1775, 1796

Panin, Nikita Ivanovich (1718–83), 1786, 1787, 1792
Peter the Great (1672–1725), 1771, 1772 (3), 1774, 1786 (2), 1787 (3), 1788 (8), 1789 (2), 1793, 1794, 1795 (2), 1796, 1798 (2), 1799
Phocion (c.402–318 BC), 1789
Pitt, William (1759–1806), 1790

Rabener, Gottlieb Wilhelm (1714–71), 1792

Retz, Jean François Paul de Gondi, Cardinal de (1614–79), 1794
Rousseau, Jean-Jaques (1712–78), 1781, 1797

Scanderbeg, King of Albania (c.1405–68), 1782, 1788
Sobieski, Jan (1624–96), 1770
Solon (c.638–c.559 BC), 1789
Stuart, Charles Edward (1720–88), 1794
Sully, Maximilien de Béthune, Duc de (1559–1641), 1770
Suvorov, Aleksandr Vasil'evich (1730–1800), 1799, 1800

Theodore I, King of Corsica (1687–1756), 1781
Theodosius the Great (c.346–95), 1767
Tikhon, Bishop of Voronezh (1724–83), 1794, 1796, 1798, 1799, 1800
Trediakovsky, Vasily Kirillovich (1703–69), 1775
Trenck, Franz, Baron von (1711–49), 1795

Ushakov, Fedor Vasil'evich (c.1749–70), 1789

Voltaire, François Marie Arouet de (1694–1778), 1786, 1787, 1791

The Walter Scott Motifs in Nikolay Gogol''s Story *The Lost Letter*

By MARK ALTSHULLER

I т is customary to believe that in his early work, the cycle *Evenings on a Farm near Dikanka*, Gogol' drew on material from Ukrainian folklore. Furthermore, reference is commonly made to the many occasions when he asks, in letters to his family, either for descriptions of Little Russian costumes ('... сельского дьячка, от верхнего платья до самых сапогов с поименованием, как это всё называлось у самых закоренелых, самых древних, самых наименее переменившихся малороссиян; равным образом название платья, носимого нашими крестьянскими девками до последней ленты ...' х. 141),[1] or for stories of ghosts, goblins, mermaids, local festivals (Christmas carolling (*kolyady*), St John's Day), and suchlike (ibid.). With characteristic persistence he forces his mother to set down for him 'поверия, страшные сказания, предания, разные анекдоты, которых множество носится между простым народом' (ibid.). Such requests are repeated again and again with great persistence (x. 144, 166, 208–9). However, these requests tend to indicate that Gogol' was not well acquainted with the traditions of the Ukraine, and presumably had had no particular interest in them as a young man, a fact that was justifiably pointed out (contrary to the accepted opinion) by V. Gippius, one of the greatest researchers into Gogol'.[2]

Gogol''s sister once began collecting Little Russian stories and songs (x. 208–9), but he himself evidently took no part in this. It was precisely because Gogol', who lived in the Poltava region, had not read any records of Ukrainian folklore or listened to any songs or tales, but had at best merely observed the realities of Ukrainian life from the perspective of the manor-house, that he was later forced to turn to a source as unreliable as the notes of his mother and sister. 'Вопросы его показывают, что представления его очень смутны — он не только не знает, какие есть "духи", кроме русалок, но не знает название платья, носимого крестьянскими "девками", и думает, что видел в церкви девушку в платье времен до гетманских.'[3]

This article has been translated by Mark Shuttleworth.

[1] N. V. Gogol', *Polnoe sobranie sochinenii*, i–xiv (1937–52). All references in the text are to this edition.

[2] V. Gippius, *Gogol'* (L., 1924).   [3] Ibid. 28.

The romantic tendencies which prevailed in St Petersburg at the beginning of the 1830s prompted a search for exotic lands which had been untouched by the unifying effects of civilization. In this way the Ukraine, Russia's closest and yet still somewhat alien southern neighbour, could also appear in a kind of romantic haze; so, influenced by these tendencies, Gogol' also turned to the folklore and ethnography of the 'Slavonic Ausonia'. This superficial, picturesque use of ethnography was completely to the taste of the reading public, who liked to see works containing local colour, one of the quintessential features of romanticism: 'Здесь так занимает всех всё малороссийское...' Gogol' wrote to his mother on 30 April 1829 (x. 142).

A distant, warmer and more colourful Ukraine, and yet one which the northern capital did not properly understand, could have been viewed as a beautiful, fairy-tale world, well suited to romantic portrayal. Gogol' had apparently read the Russian translation of Walter Scott's article 'On the Supernatural in Fictitious Composition',[4] published in 1829 in *Syn otechestva* (nos. 44–6). In this article the famous novelist, while discussing the problem of the mysterious and the supersensual in literature, speaks of the peculiar appeal of the ancient legends of hoary, superstitious antiquity, which acquire their particular attraction as a result of their 'ragged simplicity'.[5] Gogol' was aiming to create precisely that kind of simplicity and naivety which supposedly characterized traditional Ukrainian life with its superstitions and legends. However, he was not concerned with faithfully reproducing the realities of this life, and even less so with exploiting genuine sources of folklore. For this reason, G. A. Gukovsky is absolutely correct when he refers to the country depicted by Gogol' in his *Evenings* as the Ukrainian Island of Utopia and the fabulous Abbey of Thélème.[6]

As is well known, Gogol' quite often needed a certain distance from the object he was depicting in order to force his powerful creative imagination into activity. Thus, his first published poem was called 'Italy', and in it the pupil of the Nezhin Lyceum described the beauties of a distant southern country, while later on, in the sumptuousness of Italy, while writing *Dead Souls*, he recreated the face of a 'sad', poverty-stricken Russia. From rainy, damp St Petersburg, and from the squalid, unheated flat of a poor civil servant dreaming of fame, his native Ukraine with its blue sky, mild, warm climate, and splendid gardens could only have seemed like a Promised Land which the rich romantic imagination of the budding writer had no difficulty in depicting in the richest of colours.

[4] Ibid. 29.

[5] W. Scott, 'On the Supernatural in Fictitious Composition, and Particularly on the Works of Ernest Theodore William Hoffman', in: *The Prose Works of Sir Walter Scott*, xviii (Edinburgh, n.d.), 281 (published here under the title 'Novels of Ernest Theodore Hoffman').

[6] G. A. Gukovsky, *Realizm Gogolya* (M.-L., 1959), 35.

It is therefore not surprising that none of the attempts to discover any pieces of folklore which significantly parallel Gogol''s Ukrainian stories have met with success. As the author of the definitive work on Gogol''s relationship to folklore is forced to admit, 'Для повестей, вошедших в этот цикл [sc. *Evenings on a Farm near Dikanka*] не представляется возможным определить те непосредственные народные источники, которые легли в их основу.'[7]

On the other hand, we know that, like many other writers, Gogol' frequently not only required some creative stimulus for the formation of an idea, but sometimes even needed the thematic skeleton of a future work, which, once it had been transformed into a perfect artistic creation, could then be given the flesh and bones of a plot. 'Сделайте милость,' he wrote to Pushkin on 7 October 1835, 'дайте какой-нибудь сюжет, хоть какой-нибудь смешной или не смешной, но русский чисто анекдот. Рука дрожит написать тем временем комедию.' (x. 375).

As we know from Gogol''s own admission, Pushkin gave him the 'plot' of *Dead Souls* and the 'idea' of *The Government Inspector* (x. 440). There are further instances which are known to us of Gogol' drawing his literary ideas from sources which were to be found not in folklore but in other works of literature. Thus, the plot of the *Story of how Ivan Ivanovich Quarreled with Ivan Nikiforovich* goes back to V. T. Narezhny's story *Dva Ivana, ili strast' k tyazhbam*. It can also hardly be doubted that the church scenes in the story *Viy* are thematically linked with Robert Southey's ballad 'The Old Woman of Berkeley. A Ballad, Shewing How an Old Woman Rode Double, and Who Rode Before Her', which was very well known in Russia in V. Zhukovsky's excellent translation 'Ballada, v kotoroi opisyvaetsya, kak odna starushka ekhala na chernom kone vdvoem i kto sidel vperedi' (1835). According to S. Karlinsky's perceptive conjecture, the very name Viy is formed by grammatical analogy with the name of the ruler of the waters in Zhukovsky's fairy-tale *Undina*, who is called Struy.[8] One could add to the number of such examples.

There would therefore appear to be no real future in the systematic search for folklore motifs in Gogol''s stories. A comparison with works of Russian and Western literature may turn out to be more fruitful. We shall now consider one such parallel, which has gone unnoticed by researchers. This is the interpolated novella in Walter Scott's novel *Redgauntlet*. We shall be concerned not with the similarity between isolated motifs, but with the consistent thematic parallel which can be found between this novella and Gogol''s story *The Lost Letter*.

[7] V. I. Eremina, 'N. V. Gogol'', in: *Russkaya literatura i fol'klor (pervaya polovina 19 veka)* (L., 1976), 251.

[8] Simon Karlinsky, *The Sexual Labyrinth of Nikolay Gogol* (Cambridge, Mass., 1976), 97–103. For the many interpretations of the name Viy, see Natalie K. Moyle, 'Folktale Patterns in Gogol's *VIJ*', *Russian Literature*, vii (1979), 665–8.

Before comparing the two works we should first of all ascertain that Gogol' was indeed acquainted with the text of Walter Scott's novel (which was published in 1824). It is well known that in his youth Gogol' had a very poor knowledge of foreign languages. He had absolutely no knowledge of English, which was not taught in the Nezhin Lyceum. He knew French badly. Memoirists confirm this with such remarks as: 'Пренебрегал изучением языков', 'Особенно плох был по языкам', 'Едва ли мог понимать без пособия словаря книгу на французском языке'.[9]

A knowledge of the original or the French translation of the novel *Redgauntlet* can therefore be almost excluded. But at the same time we know that, even while still a student at the Lyceum (1821–8), Gogol' was an extremely avid reader who spent all his pocket money on books and was even elected by his comrades to be the custodian of their joint library, which consisted of books bought out of common funds.[10] Also, the library of the Nezhin Lyceum itself would no doubt have contained all of the small number of important Russian books and journals which were appearing at that time.

In 1825 in the journal *Syn otechestva* there appeared, translated from the French by Orest Somov, the *Kvitantsiya posle smerti. Povest', rasskazannaya slepym skripachom. (Iz Redgontleta, romana S. Val'tera Skotta)*. It is impossible to imagine that a sixteen-year-old boy who was passionate about literature and dreamed of becoming a writer would not have read a story by the already universally celebrated writer, which was furthermore published in one of the most popular journals of the 1820s. A complete Russian translation of *Redgauntlet* (translated from the French) appeared in 1828. Gogol' came to St Petersburg at the end of that year and tried as hard as he could to establish himself in the world of letters. The appearance of each of Walter Scott's novels was becoming a literary event, and so the young man of letters would doubtless have read the newly published book immediately; in so doing, at the very time in which he was writing the *Evenings*, he would have been refreshing the impressions he had gained from the fragment which he had most likely read several years previously. That Gogol' was acquainted with the text in question can consequently be held to be almost beyond doubt.

The interpolated novella, known in the Russian translation as the *Kvitantsiya posle smerti*, tells of a forebear of the main hero and has little bearing on the main subject of the novel. The storyteller's grandfather, Steenie Steenson, a daring fellow and an excellent piper (102),[11] is a tenant of the Laird Robert Redgauntlet. One day he brings his rent to his sick, dying landlord. Redgauntlet is sitting in his

---

[9] V. Veresaev, *Gogol' v zhizni* (M.-L., 1933) (repr. Ann Arbor, 1983), 60–3, 70.

[10] Ibid. 52–3, 56, 63, 65.

[11] *Syn otechestva* (1825), part 103, no. 18 (page references are in the text).

room, accompanied only by his favourite, a hideous ape. He starts to count the money in order to write out the receipt, and Steenie goes out with the valet to drink a glass of brandy. Suddenly there comes a cry from the laird's room. The servants find him on the point of death; the receipt and the money have disappeared. The heir demands of Steenie that he either pay the debt or produce his father's receipt, and threatens to throw the luckless tenant off his land. Steenie is unable to prove anything; he cannot understand what has happened, and supposes his money to be in hell, where the old sinner Redgauntlet has doubtless ended up.

The distraught Steenie stops for a moment at an inn and drinks a toast to the health of the Devil (121), asking him for help in his troubles. He is in despair. The road then passes through a thick, dark forest. Suddenly a horseman appears alongside Steenie and invites him to a meeting with his dead landlord, at which he is to be given the receipt. The stranger leads Steenie to an enormous house where a banquet is taking place. Steenie's old landlord is sitting at table in the company of other deceased people.

Redgauntlet tells Steenie that he will give him the receipt if he will play a tune. Steenie replies that he has not brought his bagpipes with him. An instrument is provided, and Steenie notices that the steel pipes are red-hot. He refuses a second time, saying that he feels weak and frightened. The Laird offers him something to eat and drink. Fearing the hospitality of hell, Steenie once again refuses, and insistently begins demanding the receipt. The Laird gives it to him, whereupon Steenie speaks God's name, and immediately plunges to the ground in the family graveyard of the Redgauntlets. He returns the receipt to the heir; it turns out that the ape had stolen the money, and the whole affair ends to everyone's satisfaction.

Even in this brief retelling it is not difficult to observe a certain similarity of motifs in the stories of Scott and Gogol'. Let us look at these parallels in greater detail. In both cases we read of the hero's journey into hell for a missing document. Usual features of stories in which a man meets the devil are the sale of the man's soul and the receipt which he gives to Satan. This is the case in all the variants of the Faust story and in the seventeenth-century Russian tale of Savva Grudtsyn. In 1829 in the almanac *Karmannaya knizhka dlya lyubitelei russkoi stariny* . . . there appeared V. Olin's story *Kumova postelya. Povest', zaimstvovannaya iz suevernykh narodnykh rasskazov*.[12] V. Gippius pointed this out as a possible source of *The Lost Letter*. However, here too we read 'о крестьянском парне, которого мать во время трудных родов продала черту, а великодушный работник — кум Бельзевула —

---

[12] *Karmannaya knizhka dlya lyubitelei russkoi stariny i slovesnosti na 1829 god.* See N. Smirnov-Sokol'sky, *Russkie literaturnye al'manakhi i sborniki 18-19 vv.* (M., 1965), 140.

впоследствии спас, сведя в ад и уничтожив "рукописание".[13] The main difference between, on the one hand, these works concerning the selling of a soul to the devil, and, on the other, *The Lost Letter* and *Kvitantsiya posle smerti*, consists in the fact that in the stories of Scott and Gogol' a *neutral business* document has to be recovered.

Walter Scott in his story made use of Scottish legends which circulated widely in versions which were very close to the novel *Redgauntlet* (a missing receipt of payment, a journey into hell, and so forth).[14] It has not been possible to find any points at which Russian or Ukrainian folklore corresponds to this central episode in the stories of Gogol' and Scott.

A further comparison of the two stories reveals other parallels as well. In both instances we read about the storyteller's grandfather, and the two grandfathers are similar. The Russian translation of Scott has an 'удалой детина' who 'порыскал по свету' (102), while in Gogol' we read: 'Дед живал в свете не мало, знал уж, как подпускать турусы и при случае, пожалуй, и перед царем не ударил бы лицом в грязь' (i. 187). Both heroes lose a vital business document: Steenie a receipt of payment of rent, and Foma Grigor'evich's grandfather a letter from the Hetman to the Tsarina. Both are certain that the document is to be found in hell (taken there by Redgauntlet/stolen by the devil along with the soul of the Zaporozhian). Steenie visits an inn to drink to the 'здоровье врага человеческого, лишь бы он отдал ... мешок с деньгами или сказал, где он девался' (121). Gogol''s Cossack seeks the advice of the other visitors to a tavern as to how to find the lost letter. A stranger shows both heroes the way to hell. In the Scott story it is an unknown horseman, clearly a messenger from hell, who leads Steenie to Redgauntlet's home beyond the grave, while in the Gogol' story it is the silent publican, who for a certain price points out the path that leads to hell. Both heroes find their way into the very depths of a thick, dark, almost impenetrable forest.

When at last the heroes reach the other world, in both cases they find a lavish banquet in progress. '... все комнаты в доме освещены ... там играли на скрипках и волынках и, казалось, плясали и веселились ... все были за столом: вино лилось рекой, клятвы и застольные песни раздавались перекатным громом ...' (*Kvitantsiya*, 124–5). In spite of the fact that Gogol''s story is many times shorter than that of the invariably verbose Scott, the Russian author at this point spares neither time nor colour to describe the central episode of the story, the merry banquet in the Ukrainian hell. It is, moreover, his narrative which is the brighter and more vivid, and which contains a much greater degree

---

[13] V. Gippius, *Gogol'* (n. 2), p. 20.
[14] Coleman O. Parsons, *Witchcraft and Demonology in Scott's Fiction* (Edinburgh–London, 1964), 179–84.

of local colour than that of his predecessor; furthermore, dances and musical instruments are present in Gogol' as well as in Scott (tambourines and French horns instead of violins and bagpipes):

Ведьм такая гибель, как случается иногда на Рождество выпадает снегу: разряжены, размазаны, словно панночки на ярмарке. И все, сколько их было там, как хмельные, отплясывали какого-то чертовского трепака. Пыль подняли, боже упаси, какую! Дрожь бы проняла крещеного человека при одном виде, как высоко скакало бесовское племя. Деда, несмотря на страх весь, смех напал, когда увидел, как черти с собачьими мордами, на немецких ножках, вертя хвостами, увивались около ведьм, будто парни около красных девушек; а музыканты тузили себя в щеки кулаками, словно в бубны, и свистали носами, как в волторны ... 'Ну, это еще не совсем худо', подумал дед, завидевши на столе свинину, колбасы, крошеный с капустой лук и много всяких сластей ... (i. 187–8).

Both heroes have to pass a thrice-repeated test. Scott's Steenie refuses to play the first time he is asked ('не принес своей волынки', 128). The second time, in order to avoid touching the searing-hot pipes, he excuses himself by saying he feels frightened and weak (129). The third time he refuses the refreshment offered to him ('молвил, что пришел не есть и не пить', 129). A parallel to these pipes which cannot be touched and to the refusal of the diabolical food may perhaps be seen in the unsuccessful attempt made by Gogol''s hero to eat something in hell: as soon as he extends his lips to the fork with sliced lard and ham on it, the food which he intended for himself is eaten by devils (i. 188).

In the Gogol' story, the actual thrice-repeated test takes the form of three hands of the card-game *duren'*. The hero has to win at least one hand. He loses the first time, and also the second. In the third hand the grandfather makes the sign of the cross over the cards and immediately gains the advantage in the game: his cards turn out to be aces and kings, all trumps. He then raises his hand to make the sign of the cross over the devils and witches, whereupon he receives back the letter and gallops out of hell on a devilish horse. Steenie resolutely demands the receipt, speaks the name of God and instantly disappears from the infernal house. Consequently, the sign of the cross in Gogol''s story is the equivalent of the name of God in Scott's.

The two heroes' arrival back on earth after escaping from hell coincides in the two stories almost word for word. Hardly has Steenie spoken the name of God, 'как вдруг очутился в густом сумраке и так со всех ног рухнулся о землю, что дух у него заняло и память отшибло' (130). The grandfather in *The Lost Letter*, leaping from his horse, 'через пни, через кочки полетел стремглав в провал и так хватился на дне его о землю, что, кажись, и дух вышибло' (i. 190).

Laird Redgauntlet demands that Steenie should present himself in hell again in a year's time to thank his lordship for returning the receipt. This demand worries him greatly, and he spends the whole year doing penance by refraining from playing the bagpipes and by abstaining from strong drink. The period of a year is reflected in Gogol''s story: 'Ровно через каждый год и именно в то самое время'— the grandfather's wife would feel an urge to dance, and even in her sleep would leap up with her spindle and comb (i. 190–1). In the draft version the furniture also dances: 'Печь ездила по всей хате, выгоняя лопатою вон горшки, лоханки, ушаты' (i. 403).

However, this dancing furniture has a different literary source. In 1825 there appeared in *Syn otechestva* a translation of Washington Irving's story *The Bold Dragoon, or the Adventure of My Grandfather* (from the book *Tales of a Traveller*), in which the wild dance of the furniture in a hotel room is depicted very vividly and picturesquely.[15] This striking episode about the dance of chairs, a stool, a chest of drawers, fire-tongs, and a coal-shovel was cited by Scott in his article 'On the Supernatural . . .', which was published in Russian translation, as we have already mentioned, in 1829. The story attracted much attention. V. Kyukhel'beker mentions dancing furniture twice in his diary.[16] Maybe it was precisely because this motif was in his readers' memory, that Gogol' removed the dancing stove from the final version of *The Lost Letter*.

Little attention has been given until now to the links between the works of Gogol' and Walter Scott, and it is really only the pseudo-historical story *Taras Bulba* which has been discussed at all.[17] I believe that the present article is the first to introduce the question of Gogol' and Walter Scott into the realm of concrete literary comparison.

---

[15] *Syn otechestva* (1825), part 102, no. 15, pp. 232–3.

[16] V. K. Kyukhel'beker, *Puteshestvie. Dnevnik. Stat'i*, ed. V. D. Rak [M. G. Al'tshuller], N. V. Koroleva (L., 1973), 288, 322.

[17] See, for example, the brief notes on this question by S. M. Petrov, 'Istoricheskii roman', in *Istoriya russkogo romana*, i (M.-L., 1962), 203–50; and Ya. L. Levkovich, 'Istoricheskaya povest'', in *Russkaya povest' 19 veka* (L., 1973), 108–34. For the links between *Dead Souls* and the traditions of Walter Scott, see Anna Yelistratova, *Nikolai Gogol' and the West European Novel* (M., 1984), 43–53.

M. E. Saltykov-Shchedrin in English: a Bibliography

By I. P. FOOTE

THE centenary of the death of M. E. Saltykov-Shchedrin—he died on 28 April (O.S.) 1889—is a suitable occasion to record the translations of his works and comment on them that have appeared in English. For a writer widely—and with some justice—regarded as 'unexportable' ('an eminently national writer, never to be comprehended abroad' was the verdict of his American obituarist Isabel Hapgood), Saltykov has fared, in fact, reasonably well in English-speaking countries, though, it must be said, less well than in some other countries no less disadvantaged by their remoteness from the contemporary issues of Russian society which were the dominant theme of his works. His merits as a social commentator and literary artist have been recognized in a now sizeable number of translations from a small, but growing range of his works (including reprints and translations published in the Soviet Union, the present tally is 84).

The translation of Saltykov into English began creditably early, with the publication in 1861 of 'Frederic Aston's' *Tchinovnicks* (A.1),[1] a compilation of chapters (with extensive commentary) from Saltykov's first cycle of sketches *Gubernskie ocherki* (1856–7). This early initiative—which came from an Englishman who happened to be in Russia at the time of Saltykov's early fame as a writer of the 'denunciatory' school of literature—was not, however, sustained and it was not until the year of his death, nearly thirty years later, that the next translations of Saltykov appeared. Since the 1890s there has been a steady, if modest, output of translations, chiefly from the narrow range of his more accessible works. The majority of the early translations, all of shorter works or extracts, were published in periodicals or books with a 'Russian' context—*Free Russia*, the journal of the Society of Friends of Russian Freedom (A.4, etc.), Ethel Voynich's *The Humour of Russia* (A.9–11), for instance—and this trend continued with the publication of short pieces by him in a succession of anthologies until the last two or three decades. His prose-fables (*Skazki*) proved a particularly popular source of these short pieces—not surprisingly, since the brevity and pointedness of the fables make them admirable anthology material. 'The Tale

---

[1] References here and below are to the Bibliography which follows.

of how One Peasant Fed Two Generals' outstrips all other works of Saltykov in the number of times it has been published in English translation, its only near rival being *Gospoda Golovlevy*.

The latter, the novel on which Saltykov's literary reputation (certainly abroad) mainly depends, did not appear in English until 1916 (there had been a translation into German in 1886, into French in 1889). This first English version (A.19), translated by Athelstan Ridgway and published in London, was followed a year later by a second (A.23), by Avram Yarmolinsky and published in New York. Reviews of the London edition were reserved, those of the New York edition more favourable, but neither translation appears to have aroused any lasting interest—Edward Garnett in his introduction to Natalie Duddington's translation of *Gospoda Golovlevy* (the next to be published, in 1931) described it as 'the last of the great Russian novels that has been awaiting translation into English', clearly unaware that two translations already existed. The publication of Duddington's translation and, in the same year, of *Fables* (A.41: twenty-two of the *Skazki* translated by Vera Volkhovsky, whose father Feliks Volkhovsky had been an editor of *Free Russia* and a pioneer translator of the *Skazki* in the 1890s) did much to raise Saltykov from the status of an anthology author and define him in the eyes of the English reading public as a major literary figure. The two books prompted a substantial review article in *The Times Literary Supplement*, and both volumes have been reprinted a number of times over the years. The 'classic' status of *Gospoda Golovlevy* was acknowledged by the reprint of Duddington's translation in Everyman's Library in 1934 (A.45).

From the 1920s to the 1950s shorter pieces by Saltykov continued to find a place in periodicals and anthologies. For the most part, these were fables from *Skazki*, but others came from an increasing range of other works: *Gubernskie ocherki*, *Nevinnye rasskazy*, *Pompadury i pompadurshi*, *Melochi zhizni*, *Za rubezhom*. A first translation of Saltykov's play *Smert' Pazukhina* (A.36) was published in 1924 in a series issued on the occasion of the tour of the Moscow Art Theatre in the United States.

Since the 1950s the signs are that Saltykov has emerged from his role as primarily an anthology author. Shorter pieces (chiefly fables) and extracts have continued to appear, but the number of them has declined sharply—due, no doubt, in part to the relative decline in popularity of the 'anthology' genre in this period. Whereas 49 of the 58 translations published before 1955 were in this category, only eight of the 26 published since have been (four of those in Moscow editions): the 'whole work' translations since 1955 include eleven issues of *Gospoda Golovlevy* (four of them new translations), two of *Istoriya odnogo goroda* (A.76, 77), one of *Pompadury i pompadurshi* (A.78) (both works previously untranslated), a new translation of *Smert' Pazukhina* (A.72), and three substantial selections of *Skazki* (Volkhovsky's *Fables* twice reprinted and Rottenberg's Moscow-published *Tales from M. Saltykov-Shchedrin* (A.60)). The—albeit modest—increase in the range of titles available has provided English readers with the opportunity to gain a broader picture of Saltykov as a writer, though the number of readers who have availed themselves of this opportunity is probably not large. *Gospoda Golovlevy* is clearly now well established in the canon of classic Russian novels, but Saltykov has still to attain the full measure of recognition which is his due. He is, however, reaching a wider public—and not only in print: the last year has seen the first broadcasts of his works—radio dramatizations by Jack Winter of three fables and *Gospoda Golovlevy* were transmitted by B.B.C. Radio 3 (in November 1987 and April 1988) and an abridged version of the *Gospoda Golovlevy* adaptation has been broadcast by the Australian Broadcasting Corporation. An enthusiastic discussion of one of the fable broadcasts overheard by the present writer *in a public bar* suggests that Saltykov has a larger public ready to receive him, if a means of introduction is provided.

The prospect of more of Saltykov's works appearing in English translation is uncertain. The distinctly national and contemporary interest of most of the works still untranslated remains a serious obstacle to their finding favour with the general reader (much less with publishers who commission translations), but some additions might reasonably be made to the present list—perhaps *Poshekhonskaya starina*, a major work that suffers less than others from any disabling concern with the complex issues of Saltykov's own time, might be next in line for the attention of translators.

In addition to translations, a few editions of Saltykov's works in Russian have also been published in Britain and America for the benefit of *émigré* readers or students of Russian: although not 'in English', these are included in the Bibliography.

The first critical responses to Saltykov in English were the reviews of 'Frederic Aston's' *Tchinovnicks* in 1861 (see A.1). A contemporary view of him (and of the 'denunciatory' school of literature then flourishing) was provided in 1863 in the English-language *Nevsky Magazine* (C.1), published in St Petersburg, but thereafter, apart from Turgenev's review of *Istoriya odnogo goroda* (C.2) in *The Athenaeum* in 1871 and occasional references to his current work in journal surveys of Russian literature, Saltykov passed without notice until his death, when Isabel Hapgood (who had attended his funeral) gave the first general assessment of his literary career in English in the New York *Nation* (C.10). For the next forty years critical comment on Saltykov was more or less confined to general studies of Russian literature and reference works. The accounts given of him in these are rarely of much substance or originality, but some are of interest—among them those of Brückner ('English' only in translation), Baring, and Mirsky. When the translations of *Gospoda Golovlevy* and selected *Skazki* of the 1930s brought Saltykov to the attention of a wider reading public, detailed assessments of his significance as a literary figure were given in the *Times Literary Supplement* review of 1931 and the review by D. J. Enright of the *Fables* reprint of 1941. The year 1940 saw the publication of the only monograph on Saltykov in English to date: Nikander Strelsky's *Saltykov and the Russian Squire* (C.30), devoted to *Gospoda Golovlevy* and *Poshekhonskaya starina*, and three years later the same author published the first scholarly journal article on his work (C.32: again, on *Poshekhonskaya starina*). A valuable study of *Gospoda Golovlevy* ('The Hypocrite', on Judas Golovlev) appeared in 1946 in V. S. Pritchett's *The Living Novel* (C.33), in which, for the first time, Saltykov's work was viewed outside its specifically Russian context. Since the 1950s the development of critical writing on Saltykov has roughly paralleled the growth and increasing range of translating activity in the same period: a dozen or so articles have appeared in academic journals devoted to Russian studies or general literature. The main focus of these has been on *Gospoda Golovlevy* (for example, Kramer (C.59), Todd (C.62), and Ehre (C.63)), but, as with the translations of this period, the scope of interest has widened to include other works by him—early stories (Neuhäuser (C.66)), *Istoriya odnogo goroda*, *Ubezhishche Monrepo* (Foote (C.55, 65)), and other aspects of his social and political outlook (Tschebotarioff Bill (C.38), Grishin (C.42), Bartholomew (C.68)). These articles apart, the last three decades have seen the publication of further accounts of Saltykov in general studies of Russian literature and reference works, the most noteworthy being those of Charles A. Moser (C.70) and Henry Gifford (C.47: on *Gospoda Golovlevy*). New translations have been reviewed widely and at a serious level in literary journals and the press.

Although there have been a number of scholarly articles on Saltykov, academic interest in him—despite the major development of Russian studies in British and American universities in recent times—has been slight. Since Strelsky's dissertation of 1939 (which became his book *Saltykov and the Russian Squire*) only three more dissertations devoted solely to Saltykov have been completed in the universities of Great Britain and the United States. Here again the 'national' interest of his work seems to be in evidence: of the total four dissertation-writers three have been of Russian origin (and one of the dissertations was even written in Russian). There is clearly much scope and need for the development of scholarly interest in this major writer, whose works, apart from their literary significance, provide a unique and valuable record of the issues and moods of a key period of Russian history—and a lasting repository of much human wisdom. There is still no general study of Saltykov in English and the filling of that gap must be regarded as the most urgent need.

BIBLIOGRAPHY

The Bibliography is divided into four sections: A. Translations of Saltykov's works into English; B. Russian-language editions of his works published in Britain and America; C. Criticism and information relating to Saltykov in books, periodicals, and works of reference; D. Dissertations on Saltykov approved for higher degrees in British and American universities. Reviews of the translated works are listed in section A following the translation to which they refer. The list of encyclopaedia references in section C is not exhaustive: all encyclopaedia articles of substance are recorded; others of slighter content are included selectively to indicate the growth and range of Saltykov's reputation as a significant literary figure. No individual reference is made to the prefatory notes which accompany a number of the translations of shorter works and extracts printed in anthologies and periodicals. Reprints of translations are listed (as separate items) when they appear in a new publication; in the case of anthologies containing works by Saltykov which have been reprinted, only the original edition is recorded.

A major source of information on pre-1934 publications has been the bibliography of Saltykov in English compiled by S. A. Makashin and published as part of his 'Materialy dlya bibliografii perevodov sochinenii Shchedrina na inostrannye yazyki i kriticheskoi literatury o nem za 1861–1933 gg.', *Literaturnoe nasledstvo*, xiii/xiv (M., 1934), 679–82. I am much indebted to J. S. G. Simmons for the expert advice and information he has given, to Garth M. Terry for supplying details of recent work on Saltykov, and to Christine Glenday and Professor J. V. Haney for their kindness in checking details of American publications not accessible to me.

A. TRANSLATIONS

1861

A.1 *Tchinovnicks. Sketches of provincial life, from the memoirs of the retired Conseiller de Cour Stchedrin (Saltikow)*. Translated, with notes, from the Russian by Frederic Aston. (London: L. Booth, 1861), [viii], 240 pp.

(Extracts from *Gubernskie ocherki*: 'Porfiry Petrovich'; '1-yi rasskaz pod"yachego'; '2-oi rasskaz pod"yachego'; 'Ozorniki'; 'Nadorvannye'; 'Knyazhna Anna L'vovna'; 'Priyatnoe semeistvo'; 'Nepriyatnoe poseshchenie (bal u Zhelvakova)')

Reviews: *Morning Post*, 15 Jan. 1861; *Literary Gazette*, 26 Jan. 1861; *Spectator*, 26 Jan. 1861; *Standard*, 5 Feb. 1861; *Athenaeum*, 16 Feb. 1861; *Examiner*, 2 Mar. 1861; *Saturday Review*, 2 Mar. 1861.

See also C.67.

1888

A.2   'The Lost Conscience'. Transl. M. Wright.

(*Skazki*: 'Propala sovest'')

Longman's Magazine, lxviii (June 1888), pp. 163–73.

(Translated from the French version of Ed. O'Farell [i.e. Alfred Léo] 'Conscience perdue' in: *Trois contes russes de Chtchédrine* (Paris, 1881))

1889

A.3   [Extracts (exemplifying 'Russian characteristics') beginning] (i) 'What is your view of the immortality of the soul . . .'; (ii) 'It has been ordained . . . that if a man is uneducated . . .'; (iii) 'Roguery is one of the forms of social life . . .'; (iv) 'If you manage the estate of another . . .'; (v) 'On the perron of a solitary house . . .'; (vi) 'Nay do but listen to the way he fooled the German . . .'; (vii) 'Why does our peasant go in bast shoes instead of leather boots?'; (viii) 'The common Russian man not only suffers . . .'; (ix) 'It has been observed . . . that the genuine Russian man is ever ready to lie'. Transl. E. J. Dillon.

(*Sovremennaya idilliya*: extracts from Chapter 2: (i) M. E. Saltykov-Shchedrin, *Sobranie sochinenii v 20-i tomakh* (henceforward *SS*) (M., 1965–77), xv(1), pp. 27–8; (ii) ibid., p. 24; *Blagonamerennye rechi*: extracts from 'V doroge': (iii) *SS*, xi, p. 29; (iv) ibid., p. 30; (v) ibid., pp. 31–2; (vi) ibid., pp. 34–5; *Pis'ma o provintsii*: extracts from Letter 6: (vii) *SS*, vii, p. 247; (viii) ibid., pp. 249–50; extract from Letter 1: (ix) *Otechestvennye zapiski*, 1868 no. 2, 'Sovremennoe obozrenie', pp. 358–9 (original text, not in *SS*)

(i)–(vi) in: E. B. Lanin [i.e. E. J. Dillon], 'Russian Characteristics', *The Fortnightly Review*, N.S. xlvi, no. 273 (September 1889), pp. 412–13, 422, no. 276 (December 1889), pp. 856–8; (i)–(ix) in: idem, *Russian Characteristics* (London: Chapman and Hall, 1892), pp. 13–14, 49–50, 67, 83–4, 149, 150–2.

1890

A.4   'The fool'. Transl.?

(*Skazki*: 'Durak')

Free Russia (London), [i], no. 5 (December 1890), pp. 16–19; ibid. (New York), [i], no. 5 (December 1890), pp. 16–19.

1891

A.5   'The Deceitful Editor and the Credulous Reader'. Transl.?

(*Skazki*: 'Obmanshchik-gazetchik i legkovernyi chitatel'')

Ibid. (London), ii, no. 4 (April 1891), pp. 13–14; ibid. (New York), [i], no. 9 (April 1891), pp. 13–14.

1892

A.6   'The Lost Conscience'. Transl. Mrs William Sharp.

(*Skazki*: 'Propala sovest'')

Short Stories (New York), ix, no. 1 (January 1892), pp. 33–42.

(Translated, without acknowledgement, from the French version of Ed. O'Farell, see A.2)

A.7   'Story of how one Peasant saved two Generals'. Transl.?

(*Skazki*: 'Povest' o tom, kak odin muzhik . . .')

Free Russia (London), iii, no. 1 (January 1892), pp. 13–15; ibid. (New York), ii, no. 6 (January 1892), pp. 14–16.

1893

A.8   'Misha and Vania: a forgotten story'. Transl.?

(*Nevinnye rasskazy*: 'Misha i Vanya')

Ibid. (London), iv, no. 1 (January 1893), pp. 13–15, (continued) iv, no. 2 (February 1893), pp. 28–31; ibid. (New York), iii, no. 6 (January 1893), pp. 13–15, (continued) iii, no. 7 (February 1893), pp. 13–14.

1895

A.9   'The Recollections of Onésime Chenapan'. Transl. E. L. Voynich.

(*Pompadury i pompadurshi*: extract from 'Mneniya znatnykh inostrantsev o pompadurakh': *SS*, viii, pp. 244–57)

In *The Humour of Russia*. Translated by E. L. Voynich, with an introduction by Stepniak (London: Walter Scott; New York: Charles Scribner and Sons, 1895), pp. 185–204.

A.10   'The Self-sacrificing Rabbit'. Transl. E. L. Voynich.

(*Skazki*: 'Samootverzhennyi zayats')

In: ibid., pp. 309–16.

See also A.32.

A.11   'The Eagle as Mecaenus [*sic*]'. Transl. E. L. Voynich.

(*Skazki*: 'Orel-metsenat')

In: ibid., pp. 335–49.

Review of *The Humour of Russia* and reference to 'The Eagle as Mecaenus': *Bookman* (London), viii, no. 44 (May 1895).

1899

A.12   'The Virtues and the Vices'. Transl. F[eliks] V[olkhovsky].

(*Skazki*: 'Dobrodeteli i poroki')

Free Russia (London), x, no. 11 (November 1899), pp. 76–8.

1900

A.13   'Easter Eve: a legend'. Transl. F[eliks] V[olkhovsky].

(*Skazki*: 'Khristova noch'')

Ibid. (London), xi, no. 4 (April 1900), pp. 42–4.

1902

A.14 'Conscience'. Transl.?

(*Skazki*: 'Propala sovest'')

Ibid. (London), xiii, no. 11 (November 1902), pp. 98–100.

A.15 'From "Beyond the Border"'. Transl.?

(*Za rubezhom*: 'Torzhestvuyushchaya svin'ya' and adjacent passages: *SS*, xiv, pp. 197–202)

In: Leo Wiener, *Anthology of Russian Literature from the earliest period to the present time* (New York and London: G. P. Putnam's Sons, 1902–3), ii, pp. 379–85.

1906

A.16 'Story of the Lost Conscience'. Transl.?

(*Skazki*: 'Propala sovest'')

Current Literature (New York), xl, no. 3 (March 1906), pp. 340–3.

1916

A.17 'The Old Governor's Favourite'. Transl.?

(*Pompadury i pompadurshi*: 'Staraya pompadursha')

Twentieth Century Russia (London), i, no. 3 (April 1916), pp. 188–207.

A.18 'Saltikov's "Fairy-tale of a Peasant and two Generals"'. Transl. C. E. Bechhöfer.

(*Skazki*: 'Povest' o tom, kak odin muzhik . . .')

New Age (London), 11 May 1916, pp. 37–8.

See also A.22.

A.19 *The Gollovlev Family*. Translated by Athelstan Ridgway. (London: Jarrold and Sons, [1916]). 283 pp.

(*Gospoda Golovlevy*)

Reviews: *Athenaeum*, May 1916; *Nation* (London), 27 May 1916; *New Statesman*, 1 July 1916 (Gerald Gould).

1917

A.20 'How a Muzhik fed two Officials'. Transl. Thomas Seltzer.

(*Skazki*: 'Povest' o tom, kak odin muzhik . . .')

In: *Best Russian Short Stories*. Compiled and edited by Thomas Seltzer. (New York: Boni and Liveright, [1917]), pp. 88–96.

See also A.21, 40, 53, 57.

A.21 'The Hungry Officials and the Accommodating Muzhik'.

Reprint of A.20 (with changed title) in: *Current Opinion* (New York), lxiii, no. 3 (September 1917), pp. 200–2.

A.22 'The Fairy-Tale of a Peasant and two Generals'.

Reprint of A.18 in: *A Russian Anthology in English*. Edited by C. E. Bechhofer. (London: Kegan Paul, Trench, Trubner; New York: E. P. Dutton, 1917), pp. 175–85.

A.23 *A Family of Noblemen*. Translated by A. Yarmolinsky. (New York: Boni and
      Liveright, 1917). [iv], 422 pp.

(*Gospoda Golovlevy*)

Reviews: *Bookman* (New York), xlvi (December 1917); *New York Times*, 9 Dec.
1917.

1918

A.24 'Konyaga'. Transl. Beatrix L. Tollemache.

(*Skazki*: 'Konyaga')

In: *The Village Priest and other stories, from the Russian of Militsina and Saltikov*.
Translated by Beatrix L. Tollemache, with an introduction by C. Hagberg
Wright. (London: T. Fisher Unwin, 1918), pp. 69–81.

Notice and review of *The Village Priest and other Stories*: *Times Literary Supplement*,
21 Nov., 19 Dec. 1918.

See also A.39.

A.25 'A Visit to a Russian Prison: I. Arenushka; II. The Old Believer'. Transl.
      Beatrix L. Tollemache.

(*Gubernskie ocherki*: 'V ostroge: "Arinushka"'; 'Kazusnye obstoyatel'stva:
"Starets"')

In: ibid., pp. 83–155.

A.26 'The Governor'. Transl. Beatrix L. Tollemache.

(*Skazki*: 'Prazdnyi razgovor')

In: ibid., pp. 157–71.

1920

A.27 'A Christmas Sermon'. Transl. Zénaïde A. Ragozin.

(*Skazki*: 'Rozhdestvenskaya skazka')

In: *Little Russian Masterpieces*. Chosen and translated . . . by Zénaïde A. Ragozin,
with an introduction and biographical notes by S. N. Syromiatnikof. (New York
and London: G. P. Putnam's Sons, 1920), ii, pp. 5–29.

A.28 'The Peasant and the two Excellencies: a fairy tale'. Transl. Zénaïde A. Ragozin.

(*Skazki*: 'Povest' o tom, kak odin muzhik . . .')

In: ibid., pp. 31–48.

A.29 'The Lost Conscience'. Transl. Zénaïde A. Ragozin.

(*Skazki*: 'Propala sovest'')

In: ibid., pp. 49–76.

A.30 'The Eagle, Patron of Learning: a fable'. Transl. Zénaïde A. Ragozin.

(*Skazki*: 'Orel-metsenat')

In: ibid., pp. 77–99.

1923

A.31 'Two Little Moujiks'. Transl.?

(*Nevinnye rasskazy*: 'Misha i Vanya')

In: *The Masterpiece Library of Short Stories*. Edited by J. A. Hammerton. (London: Educational Book Co., [1923]), xii, pp. 136–44.

A.32 'The Self-sacrificing Rabbit'.

Reprint of A.10 in: ibid., pp. 145–50.

A.33 'The Tale of how a Peasant fed two Generals'. Transl. Vera Volkhovsky.

(*Skazki*: 'Povest′ o tom, kak odin muzhik . . .')

New Leader (London), 16 February 1923, pp. 10–11.

Reprinted in *Fables* (A.41). See also A.62.

A.34 'The Self-sacrificing Rabbit'. Transl. Vera Volkhovsky.

(*Skazki*: 'Samootverzhennyi zayats')

Ibid., 18 May 1923, pp. 88–9.

Reprinted in *Fables* (A.41).

A.35 'The Deceitful Newspaper Man and the Credulous Reader'. Transl. Vera Volkhovsky.

(*Skazki*: 'Obmanshchik-gazetchik i legkovernyi chitatel′')

Ibid., 9 November 1923, p. 10.

Reprinted in *Fables* (A.41).

1924

A.36 *The Death of Pazukhin* . . . English translation by Julian Leigh. (The Moscow Art Theatre Series of Russian Plays, ed. O. M. Saylĕr, vi (Second Series)). (New York, Brentano's, [1924]). 55 pp.

(*Smert′ Pazukhina*)

A.37 'The Ram who could not remember'. Transl. Vera Volkhovsky.

(*Skazki*: 'Baran-nepomnyashchii')

New Leader (London), 11 January 1924, p. 10.

Reprinted in *Fables* (A.41).

A.38 'The Wild Squire'. Transl. Vera Volkhovsky.

(*Skazki*: 'Dikii pomeshchik')

Ibid., 25 April 1924, p. 16.

Reprinted in *Fables* (A.41).

1929

A.39 'Konyaga'.

Reprint of A.24 in: *From Confucius to Mencken: the trend of the world's best thought as expressed by famous writers of all time*. Edited by F. H. Pritchard. (New York: Harper & Brothers; London: George G. Harrap [title: *Great Essays of all Nations*], 1929), pp. 745–50.

1930

A.40 'How a Muzhik fed two Russian Officials'.

Reprint of A.20 (with changed title) in: *The Golden Book Magazine*, xii, no. 72 (December 1930), pp. 62–5.

1931

A.41 *Fables*. By Shchedrin (M. E. Saltykov). Translated from the Russian by Vera
Volkhovsky. (London: Chatto and Windus, 1931 (The Phoenix Library)). xii,
256 pp.

Contents: Introductory: Shchedrin-Saltykov; 'The Tale of how a Peasant fed two
Generals'; 'The Very Wise Minnow'; 'The Conscience is lost!'; 'The Deceitful
Newspaper-man and the Credulous Reader'; 'The Rabbit who had the Habit of
Sound Thinking'; 'The Old Nag'; 'The Carp who was an Idealist'; 'Faithful
Trésor'; 'The Liberal'; 'The Poor Wolf'; 'An Idle Conversation'; 'A Village Fire';
'The Self-sacrificing Rabbit'; 'The Unsleeping Eye'; 'The Ram who could not
remember'; 'The Siskin's Tragedy'; 'Kramólnikov's Misadventure'; 'The
Suppliant Crow'; 'The Fool'; 'The Wild Squire'; 'Christ's Night'; 'The Virtues
and the Vices'.

(*Skazki*: 'Povest' o tom, kak odin muzhik . . .'; 'Premudryi piskar''; 'Propala
sovest''; 'Obmanshchik-gazetchik i legkovernyi chitatel''; 'Zdravomyslennyi
zayats'; 'Konyaga'; 'Karas'-idealist'; 'Vernyi Trezor'; 'Liberal'; 'Bednyi volk';
'Prazdnyi razgovor'; 'Derevenskii pozhar'; 'Samootverzhennyi zayats'; 'Nedremannoe oko'; 'Baran-nepomnyashchii'; 'Chizhikovo gore'; 'Priklyuchenie s
Kramol'nikovym'; 'Voron-chelobitchik'; 'Durak'; 'Dikii pomeshchik'; 'Khristova
noch''; 'Dobrodeteli i poroki')

Includes reprints of A.33, 34, 35, 37, 38.

Notice and review: *Times Literary Supplement*, 15, 22 Oct. 1931.

See also A.50, 71, 75.

A.42 *The Golovlyov Family*. Translated by Natalie Duddington, with an introduction by
Edward Garnett. (London: George Allen and Unwin, 1931). 336 pp.

(*Gospoda Golovlevy*)

Reviews: *Times Literary Supplement*, 15 Oct. (notice), 22 Oct. (review) 1931;
Sunday Referee, 18 Oct. 1931 (Edward Crickmay); *Spectator*, 24 Oct. 1931
(J. Rodko).

See also A.43, 45, 52, 59, 63, 66, 69, 74, and (revised version) 61, 70.

A.43 *The Golovlyov Family* (New York: The Macmillan Company, 1931), [iv], 336 pp.

Reprint of A.42.

Reviews: *American Mercury* (New York), xxv (January 1932); *Booklist* (Chicago),
xxviii (February 1932); *Boston Transcript* (Boston), 4 Nov. 1931; *New Republic*
(New York), 6 Jan. 1932; *New York Times*, 4 Oct. 1931.

A.44 'The Nostalgic Ram'. Transl. J. Chaitkin.

(*Skazki*: 'Baran-nepomnyashchii')

The Golden Book Magazine (New York), xiv, no. 82 (October 1931), pp. 217–19.

1934

A.45 *The Golovlyov Family*. (London: J. M. Dent and Sons; New York: E. P. Dutton,
1934 (Everyman's Library, no. 908)). x, 324 pp.

Reprint of A.42.

1939

A.46 'The Sophisticated Gudgeon'. Transl.?

(*Skazki*: 'Premudryi piskar'')

International Literature (Moscow), 1939, no. 6, pp. 4–8.

A.47 'The Self-sacrificing Hare'. Transl.?

(*Skazki*: 'Samootverzhennyi zayats')

Ibid., pp. 8–13.

A.48 'The Liberal'. Transl.?

(*Skazki*: 'Liberal')

Ibid., pp. 13–16.

A.49 'Boy in Pants and Boy without'. Transl. Gleb Struve.

(*Za rubezhom*: 'Mal'chik v shtanakh i mal'chik bez shtanov': *SS*, xiv, pp. 32–42)

The Slavonic and East European Review (London), xviii, no. 52 (July 1939), pp. 18–28.

1941

A.50 *Fables* (London, Chatto and Windus, 1941 (The Pelham Library)).

Reprint of A.41.

Review: D. J. Enright, 'Shchedrin: the Russian Swift', *Scrutiny* (Cambridge), x, no. 4 (April 1942).

1943

A.51 [Extract beginning] 'Why does our peasant go in bast shoes instead of leather boots?' Tranls. adapted from version of E. J. Dillon (A.3)?

(*Pis'ma o provintsii*: extracts from Letter 6: *SS*, vii, pp. 247, 249–50)

In: *The Russian Horizon: an anthology*. Compiled by N. Gangulee, with a foreword by H. G. Wells. (London: George Allen and Unwin, 1943), pp. 22–3.

A.52 [Extract headed] 'Little Judas speeds his brother on the way'. Transl. Natalie Duddington.

(*Gospoda Golovlevy*: part of 'Po-rodstvennomu': *SS*, xiii, 73–93)

In: *A Treasury of Russian Life and Humor*. Edited, with an introduction, by John Cournos. (New York: Coward-McCann, 1943), pp. 415–34.

Reprinted from A.42.

A.53 'How a Muzhik fed two Officials'.

Reprint of A.20 in: ibid., pp. 588–94.

A.54 'The Virtues and the Vices'. Transl. B. G. Guerney.

(*Skazki*: 'Dobrodeteli i poroki')

In: *A Treasury of Russian Literature*. Edited by Bernard Gilbert Guerney. (New York: The Vanguard Press, 1943; London: The Bodley Head, 1948), pp. 538–47.

1946

A.55 'Mr and Mrs Cheriozov'. Transl. E. M. Walton.

(*Melochi zhizni*: 'Cherezovy muzh i zhena')

In: *A Second Series of Representative Russian Stories: Leskov to Andreyev*. Selected and edited and with an introduction by Janko Lavrin. (London: Westhouse, 1946), pp. 64–76.

A.56 'The Ideals of a Carp'. Transl. E. M. Walton.

(*Skazki*: 'Karas'-idealist')

In: *Russian Humorous Stories*. Edited and introduced by Janko Lavrin. (London: Sylvan Press, 1946), pp. 53–67.

A.57 'How a Muzhik fed two Russian Officials'.

(*Skazki*: 'Povest' o tom, kak odin muzhik . . .')

Reprint of A.20 (with changed title) in: *Strange to Tell: Stories of the Marvelous and Mysterious*. Edited by Marjorie Fischer and Rolfe Humphries. (New York: Julian Messner, 1946), pp. 310–17.

1947

A.58 'Tale of how one Muzhik kept two Brass-hats well fed'. Transl. B. G. Guerney.

(*Skazki*: 'Povest' o tom, kak odin muzhik . . .')

In: *The Portable Russian Reader. A Collection newly translated from classical and present-day Authors*. Chosen and done into English, with a foreword and biographical notes by Bernard Gilbert Guerney. (New York: The Viking Press, 1947), pp. 190–201.

1955

A.59 *The Golovlyov Family*. (London: J. M. Dent and Sons; New York: E. P. Dutton, 1955).

Reprint of A.42 in Everyman's Library edition (A.45).

1956?

A.60 *Tales from M. Saltykov-Shchedrin*. Translated by Dorian Rottenberg, edited by John Gibbons. (Moscow: Foreign Languages Publishing House, [1956?] (Classics of Russian Literature)). 199 pp.

Contents: 'How one Plain Peasant fed two High Officials'; 'The Wild Gentleman'; 'The Sapient Minnow'; 'The Selfless Rabbit'; 'The Virtues and the Vices'; 'Bears in Government'; 'The Deceitful Newsmonger and the Credulous Reader'; 'The Eagle—Patron of Arts'; 'The Idealistic Crucian'; 'The Siskin's Calamity'; 'The two Neighbours'; 'The Rational Rabbit'; 'The Liberal'; 'The Old Nag'; 'Idle Talk'; 'The Mighty Bogatyr'; 'The Crow that went in Search of Truth'; 'Kramolnikov's Misfortune'; 'A Tale of the Zealous Governor whose Industry caused his Superiors Concern'.

(*Skazki*: 'Povest' o tom, kak odin muzhik . . .'; 'Dikii pomeshchik'; 'Premudryi piskar''; 'Samootverzhennyi zayats'; 'Dobrodeteli i poroki'; 'Medved' na voevodstve'; 'Obmanshchik-gazetchik i legkovernyi chitatel''; 'Orel-metsenat'; 'Karas'-idealist'; 'Chizhikovo gore'; 'Sosedi'; 'Zdravomyslennyi zayats'; 'Liberal'; 'Konyaga'; 'Prazdnyi razgovor'; 'Bogatyr''; 'Voron-chelobitchik'; 'Priklyuchenie s Kramol'nikovym'; *Sovremennaya idilliya*: extract from Chapter 20: 'Skazka o retivom nachal'nike')

See also A.79, 81, 82, 83.

1957

A.61 *Judas Golovlyov*. Edited by Olga Shartse. (Moscow: Foreign Languages Publishing House, [1957] (Classics of Russian Literature)). 366 pp.

(*Gospoda Golovlevy*)

Reprint of A.42 (revised). See also A.70.

1958

A.62 'How a Muzhik fed two Officials'.

Reprint of A.33 in: *Great Russian Short Stories*. Edited and introduced by Norris Houghton. (New York: Dell Publishing Co., 1958), pp. 85–93.

1961

A.63 *The Golovlovs*. Translated by Andrew R. MacAndrew, with an afterword by William E. Harkins. (New York: The New American Library, 1961 (Signet Classics)). 317 pp.

(*Gospoda Golovlevy*)

1962

A.64 *The Golovlyov Family*. (London: J. M. Dent and Sons; New York: E. P. Dutton, 1962).

Reprint of A.42 in Everyman's Library edition (A.45).

1965

A.65 'The Eagle Patron'. Transl. John W. Strachan.

(*Skazki*: 'Orel-metsenat')

In: *15 Great Russian Short Stories*. Translated by John W. Strachan and Rosalind A. Zoglin. (New York: Washington Square Press, 1965), pp. 47–62.

1968

A.66 *The Golovlyov Family*. (London: Heron Books, 1968; also issued later undated and without Heron Books imprint (The Greatest Masterpieces of Russian Literature)).

Reprint of A.42.

1974

A.67 'Porfiry Petrovich'. Transl. William Edward Brown.

(*Gubernskie ocherki*: 'Porfiry Petrovich')

Russian Literature Triquarterly (Ann Arbor, Michigan), x (Fall, 1974), pp. 79–91.

A.68 'Zubatov'. Transl. David Lapeza.

(*Nevinnye rasskazy*: 'Zubatov')

Ibid., pp. 67–76.

A.69 *The Golovlyov Family*. (London: J. M. Dent and Sons; New York: E. P. Dutton, c.1974).

Reprint of A.42 in Everyman's Library edition (A.45).

1975

A.70 *The Golovlyovs*. Translated by Olga Shartse, with an introduction by S. Makashin. (Moscow: Progress Publishers, 1975). 326 pp.

Reprint of A.61 (with changed title). Olga Shartse incorrectly named as *translator*, cf. A.61 = (unattributed Duddington) translation '*edited* by Olga Shartse'.

1976

A.71 *Fables* (Westport, Connecticut: Greenwood Press, 1976).

Reprint of A.41.

A.72 *Pazukhin's Death*. Transl. Laurence Senelick.

(*Smert' Pazukhina*)

Russian Literature Triquarterly (Ann Arbor, Michigan), xiv (Winter, 1976), pp. 321–76.

1977

A.73 *The Golovlyov Family*. Translated by Samuel D. Cioran, with an introduction by Carl D. Proffer. (Ann Arbor, Michigan: Ardis, 1977). xxxiv, 251 pp.

(*Gospoda Golovlevy*)

Review: *Canadian Slavonic Papers*, xx, no. 4 (1978) (Barbara Sharratt).

A.74 *The Golovlyov Family*. (Westport, Connecticut: Hyperion Press, 1977 (The Hyperion Library of World Literature)).

Reprint of A.42.

A.75 *Fables* (Westport, Connecticut: Hyperion Press, 1977 (The Hyperion Library of World Literature)).

Reprint of A.41.

1980

A.76 *The History of a Town*. Translated, with introduction and notes, by I. P. Foote. (Oxford: Willem A. Meeuws, 1980). xv, 192 pp.

(*Istoriya odnogo goroda*)

Reviews: *Sunday Times*, 13 Apr. 1980 (Bernard Levin); *Times Literary Supplement*, 23 May 1980 (Edwin Morgan); *Sunday Telegraph*, 25 May 1980 (A.W.); *Observer*, 22 June 1980 (Anthony Burgess), reprinted as 'Gloopy Glupov' in: Anthony Burgess, *Homage to Qwert Yuiop: selected journalism, 1975–1985* (London: Hutchinson, 1986); *London Review of Books*, ii, no. 17 (4–17 Sept. 1980) (Virginia Llewellyn Smith); *New York Review of Books*, xxvii, no. 14 (25 Sept. 1980) (V. S. Pritchett); *Slavic and East European Journal*, xxv, no. 3 (1981) (Keith Armes); *Russkaya literatura*, 1982, no. 2 (N. M. Keleinikova, 'Khronika goroda Glupova po-angliiski').

1982

A.77 *The History of a Town*. Translated and edited by Susan C. Brownsberger. (Ann Arbor, Michigan: Ardis, 1982). 219 pp.

(*Istoriya odnogo goroda*)

Review: *Times Literary Supplement*, 9 July 1982 (Geoffrey A. Hosking).

1985

A.78 *The Pompadours: a satire on the art of government*. Translated, with an introduction, by David Magarshack. (Ann Arbor, Michigan: Ardis, 1985). xiv, 280 pp.

Review: *Times Literary Supplement*, 29 Aug. 1986 (D. J. Enright).

A.79 'The Sapient Minnow'.

(*Skazki*: 'Premudryi piskar'')

In: *Anthology of Russian Short Stories*, i (Moscow: Raduga, 1985), pp. 276–81.

Reprinted from A.60.

1986

A.80 *The Golovlevs*. Translated, with introduction and notes, by I. P. Foote. (Oxford and New York: Oxford University Press, 1986 (World's Classics)). xix, 316 pp.

(*Gospoda Golovlevy*)

Reviews: *Times Literary Supplement*, 29 Aug. 1986 (D. J. Enright); *Slavonic and East European Review*, lxvi, no. 1 (January 1988) (Richard Freeborn).

1987

A.81 'How one Plain Peasant fed two High Officials'.

(*Skazki*: 'Povest' o tom, kak odin muzhik . . .')

In: *In the Depths: Nineteenth-Century Russian Stories* (Moscow: Raduga, 1987), pp. 188–93.

Reprinted from A.60.

A.82 'The Wild Squire'.

(*Skazki*: 'Dikii pomeshchik')

In: ibid., pp. 193–9.

Reprinted from A.60.

A.83 'The Old Nag'.

(*Skazki*: 'Konyaga')

In: ibid., pp. 199–203.

Reprinted from A.60.

1988

A.84 *The Golovlyov Family*. Translated and with an introduction by Ronald Wilks. Introductory essay by V. S. Pritchett. (Harmondsworth: Penguin Books, 1988 (Penguin Classics)). 286 pp.

(*Gospoda Golovlevy*)

Introductory essay = 'The Hypocrite' (C.33).

Index of Translations

References in italic indicate that the translation is a reprint, those in parentheses that the translation is of only part or parts of the work referred to. Translations of individual *skazki* are listed separately under *Skazki*. * signifies a revised version of an earlier translation.

B. EDITIONS OF SALTYKOV'S WORKS IN RUSSIAN

B.1 M. E. Saltykov, *Gubernskie ocherki*: 'Vvedenie'. In: *Third Russian Book. Extracts from Aksákov, Grigoróvich, Hérzen, Saltykóv.* Accented and edited . . . by Nevill Forbes. (Oxford: Clarendon Press, 1917), pp. 113–27.

B.2 M. E. Saltykov-Shchedrin, *Bogomol'tsy, stranniki i proezzhie. Proshlye vremena* (Oksford: Tipografiya Klarendon, 1917; on cover: Saltykov. *Pilgrims and Wayfarers. Bygone Times* (Oxford: Clarendon Press); at head of cover: 'Oxford Russian Plain Texts'). 80 pp.

(Extracts from *Gubernskie ocherki*: 'Bogomol'tsy, stranniki i proezzhie: "Obshchaya kartina"'; 'Proshlye vremena: "Pervyi rasskaz pod"yachego"; "Vtoroi rasskaz pod"yachego"')

B.3 M.Ya. (*sic*) Saltykov-Shchedrin, *Skazki* (N'yu-Iork: Knizhnyi sklad M. Gurevicha, 1919; first issued in 6 parts in the series 'Biblioteka russkikh pisatelei', *c.*1919). 190 pp.

Contents: 'Premudryi piskar''; 'Karas'-idealist'; 'Bednyi volk'; 'Zdravomyslennyi zayats'; 'Vernyi Trezor'; 'Baran-nepomnyashchii'; 'Kisel''; 'Dobrodeteli i poroki'; 'Nedremannoe oko'; 'Durak'; 'Konyaga'; 'Khristova noch''; 'Rozhdestvenskaya skazka'; 'Putem-dorogoyu'; 'Sosedi'; 'Liberal'; 'Giena'; 'Dikii pomeshchik'; 'Samootverzhennyi zayats'; 'Povest' o tom, kak odin muzhik dvukh generalov prokormil'.

B.4　M. E. Saltykov-Shchedrin, *Selected Satirical Writings*. Edited by I. P. Foote. (Oxford, Clarendon Press, 1977). 284 pp.

(Extracts from *Blagonamerennye rechi*; *Dnevnik provintsiala v Peterburge*; *Gospoda Tashkenttsy*; *Gubernskie ocherki*; *Istoriya odnogo goroda*; *Kruglyi god*; *Melochi zhizni*; *Pis'ma k teten'ke*; *Pompadury i pompadurshi*; *Satiry v proze*; *Skazki*; *Sovremennaya idilliya*; *Ubezhishche Monrepo*; *V srede umerennosti i akkuratnosti*; *Za rubezhom*)

Reviews: *Times Literary Supplement*, 26 Aug. 1977 (Richard Freeborn); *Slavic Review*, xxxvii, no. 2 (1978) (C. Kulesov); *Slavonic and East European Review*, lvi (1978) (Arnold B. McMillin); *Journal of Russian Studies*, no. 35 (1978) (C. R. Pike); *Russian Language Journal*, xxxiii, no. 115 (1979) (H. Gamburg); *Modern Language Review*, lxxiv, no. 1 (1979) (D. C. Offord).

C. CRITICISM

1863

C.1　Unsigned, 'Stchedrin and his School', *Nevsky Magazine* (St Petersburg), i (1863), pp. 579–92.

1870

C.2　I. Tourguèneff [I. S. Turgenev], 'History of a Town. Edited by M. E. Saltykoff. (*Istoriya odnogo goroda*). St Petersburg: 1870', *The Academy*, 1 March 1871, pp. 151–2.

1874

C.3　Eugene Schuyler, [Annual review of Russian literature], *The Athenaeum*, 3 January 1874.
　　(For Saltykov, see p. 17.)

1881

C.4　Nicholas Storojenko [N. I. Storozhenko], [Annual review of Russian literature], ibid., 31 December 1881.
　　(For Saltykov, see p. 893.)

1883

C.5　Idem, [Annual review of Russian literature], ibid., 29 December 1883.
　　(For Saltykov, see p. 855.)

1884

C.6　*Daily News*, 22 October, 24 November 1884.
　　(22 October: report by the *Daily News* Odessa correspondent claiming that

student riots in Kiev had been caused by the rejection of Saltykov's nomination as their representative, and that he, as one of the 'Russian Republican party' had been 'several times under arrest on charges of sedition'; 24 November: these claims denied by Saltykov in letter to the Editor.)

1885

C.7 *The Scottish Review*, April 1885, pp. 387–9; July 1885, pp. 193–5.
     (References to Saltykov's *Pestrye pis'ma* (published in *Vestnik Evropy*) in summaries of foreign journals.)

1887

C.8 Serge [A.] Varsher, [Annual review of Russian literature], *The Athenaeum*, 2 July 1887.
     (For Saltykov, see p. 15.)

1888

C.9 P. Kropotkin, [Annual review of Russian literature], ibid., 7 July 1888.
     (For Saltykov, see p. 26.)

1889

C.10 I. F. Hapgood, 'A Russian Satirist', *The Nation* (New York), xlix, no. 1253, 4 July 1889, pp. 8–10.
      (Obituary.)

1891

C.11 Unsigned, 'Recent Russian Literature. A Quarterly Causerie by our St Petersburg Correspondent', *The Review of Reviews*, iii, no. 16 (April 1891).
      (For Saltykov, see p. 386.)

1893

C.12 [S. N. Krivenko], 'Saltykov (Shchedrin). From a Biography by S. N. Krivenko', *Free Russia* (London), iv, no. 5 (May 1893), pp. 72–5.
      (Characterization of Saltykov based on S. N. Krivenko, *M. E. Saltykov . . . Biograficheskii ocherk* (Spb., 1891))

1900

C.13 K. Waliszewski, *A History of Russian Literature* (London: William Heinemann, 1900).
      (For Saltykov, see pp. 309–18.)

1902

C.14 G[eorge] D[obson], 'Saltykoff (Stchedrin), Michael Evgrafovich', in: *The Encyclopaedia Britannica*, 10 ed., xxxii (New Volumes, viii) (Edinburgh and London, 1902), p. 394.

1905

C.15 P. Kropotkin, *Russian Literature* (London: Duckworth, 1905 and later editions) [Spine-title: *Ideals and Realities in Russian Literature*].
(For Saltykov, see pp. 282–4.)

1908

C.16 A. Brückner, *A Literary History of Russia*. Edited by Ellis H. Minns, translated [from the German] by H. Havelock (London and Leipsic: T. Fisher Unwin, 1908).
(For Saltykov, see chapter 16 'Satire. Saltykóv', pp. 452–75.)

1911

C.17 Unsigned, 'Saltykov, Michael Evgrafovich', in: *Nelson's Encyclopaedia* (London, etc.: Thomas Nelson and Sons, 1911), xx, p. 92.

1913

C.18 Unsigned, 'Saltykov, Michael Evgrafovich', in: *The Everyman Encyclopaedia* (London: J. M. Dent and Sons; New York: E. P. Dutton, 1913), xi, p. 275 (revised entry 4 ed. (1958), xi, p. 59).

1914/15

C.19 M. Baring, *An Outline of Russian Literature* (London: Williams and Norgate; New York: Henry Holt, 1914/15 (Home University Library of Modern Knowledge)).
(For Saltykov, see pp. 184–9.)

1916

C.20 A. Bennett, 'Some Adventures among Russian Fiction', in: *The Soul of Russia*, ed. Winifred Stephens (London: Macmillan, 1916).
(For *Gospoda Golovlevy*, see p. 88.)

C.21 S. Naumoff, 'Shtedrine on Germany', *Twentieth Century Russia*, i, no. 4 (July 1916), pp. 312–16.

1921

C.22 M. J. Olgin, *A Guide to Russian Literature, 1820–1917* (London: Jonathan Cape, 1921).
(For Saltykov, see pp. 126–8.)

1924

C.23 Previews, reviews, and comment on Moscow Art Theatre production of *Smert' Pazukhina* in America, 1924: *Tribune*, 10 Feb. 1924; *World*, 10 Feb. 1924; *American*, 12 Feb. 1924 (A. Dale); *Herald*, 12 Feb. 1924 (A. Woolcott); *New Plays*, 12 Feb. 1924 (two items: (i) R. G. Welsch, (ii) 'Playgoer'); *Tribune*, 12 Feb. 1924; *Telegraph*, 12 Feb. 1924 (A.W.); *World*, 12 Feb. 1924 (E. W. Osborn); ibid., 13 Feb. 1924; *Times*, 13 Feb. 1924 (J. Corbin); *Telegraph*, 17 Feb. 1924.

1925

C.24 D. S. Mirsky, *Modern Russian Literature* (London: Oxford University Press, 1925).
(For Saltykov, see pp. 37–8.)

1927

C.25 J. Lavrin, *Russian Literature* (London: Ernest Benn, 1927 (Benn's Sixpenny Library)).
(For Saltykov, see p. 42.)

C.26 D. S. Mirsky, *A History of Russian Literature from the beginnings to the death of Dostoyevsky (1881)* (London: George Routledge and Sons, 1927).
(For Saltykov, see pp. 358–62.)

1931

C.27 Unsigned [R. D. Charques], 'A Russian Satirist', *The Times Literary Supplement*, 22 October 1931, pp. 809–10.
(Review article on Saltykov in connection with the publication of *The Golovlyov Family* (A.42) and *Fables* (A.41).)

1935

C.28 Unsigned, 'Saltykov, Mikhail Evgrafovich', *The Columbia Encyclopedia* (New York: Columbia University Press; London, etc.: George C. Harrap, 1935), p. 1561.

1939

C.29 A. Lavretsky, 'Saltykov-Shchedrin—Great Russian Satirist', *International Literature* (Moscow), 1939, no. 6, pp. 72–8.

1940

C.30 N. Strelsky, *Saltykov and the Russian Squire* (New York: Columbia University Press, 1940). xii, 176 pp.
Reviews: *The Russian Review* (New York), i, no. 1 (November 1941), pp. 119–20 (Gilbert Highet); *Slavonic and East European Review*, xx (American Series, i) (1941), pp. 347–54 (Wacław Lednicki). See also Theodore Dreiser, letter to N. Strelsky, 9 Oct. 1939 (*Letters of Theodore Dreiser, a selection*, ed. R. H. Elias (Philadelphia, 1959), iii, pp. 846–8).
Reprinted 1966; see C.50.

1942

C.31 J. Lavrin, *An Introduction to the Russian Novel* (London: Methuen, 1942).
(For Saltykov, see pp. 82–7.)

1943

C.32 N. Strelsky, 'A New Light on Saltykov's Philosophy', in: A. Kaun and E. J. Simmons (eds.), *Slavic Studies [in Honor of George Rapall Noyes]* (Ithaca, N.Y.: Cornell University Press, 1943), pp. 199–212.

1946

C.33 V. S. Pritchett, *The Living Novel* (London: Chatto and Windus, 1946).
(For *Gospoda Golovlevy*, see 'The Hypocrite', pp. 226–32.)
'The Hypocrite' reprinted in A.84.

1947

C.34 R. Hare, *Russian Literature from Pushkin to the Present Day* (London: Methuen, 1947 (Home Study Books)).
(For Saltykov, see pp. 94–7.)

1950

C.35 Unsigned, 'Saltykov, Mikhail Evgrafovich', in: *Chambers's Encyclopaedia*, New Edition (London: George Newnes, 1950), xii, p. 172.

1953

C.36 J[anko] L[avrin], 'Saltykov-Shchedrin, Mikhail Evgrafovich', in: *Cassell's Encyclopaedia of Literature*, ed. S. H. Steinberg (London: Cassell, 1953), ii, p. 1444.

C.37 M. Slonim, *Modern Russian Literature. From Chekhov to the Present* (New York: Oxford University Press, 1953).
(For Saltykov, see pp. 31–9.)

1956

C.38 V. Tschebotarioff Bill, 'The Dead Souls of Russia's Merchant World', *The Russian Review* (Hanover, New Hampshire), xv, no. 4 (October 1956), pp. 245–58.
(On the merchant world in the works of Ostrovsky, Saltykov, and Gor'ky.)

C.39 W. E. Harkins, 'Saltykov, Mikhail Yevgrafovich', in: idem, *Dictionary of Russian Literature* (New York: Philosophical Library; London: George Allen and Unwin, 1956), pp. 343–5.

1957

C.40 H. Muchnic, Review of: Kyra Sanine, *Saltykov-Chtchédrine: sa vie et ses œuvres* (Paris, 1955) in: *The Russian Review* (Hanover, New Hampshire), xvi, no. 4 (October 1957), pp. 79–80.

1958

C.41 M. Slonim, *An Outline of Russian Literature* (London, New York, etc.: Oxford University Press, 1958 (The Home University Library of Modern Knowledge, 236)).
(For Saltykov, see pp. 129–31.)

1959

C.42 D. V. Grishin, 'The Problem of Dictatorship in the work of Dostoevsky and S. Schedrin', *The Australian Quarterly* (Sydney), xxxi, no. 3 (September 1959), pp. 82–91.

1960

C.43 E. M. Almedingen, 'The Supernatural in Russian Literature', *Essays by Divers Hands* (Transactions of the Royal Society of Literature), N.S. xxx (1960), pp. 68–84.

(For *Gospoda Golovlevy*, see pp. 78–80.)

1961

C.44 M. Slonim, *Russian Theater from the Empire to the Soviets* (Cleveland and New York: World Publishing Co., 1961; London: Methuen, 1963).

(For *Smert' Pazukhina*, see pp. 69–70.)

C.45 S. V. Utechin, 'Saltykov, Mikhail Yevgrafovich', in: idem, *Everyman's Concise Encyclopaedia of Russia* (London: J. M. Dent and Sons; New York: E. P. Dutton, 1961), p. 471.

C.46 Unsigned, 'Saltykóv, Mikhail Yevgráfovich', in: *McGraw-Hill Encyclopedia of Russia and the Soviet Union*, ed. Michael T. Florinsky (New York, Toronto, London: McGraw-Hill Book Company, 1961), p. 495.

1964

C.47 H. Gifford, *The Novel in Russia. From Pushkin to Pasternak* (London: Hutchinson, 1964 (Hutchinson University Library)).

('Saltykov-Shchedrin: *The Golovlyov Family*', pp. 97–107.)

1965

C.48 Unsigned, 'Saltykov, Mikhail Evgrafovich', in: W. R. Benét (ed.), *The Reader's Encyclopaedia*, 2 ed. (London: Adam and Charles Black, 1965), p. 892.

1966

C.49 T. S. Lindstrom, *A Concise History of Russian Literature*, i: *From the beginnings to Chekhov* (London: University of London Press; New York: New York University Press, 1966).

(For Saltykov, see pp. 160–3.)

C.50 N. Strelsky, *Saltykov and the Russian Squire* (New York: AMS Press, 1966). Reprint of C.30.

C.51 Unsigned [I. P. Foote], 'Coded Satire', *The Times Literary Supplement*, 18 August 1966, pp. 733–4.

(Review article on Saltykov in connection with the publication of *Sobranie sochinenii v 20-i tomakh* (Moscow, 1965–77), i–iii.)

1967

C.52 D[avid] M[agarshack], 'Saltykov, Mikhail Evgrafovich', in: *Encyclopaedia Britannica* (Chicago, etc., 1967), xix, p. 961.

C.53 L[eon] R[utman] and H[arvey] A. H[arvey], 'Saltykov-Shchedrin, Mikhail (Y)evgrafovich', in: *European Authors 1000–1900: a Biographical Dictionary of European Literature*, ed. Stanley J. Kunitz and Vineta Colby (New York: The H. W. Wilson Company, 1967), pp. 827–8.

1968

C.54 I. P. Foote, 'M. E. Saltykov-Shchedrin: *The Golovlyov Family*', *Forum for Modern Language Studies* (St Andrews), iv, no. 1 (January 1968), pp. 53–63.

Reprinted in: Cherie D. Abbey and Janet Mullane (eds.), *Nineteenth-Century Literature Criticism* . . ., xvi (Detroit: Gale Research Company, 1987), pp. 359–63.

C.55 I. P. Foote, 'Reaction or Revolution: the Ending of Saltykov's *History of a Town*', *Oxford Slavonic Papers*, NS i (1968), pp. 105–25.

C.56 W. N. Hargreaves-Mawdsley, 'Saltykov-Shchedrin, Mikhail Evgrafovich', in: *Everyman's Dictionary of European Writers* (London: J. M. Dent and Sons; New York: E. P. Dutton, 1968), p. 472.

1969

C.57 Unsigned, 'Saltykov, Mikhail Yevgrafovich', in: *The Penguin Companion to Literature: Europe*, ed. Anthony Thorlby (London: Allen Lane, The Penguin Press, 1969), p. 691.

1970

C.58 P. Bitsilli, 'The Revival of Allegory', in: *Nabokov. Criticism, reminiscences, translations, and tributes*, ed. Alfred Appel and Charles Newman (Evanston, Ill.: Northwestern University Press, 1970; London: Weidenfeld and Nicolson, 1971), pp. 102–18.

(Translation of article published in Russian in *Sovremennye zapiski* (Paris), lxi (1936).)

(For Saltykov, see pp. 103–11.)

C.59 K. D. Kramer, 'Satiric Form in Saltykov's *Gospoda Golovlevy*', *The Slavic and East European Journal* (Madison, Wisconsin), xiv, no. 4 (1970), pp. 453–64.

1973

C.60 J. Lavrin, *A Panorama of Russian Literature* (London: University of London Press, 1973).

(For Saltykov, see pp. 171–3.)

1976

C.61 A. Calder, *Russia Discovered: Nineteenth-century Fiction from Pushkin to Chekhov* (London: Heinemann; New York: Barnes and Noble Books, 1976).

(For Saltykov, see pp. 104–7.)

C.62 W. M. Todd, 'The Anti-hero with a Thousand Faces: Saltykov-Shchedrin's Porfiry Golovlev', *Studies in the Literary Imagination* (Atlanta, Georgia), ix, no. 1 (1976), pp. 87–105.

1977

C.63 M. Ehre, 'A Classic of Russian Realism: Form and Meaning in *The Golovlyovs*', *Studies in the Novel* (Denton, Texas), ix (1977), pp. 3–16.

C.64 V. Setchkarev, '[Russian Literature] From the Golden to the Silver Age', in:

R. Auty and D. Obolensky (eds.), *An Introduction to Russian Language and Literature* (*Companion to Russian Studies*, ii) (Cambridge, London, etc.: Cambridge University Press, 1977).
(For Saltykov, see pp. 160–1.)

1979

C.65 I. P. Foote, 'Quintessential Saltykov: *Ubezhishche Monrepo*', *Oxford Slavonic Papers*, NS xii (1979), pp. 84–103.

1980

C.66 R. Neuhäuser, 'The Early Prose of Saltykov-Shchedrin and Dostoevskii: Parallels and Echoes', *Canadian Slavonic Papers* (Toronto), xxii, no. 3 (1980), pp. 372–87.

1981

C.67 I. P. Foote, 'Frederic Aston's *Tchinovnicks* and Mr Adams', *Oxford Slavonic Papers*, NS xiv (1981), pp. 93–106.

1984

C.68 F. M. Bartholomew, 'Saltykov, Miliutin, and Maikov: a Forgotten Circle', *Canadian Slavonic Papers* (Toronto), xxvi, no. 4 (1984), pp. 283–95.

1985

C.69 P. Merivale, '"One endless round": *Something Happened* and the Purgatorial Novel', *English Studies in Canada* (Fredericton, New Brunswick), xi, no. 4 (1985), pp. 438–49.
(Compares Joseph Heller's *Something Happened* with other novels, including *Gospoda Golovlevy*.)

C.70 C[harles] A. M[oser], 'Saltykov-Shchedrin, Mikhail Evgrafovich', in: *Handbook of Russian Literature*, ed. Victor Terras (New Haven and London: Yale University Press, 1985), pp. 381–3.

1988

C.71 Previews and reviews of *Golovlovo*, dramatized adaptation of *Gospoda Golovlevy* by Jack Winter, broadcast on BBC Radio 3, 12 April 1988: *Yorkshire Post*, 9 Apr. 1988; *Times*, 12 Apr. 1988 (P. Davalle); *Times Literary Supplement*, 15 Apr. 1988 (Z. Leader); *Financial Times*, 18 Apr. 1988 (B. A. Young); *Listener*, 21 Apr. 1988 (N. Andrew).

D. DISSERTATIONS

D.1 N. Strelsky, 'Saltykov and the Russian Squire' (Ph.D., University of Columbia, 1941).
See C.30.

D.2 C. Kulešov, 'Saltykov-Ščedrin, *Istorija odnogo goroda*: an annotated edition with an introduction' (Ph.D., University of Indiana, 1969).

D.3 S. E. Kay, 'Saltykov's theory and practice of writing: an analysis of the work of M. Ye. Saltykov-Shchedrin, 1868–84' (Ph.D., University of London, 1976).

D.4 E. Draitser, 'The comic art of Saltykov-Shchedrin' (in Russian) (Ph.D., University of California, Los Angeles, 1983).

Shakespeare and Russian Literature: Nineteenth-Century Attitudes

By YU. D. LEVIN

MY subject is too vast to be treated within the limits of a single lecture. So I have no choice but to confine myself to outlining the main trends, adding where necessary a select number of illustrations.

The name of Shakespeare first appeared in Russian letters in 1748. He was mentioned by the Russian poet Aleksandr Sumarokov in his *Epistle on Poetry*. Sumarokov placed Shakespeare among the other immortal poets dwelling on Helicon: 'Мильтóн и Шекеспи́р, хотя непросвещенный' ('Milton and Shakespeare, the latter, tho' unschooled').[1] The qualification implied that Shakespeare was ignorant of the classical rules of poetry which Sumarokov himself, especially as a dramatist, considered absolutely obligatory. Seventeen years earlier some 'excellent Hamletic and Othellonian comedies' ('преизрядные Гамлетовы и Отелоновы комедии') had been referred to in an article published in the *Comments on the St Petersburg News*.[2] The article was translated from a foreign original, and it is quite obvious that neither the translator, nor the reading public had the slightest idea of what the reference meant.

It is hardly legitimate, indeed, to speak of any interest in Shakespeare's dramatic and poetic work in eighteenth-century Russian literature. Sumarokov's adaptation of *Hamlet* (1748) and that of *The Merry Wives of Windsor* by Catherine the Great—the Russian tsarina had a marked taste for playwriting and reworked Shakespeare's comedy into a play of her own, entitling it Вот каково иметь корзину и белье (*What Comes of Having a Basket and Some Linen*, 1786)—bore very little resemblance to the English originals. The first translations—*Richard III*, an anonymous version, produced in Nizhnii Novgorod, and *Julius Caesar*, translated by Karamzin—went quite unnoticed. Even as late as in the first decade of the nineteenth century progress was slow. Such Shakespearean plays as were translated came not direct, from the English originals, but from the French adaptations by

An Ilchester Lecture given in New College, Oxford, on 20 June 1988. The author wishes to record his special thanks to Dr J. S. G. Simmons for assistance in preparing the text.

[1] *Dve epistoly Aleksandra Sumarokova* (Spb., 1748), 9.
[2] *Istoricheskie, genealogicheskie i geograficheskie primechaniya v Vedomostyakh*, lxxviii (1731), 318.

Jean François Ducis, who had re-cast the plays in accordance with the rules of French classicism.

The revelation of the real Shakespeare in Russia (as in other countries of Europe) was due to the Romantic movement. The art of classicism with its rigid patterns and strict rules no longer suited a society that at the turn of the century went through such upheavals as the Industrial Revolution in England, the French Revolution, and the Napoleonic wars. A new kind of art—more complex and diverse, more in tune with the new order of things was needed: and that kind of art proved to be the Romantic movement. While developing and coining new aesthetic ideas and forms, the Romantics sought for allies in the past. Shakespeare, they thought, was one of these—and to Shakespeare they turned. His art, which grew out of and gave expression to the tragic crisis of Renaissance humanism, seemed in a way to match their needs. And the Romantics plunged into the ocean of his poetry in the hope of finding solutions to the problems which their national literatures faced. In their approach to Shakespeare Russian Romantics pursued the aims and interests of their national— Russian—literature. And whether Russian literature assimilated Shakespeare, or, for example, Goethe, or Cervantes, or any other foreign writer, it was primarily in the interests of its own needs and problems.

The special feature of the early nineteenth century in Russian literature was that its progress depended on the development of liberation ideas in Russian society, and of finding ways to solve the most urgent national problems, of which the most pressing was the abolition of serfdom and of social oppression in general. This liberation fervour, which was typical of Russian literature, coloured the interest in, and treatment of, all foreign literary works, Shakespeare's included.

It was in the twenties and thirties of the nineteenth century—'the age of Pushkin'—that Shakespeare was brought into the Russian literary and social struggle. Progressively-minded Russian writers of the time were mostly connected with the Decembrist movement. The Decembrists were officers and noblemen, most of whom had participated in the war against Napoleon—an experience which had greatly developed their national consciousness—and had made them yearn for a distinctively Russian literature with an essentially national character and spirit. It was as a clearly original, national writer, a genius whose imagination was unhampered by imposed precepts and rules, that Shakespeare inspired these Russians. The Decembrist poet Vil'gel'm Kyukhel'beker, a friend of Pushkin, wrote of Shakespeare that he 'knew all that is to be known—hell and paradise, heaven and earth'. 'Shakespeare', he wrote, 'is a universe of scenes, feelings, ideas and wisdom; he is infinitely profound and limitlessly diverse, tough and tender, strong and sweet, formidable and fascinating!'[3] Orest Somov, a near-Decembrist writer, demanded that the Russians should create an original national poetry of their own 'independent of tales of foreign lands'. Among those who could serve as their models Somov named Shakespeare—'this genius, untrammelled by any conventions, who wrote his own rules ... who wrote as his heart and imagination dictated'.[4]

In an article translated from French by the Decembrist Aleksandr Bestuzhev we find a direct statement: 'It is not that we ought to imitate Shakespeare; we ought to write in the spirit of our age as Shakespeare did in his'.[5]

The leading role in the appreciation of Shakespeare in Russia as well as in the development of Russian literature in general unquestionably belongs to Pushkin. Pushkin had the same aims and objectives as the Decembrists; however, in this as in everything else, he far surpassed them. Pushkin's Shakespearianism was not confined to literary and aesthetic concepts only—it helped him to form and develop his historical views. Of the Decembrist uprising of 1825 Pushkin wrote to a friend: 'Let us not be superstitious or one-sided—like French tragedians: let us look at the tragedy through Shakespeare's eyes'.[6]

'Through Shakespeare's eyes' for Pushkin, no doubt, meant a rejection of fatalism, the objective historical evaluation of epochs, people, and events, and a many-sided and impartial analysis of phenomena and their interrelations. Shakespeare for him was a model playwright whose essential and distinctive features he formulated as follows: 'What does a playwright need? Philosophy, impartiality, a historian's mind, capable of seeing things through the eyes of the state, shrewdness, a lively imagination, a mind unprejudiced by long-cherished ideas. *Freedom* ...'.[7] The basic quality of Shakespeare, in Pushkin's opinion was neither Shakespeare's rejection of classical rules, nor his brilliant stage effects, but his objectivity, his realistic characters and his 'true depiction of the age' achieved by the reconstruction of its spirit and of the general historical concept of the nation. Pushkin dreamt of transforming the national theatre and making it truly popular. And in this Shakespeare was to be a great ally. Pushkin wrote: 'I am firmly convinced that the national laws of the Shakespearean drama are appropriate for any theatre, unlike the court conventions of Racine's tragedies.'[8]

This conception was realized in his historical tragedy *Boris Godunov*

[3] V. Kyukhel'beker, 'Razgovor s F. V. Bulgarinym', *Mnemozina*, iii (1824), 173.

[4] 'O romanticheskoi poezii', *Sorevnovatel' prosveshcheniya i blagotvoreniya*, xxiii, kn. 2 (1823), 160.

[5] Arto [Artaud], 'O dukhe poezii XIX veka. Per. A.B.', *Syn otechestva*, cii, no. 16 (1825), 397.

[6] [A. S.] Pushkin, *Polnoe sobranie sochinenii* (M.-L., 1937–59), xiii. 259.

[7] Ibid. xi. 419.

[8] Ibid. 141.

(1825) which he deliberately 'arranged ... according to the system of our Father Shakespeare' (по системе отца нашего Шекспира).[9] For instance, the scene where Tsar Boris, dying, takes leave of his son Fedor was no doubt suggested by the similar scene in *King Henry the Fourth*. In the last scene of Pushkin's tragedy, after the assassination of Boris's wife and her son, the boyar Mosalsky calls upon the people: Кричите: да здравствует царь Димитрий Иванович ('Cry, Long live Tsar Dimitry Ivanovich!'), but the horrified people are silent.[10] A similar situation is to be found in Shakespeare's *Richard the Third* where the Duke of Buckingham calls upon the people to shout 'God save Richard, England's royal king!' And then Buckingham says:

> ... they spake not a word;
> But, like dumb statuas or breathing stones,
> Star'd each on other, and look'd deadly pale.

(III, vii, 24–6)

However, it is not these direct parallels that are most vital—especially since some of them are merely the reflection of similar situations in plays dealing with political discord in feudal countries. Pushkin made use of those elements which were at his disposal and reworked them in accordance with his own needs. And that is why his interpretation of Shakespeare opened a new chapter in the progress of the great English playwright in Russia.

Following Shakespeare's dramatic system, Pushkin boldly transferred the action of his tragedy from the Moscow Kremlin to the Chudov Monastery, from the capital to the Lithuanian border, from Russia to Poland. His tragedy covers all seven years of Tsar Boris's reign. Various social strata are represented, but what is more important, Pushkin, like Shakespeare (and for the first time in the Russian dramatic tradition), introduced the broad masses—the people—into the action of the play. In this Pushkin transcended his great predecessor who treated the people as, in Marx's words, 'an essentially active background'.[11] With Pushkin, however, the problem of state power—the monarch, on the one hand, and the people, on the other—moves into the foreground and the people become the tragedy's driving force.

Pushkin, as he himself acknowledged, imitated Shakespeare in the latter's 'broad and free depiction of characters'.[12] Pushkin's Shakespeare studies are recorded in his notes on the characters of Shylock, Angelo, and Falstaff: 'The characters created by Shakespeare are not, like Molière's, basically types of such and such a passion, such and

---

[9] Ibid. 66.
[10] Ibid. vii. 98.
[11] K. Marx, F. Engels, *Werke*, xxix (Berlin, 1963), 597.
[12] Pushkin, *Polnoe sobranie sochinenii* (n. 6), xiv. 129.

such a vice, but living beings instinct with many passions, many vices; circumstances develop their variegated and many-sided personalities before the spectator's eyes. In Molière, the Miser is miserly—and that's all; in Shakespeare Shylock is miserly, acute, vindictive, philoprogenitive, witty', and so on.[13] It is in this many-sided approach, which contrasts with the one-sidedness of classical plays, that Pushkin strove to represent the characters in his tragedy: Boris and the Pretender, in particular; Shuisky, Marina Mniszek, and others. The same approach to complex dramatic characters is to be found in Pushkin's later plays— the so-called 'little tragedies', especially in *The Covetous Knight* and *The Stone Guest*.

Boris Godunov is unquestionably a great play. Even so it did not produce the fundamental reform of the Russian stage that Pushkin hoped it would achieve. There were a number of reasons for this which unfortunately we have no time to dwell on here. But though it failed to fulfil its reforming role, *Boris Godunov* marks an important stage in the history of Russian Shakespeareanism. Pushkin pointed the way to a broad and deep understanding of the Shakespearean poetic system that was later elaborated in Russian literature, and which can be summed up as: 'Genuineness of feelings in given circumstances'.[14] In other words, Pushkin's interpretation of Shakespeare became the fundamental law of Russian nineteenth-century drama.

The influence of *Boris Godunov* is manifest in the later progress of Russian historical drama. This followed Shakespeare's stylistic system as interpreted by Pushkin. Especially critical was the impact of *Boris Godunov* on the dramatic works of a group of writers associated with the Lyubomudrie Society of Moscow, with which Pushkin was in sympathy. Two of these writers—Mikhail Pogodin and Aleksey Khomyakov—regarded Pushkin's tragedy as a model of 'Shakespearization' well adapted to national needs and conditions. The plot of Khomyakov's tragedy *The False Dimitry* (1833) continued the story of *Boris Godunov*, taking it up at the point where it had been left by Pushkin— the coronation of the Pretender. Moreover, in Khomyakov's tragedy the Pretender recalls his rendezvous with Marina Mniszek by the fountain—a well-known scene from Pushkin's *Boris Godunov*. However, Khomyakov could never match Pushkin's power of insight. With him all the historical and social antagonisms of the time, so brilliantly depicted by Pushkin, were submerged by a moral and psychological conflict, in which the people were portrayed as a mindless, fickle mob, easily aroused and easily calmed and essentially obsequious towards the boyars and their Tsar.

Pushkin, if we may judge from his letters, was rather disappointed

---

[13] Ibid. xii. 159-60.   [14] Ibid. xi. 178.

with Khomyakov as a playwright. Pogodin also criticized *The False Dimitry*, and this is of interest because it was precisely Pogodin who attempted to develop historical drama on Pushkin's lines. In 1830 his play *Martha, the Governor of Novgorod* was published. In it Pogodin tried to depict the historical conflict which exercised the best minds of the post-Decembrist period, that is, the conflict between the interests of a centralized power, on the one hand, and local freedoms (or self-government), on the other. Pogodin developed what had only been sketched in *Boris Godunov*—the clash of two major forces: the Tsar and the people. In his drama this is represented as the clash between the Grand Prince of Muscovy, Ivan III, and the Novgorod *veche* (the Novgorod popular assembly); and the people became, in Pogodin's own words, 'the protagonist of the play'.[15] Pushkin highly appreciated the 'popular' scenes in Pogodin's *Martha*: 'All of this has a *Shakespearean* quality', he wrote to the playwright.[16] But Pushkin certainly overrated Pogodin's drama: what he appreciated was not its intrinsic merit as a play, but rather the perspectives which it suggested and which, in Pushkin's view, seemed to be a fruitful development of the Shakespearean tradition.

Among the Decembrist writers it was Vil′gel′m Kyukhel′beker who, in prison after the events of December 1825, engaged in the most serious and profound study of Shakespeare's works. To Kyukhel′beker Shakespeare became a kind of intimate and dearly loved friend. 'My Will, my incomparable Will!' he wrote in a letter and further: 'My namesake is the greatest of all people who ever lived, who live now and (I'm tempted to say) who ever *will* live.'[17] In his military prison Kyukhel′beker set about studying and translating Shakespeare's plays, selecting for translation those which had the clearest political implications—*Macbeth* and the chronicle-plays. Apart from translating Shakespeare he wrote a historical tragedy of his own—*Prokofy Lyapunov*, largely on Shakespearean lines. Here Shakespeare's influence can be traced in many areas—in the general construction of the plot, in its handling, partly in the presentation of the characters, and finally, in those scenes in which the masses are involved. However, it must be confessed that Kyukhel′beker never fully mastered what we may call the Shakespearean technique.

When speaking of the reception of Shakespeare's dramatic system in Russia, one ought to mention the work of Nikolay Polevoy, who will be referred to later as the translator of *Hamlet*.

Born of merchant stock (that is to say, of 'low birth'), a prolific and versatile writer of the Romantic school, with a very sensitive ear for the

[15] *Russkii arkhiv*, iii (1882), no. 6, 151.
[16] Pushkin, *Polnoe sobranie sochinenii* (n. 6), xi. 140.
[17] *Literaturnoe nasledstvo*, lix (M., 1954), 433.

demands of the reading public, Polevoy, in his dramatic works, tried to follow Shakespeare, but did so rather on the lines suggested by the French Romantics than in the genuinely Shakespearean manner. His 'Shakespearization' consisted mainly in rejecting the conventions of formal classicism, in introducing hyper-romantic characters, and piling up melodramatic stage effects; some situations he lifted directly from Shakespeare but handled them rather superficially. These are the distinctive features of Polevoy's pseudo-historical plays *Ugolino* (1838) and *Elena Glinskaya* (1839). In the latter, set in sixteenth-century Russia when Elena Glinskaya, mother of the future Tsar Ivan the Terrible (then a small boy), ruled the country, we find some highly spectacular scenes borrowed from *Macbeth*—for example, the scene in which a chorus of ghosts sings a song very much like that of Macbeth's witches:

> Сейте гром
> Решетом,
> Жарьте змей
> Для людей!
> Поспешите, поспешите,
> Духи тьмы![18]

> [Sow thunder
> With a sieve,
> Bake snakes
> For the human race!
> Haste, haste,
> Ye spirits of gloom!]

Enigmatic prophecies, the ghost of the Glinsky's ancestor visible only to Elena (as Banquo's ghost is visible only to Macbeth), are also present in Polevoy's play. It goes without saying that the Shakespeare imitation was utterly superficial and the play was deservedly censured by Russian literary criticism.

Chronologically, the progress of the Shakespearean dramatic system in Russian literature was limited to the period of the eighteen-twenties and thirties, and this represents, in my view, the first phase of Russian nineteenth-century Shakespeareanism.

The further development of Russian drama by the great Russian writers such as Gogol', Ostrovsky, Lev Tolstoy, and Chekhov—had no direct Shakespeare connections. Even in the historical drama of the nineteenth century, which had largely evolved from *Boris Godunov*, Shakespeare's impact manifested itself not in a direct way, but at second hand—that is to say, through Pushkin's work. And it is notable that later in the century Aleksey Konstantinovich Tolstoy in his own historical trilogy (*The Death of Ioann the Terrible, Tsar Fedor Ioannovich*,

---

[18] N. A. Polevoy, *Dramaticheskie sochineniya i perevody*, iv (Spb., 1843), 376.

and *Tsar Boris*), followed Pushkin, rejecting Shakespeare, especially Shakespeare's chronicle-plays. Discussing the scene of Lady Anne's seduction in *Richard the Third*, Aleksey Tolstoy wrote in a letter in 1858: 'Is he a *dramatic* writer at all? Are his characters, and the way they move *on the stage*, ever authentic?'[19]

Even though towards the end of the eighteen-thirties Shakespeare's dramatic system no longer made a direct impact on Russian literature, the importance of Shakespeare did not diminish in the least. On the contrary, never before or since did the author of *Hamlet* evoke such a response and play such a significant part in the Russian literary and social movement as he did in the late eighteen-forties.

By that time Shakespeare had become widely known. In the early twenties it was only the intellectual élite of Russian society who knew Shakespeare, and when his plays were staged in Russia they were in versions made from Ducis's adaptations translated at the beginning of the century, but by the late twenties and early thirties a number of Russian men of letters, independently of each other, began to translate Shakespeare from the original. In addition to Kyukhel'beker, to whom I have already referred, there were Mikhail Vronchenko, a military geodesist; Vasily Yakimov, a scientific assistant at Khar'kov University; and Petr Kireevsky, a member of the Lyubomudrie Society. All three of them aimed to make Shakespeare known to the Russian reading public.

Limitations of time prevent me from dealing with the history of Russian translations of Shakespeare. Here note only that the first translators, who rejected adaptations and were anxious to give the Russian public an authentic and reliable Shakespeare, fell into the trap of excessive literalism. Their versions were leaden and full of clumsy phrases which conveyed the English text word-for-word. Even the best of these translations (by Vronchenko) elicited the following comment from Pushkin: 'Yes, they are good, because they give a clear idea of what the original is like, but the trouble is that an iron weight hangs on every one of Vronchenko's lines'.[20] All of these translations, no matter how much they served to introduce Russian readers to Shakespeare, were quite unsuitable for the stage. The theatre, however, demanded Shakespeare. So the actors themselves set to work, among them Yakov Bryansky, Vasily Karatygin and others. Their translations, though they reached the stage, were, alas, far from successful.

The decisive step in the establishment of Shakespeare on the Russian stage, and, generally, in the consciousness of Russian society, was made in January 1837 when *Hamlet* was published and staged in the translation provided by Nikolay Polevoy (to whom I have already

---

[19] A. K. Tolstoy, *Sobranie sochinenii v 4 tomakh*, iv (M., 1964), 103.
[20] *Zapiski K. A. Polevogo* (Spb., 1888), 274.

referred). By present-day standards his was a free and an inaccurate version, but it was for the first time that Shakespeare's characters could be heard speaking lively, emotional, and—what was still more important—*up-to-date* Russian. In Polevoy's version the image of Hamlet was somewhat distorted, his state of spiritual loss, his frustration, his despair over man's wretchedness were intensified and stressed. This, however, brought Shakespeare's hero still closer to the public. Through Hamlet's sufferings Polevoy expressed the tragic lot of his own generation. This was the reason why Polevoy—to use the words of Belinsky, the leading Russian literary critic of the nineteenth century— was able to 'establish the glory of Shakespeare's name in Russia, to establish and spread it not only in literary circles but among the reading and theatre-going public, to dismiss the false notion that Shakespeare is unfitted for the stage, and to prove that, on the contrary, it is Shakespeare who fits it best . . .'[21]

The reign of Tsar Nicholas I (1825–55) was a sombre period in Russian history. The power of the autocracy had crushed the revolutionary movement of the Decembrists and was ruthless in suppressing democratic aspirations. Polevoy, using Shakespeare's dramatic images, was, in fact, portraying a contemporary Russian society which was living in constant dread of reality. Judging from his own words he himself was aware of this: '. . . We love Hamlet', he said, 'as our own kin, because his weaknesses are our weaknesses; he feels with our heart and he thinks with our head' and 'We mourn with Hamlet and we mourn for ourselves.'[22]

The tragic note in Shakespeare's art struck a chord in the hearts of the progressive members of the contemporary Russian society. This developed later to explain the remarkable significance which Shakespeare had for the intellectual climate of Russia throughout the eighteen-forties. The critic Pavel Annenkov made a profound and penetrating observation: 'Shakespeare', he wrote, 'allowed a whole generation of Russian people to feel that they were intelligent human beings capable of comprehending the historical process and the essential conditions of human existence. And all this at a time when indeed a whole generation had no real social integration and no voice, even in the slightest affairs of civil existence.'[23]

The generation of Belinsky, Herzen, and Turgenev were enthusiastic Shakespeare readers, and for them his works offered profound insights into the secret recesses of the human heart. In Shakespeare they sought and found the affinity with their own tragic perception of the world.

---

[21] V. G. Belinsky, *Polnoe sobranie sochinenii* (M., 1953–9), ii, 426–7.

[22] S. P. Solov'ev, 'Dvadtsat' let iz zhizni Moskovskogo teatra', *Teatral'naya gazeta*, 1877 no. 81, p. 255; no. 84, p. 266.

[23] P. Annenkov, *Aleksandr Sergeevich Pushkin v Aleksandrovskuyu epokhu* (Spb., 1874), 298.

Thus the second stage of Russian Shakespeareanism began. Transferred to the contemporary world, Shakespeare's characters threw light on its contradictions, thereby acquiring a vital social significance. This is well illustrated by Belinsky's statement in 1847: '. . . our acquaintance with Shakespeare's plays showed that any human being, no matter how low his position in society and even human dignity, has every right to artistic attention, for the simple reason that he is a human being'.[24] In saying this, the radical critic emphasized in Shakespeare what appealed to the democratic trend in Russian literature of the forties known as 'the natural school', of which Belinsky was the most prominent intellectual leader.

Another Russian writer and radical thinker, Aleksandr Herzen, recognized in Shakespeare the concept of the clash between two worlds, and of historical crisis. In Herzen's works there are many references to Shakespeare, used mainly to stress the tragic quality of an event or episode. For example, the suppression of revolutionary uprisings is personified in the figure of Macbeth; the ghost of Hamlet's father is called on to remind readers of the responsibilities bequeathed to survivors. Here is the passage from Herzen's *My Past and Thoughts* in which the arrival in England of the Italian revolutionary leader Garibaldi is described: 'A kind of Shakespearean fantasy seems to have flashed before our eyes against England's grey background; with a genuinely Shakespearean juxtaposition of the grand and the vile, of that which pierces the soul and that which sets the teeth on edge . . . Familiar shades flit before our eyes in other forms—from Hamlet to King Lear, from Goneril and Cordelia to *honest* Iago. These Iagos are all tiny, but how many of them there are and how honest they are!'.[25] This passage demonstrates how Shakespearean imagery is used by Herzen to depict an event in a vivid, expressive and meaningful way.

Generally, it was characteristic of this generation of Russians to perceive the tragedy of their time and fate in Shakespearean terms and this led to the phenomenon known as 'Russian Hamletism'. The basic tragic conflict of the play lies in the fact that while being fully aware of the inhuman and hostile nature of his surroundings and clearly seeing that his moral duty is to fight against it, Hamlet feels himself to be unequal to the task. This makes him question the meaning of human existence and to consider suicide. This in my view lies at the heart of the tragedy. But what reasons underlie the tragic contradiction? Are they rooted within the character or are they external to him? What exactly are the inward motives and the outward circumstances? Over the last two centuries many and various answers to the problem have been proposed: and some of these have given birth to the phenomenon of

[24] Belinsky, *Polnoe sobranie sochinenii* (n. 21), x. 242.
[25] A. I. Herzen, *Sobranie sochinenii v 30 tomakh*, xi (M., 1957), 254.

'Hamletism'—the sufferings of the hero being regarded as an expression of the intellectual experience of a certain generation, a certain social group, sometimes even a whole nation, undergoing a critical stage in its history.

I have already quoted Annenkov's remark on the significance of Shakespeare for progressively-minded Russians of the 1830s who suffered as the result of the contrast between their intellectual demands and capacities, on the one hand, and their lack of political rights, on the other. It is here that the key to how Russian Hamletism came about is to be found.

The first Russian to exhibit the phenomenon was Polevoy. He made Hamlet sound like a Russian intellectual—helpless when faced with political oppression and painfully tormented by his helplessness. This parallel, suggested by Polevoy in his Russian version of Hamlet, was immediately taken up by Belinsky. In his article on the staging in Moscow of *Hamlet* in Polevoy's translation he wrote as follows: 'Hamlet! . . . here is the life of man, man himself, you and me, every one of us, more or less, lofty and ridiculous, but always in a sad and pathetic sense'.[26] Later, when formulating his conception of *Hamlet*, Belinsky was to condemn as 'shameful' the hero's irresolution when 'he growes pale at the thought of the terrible challenge that faces him, hesitates and only *talks*, but never *acts*'.[27]

Criticism of *Hamlet* in Russia eventually developed into self-criticism. In this reproach one recognizes the regret of the radical thinker and fighter who sees no opportunity of engaging in 'open and fearless conflict' with an 'unjust' power. In Belinsky's letter of 1840 to his friend Vasily Botkin, a critic and translator, we find a rather typical statement: 'There is reflected in us', he wrote, 'one of the hardest moments in the history of society . . . The situation is really tragic! . . . We cannot move a step without reflection . . . As a consolation (though it's a poor one!) we may say that though Hamlet (as a human character) is contemptible, we are all more in sympathy with him than with the giant Othello and the other heroes of Shakespeare's plays. He is weak and self-disgusted; however, only those who are themselves low and trivial can call him low and trivial, overlooking the splendour and magnificence of his worthlessness.'[28]

Other Russian thinkers of the forties—for example, Herzen, Ogarev, as well as Botkin and Turgenev—also felt affinities with Hamlet's spiritual torment. Botkin, for example, wrote to Ogarev: '. . . life seemed to me, in Hamlet's words, an unweeded garden that is going to seed and over which death hovers. It is a frightful prospect, Ogarev, is it

---

[26] Belinsky, *Polnoe sobranie sochinenii* (n. 21), ii. 254.
[27] Ibid. vii. 313.
[28] Ibid. xi. 526–7.

not?'[29] Belinsky's view of Hamlet was developed by Turgenev, who offered an original interpretation of 'Hamletism' in his article 'Hamlet and Don-Quixote' (1860).

By the sixties the liberation movement in Russia had entered a new phase. At the end of the fifties a revolutionary situation loomed, the struggle for the abolition of serfdom reached its climax, and a new social force—the democratic revolutionaries or *raznochintsy* (intellectuals of non-noble origin)—emerged. Developing the self-critical study of Hamlet, started by Belinsky, Turgenev, who was very sensitive to social change, showed that in the new historical context the 'Hamlets' of the forties had degenerated into the so-called 'superfluous men'. In other words, 'Hamletism' became identified with self-centred individualism. 'So what is Hamlet?', Turgenev wrote, 'Analysis and egotism, and therefore lack of faith. He lives for himself alone . . . He is a sceptic—always reflecting and brooding upon his own self; always concerned with his situation and never with his responsibilities . . .'. Further, he wrote: 'Hamlets discover nothing, invent nothing, and leave nothing behind them except their own personalities; they leave no actions behind. They possess neither love, nor faith. So what can they discover?'[30]

This interpretation was intended to be a warning against self-centred reflection and scepticism, which Turgenev looked upon as futile and socially negative. 'Hamlets' of this type were portrayed in many of Turgenev's characters beginning with his short story *The Hamlet of Shchigri District* (1849) and ending with his novel *Virgin Soil* (1876).

Turgenev's conception of Hamlet was, then, in harmony with the social tendencies of his time; in other words, it was historically determined. It should not be overlooked, though, that the Russian author had considerably deviated from Shakespeare's original—both in the letter and in the spirit. None the less, the identification of Hamlet with the 'superfluous man' was accepted both by Russian democratic literary criticism and by the later literary tradition, in which many Hamlet-like characters, even further distanced from the English original, appeared.

In the 1880s numerous 'Hamlets' and 'quasi-Hamlets' made their appearance, especially in works that reflected the crisis of the democratic social movement of *narodnichestvo* (Populism). However, their prototype was not Shakespeare's Hamlet, but Turgenev's populist Nezhdanov, the hero of *Virgin Soil*, who exclaimed in a spirit of self-contempt: 'O Hamlet, Hamlet, Prince of Denmark, how can one escape from the shadow of your spirit! How can one stop imitating you in everything, even in the vile

[29] *Russkaya mysl'*, 1891 no. 8, p. 3.
[30] I. S. Turgenev, *Polnoe sobranie sochinenii i pisem v 30 tomakh. Sochineniya*, 2 ed., v (M., 1980), 333, 338.

enjoyment of one's own self-depreciation?'[31] A few apostates from the populist movement tried to dignify their heroes by assimilating them to Hamlet, and it is these figures that the then well-known populist literary critic Nikolay Mikhailovsky characterized as 'Hamletized piglets'. The bright halo of Hamlet's name had tarnished by the time that the hero of Chekhov's play *Ivanov* (1887) declares himself ashamed by the comparison: 'I nearly die of shame when I think what a strong, healthy man like myself has become—heaven only knows what—a Manfred or a Hamlet, a superfluous man! . . . There are some miserable creatures who feel flattered when people call them Hamlets or "superfluous", but to me that is an insult.'[32]

Such was the historical outcome of Russian Hamletism. However, there were other interpretations of Shakespeare. A most original and impressive one is Dostoevsky's. We have evidence for it in his notes: 'Shakespeare is a prophet', he wrote, 'sent by God to reveal to us the mystery of man, of the human soul.'[33] These words seem to express Dostoevsky's own artistic ideal, for he wrote shortly before his death: 'They call me a psychologist, but it is not true—I'm only a realist, in the loftiest sense of the word, that is to say, I portray the hidden depths of the human soul.'[34] In some of his other notes there are suggestions of the way in which Dostoevsky related Shakespeare to the contemporary world. Together with Goethe and Cervantes, Shakespeare is viewed by him as a poet of a new age, who pictured man's despair in the face of the chaos of life. As Dostoevsky wrote in 1876: 'Classical tragedy is a liturgy; Shakespeare's is a despair.' And further: 'A Shakespeare of our time would also bring us despair.'[35] These words show that Dostoevsky found affinities between Shakespeare and himself.

Shakespeare's heroes were permanently present in his mind. In his works and drafts there are frequent references to Romeo and Juliet, Beatrice and Benedick, Prince Harry and Falstaff. But three Shakespearean heroes—Hamlet, Othello, and Falstaff—especially arouse the interest and attention of the author of *The Brothers Karamazov*. Shakespeare did not link these three heroes of three separate plays, but Dostoevsky, who regarded Shakespeare as a poet of despair, treated them as personifications of three possible attitudes to the chaos of life. Hamlet, in Dostoevsky's eyes, was a tormented, embittered soul, full of rancour both against himself and against the world, full of blank despair; a mind that questioned all values; a heart conscious of its total solitude. Like Turgenev, Dostoevsky applied Hamlet's traits to many of

[31] Ibid. ix. 233.
[32] A. P. Chekhov, *Polnoe sobranie sochinenii i pisem v 30 tomakh. Sochineniya*, xii (M., 1978), 37.
[33] F. M. Dostoevsky, *Polnoe sobranie sochinenii v 30 tomakh* (L., 1972–88), xi. 237.
[34] *Biografiya, pis'ma i zametki iz zapisnoi knizhki F. M. Dostoevskogo* (Spb., 1883), 373.
[35] Dostoevsky, *Polnoe sobranie sochinenii* (n. 33), xxiv. 160.

his own literary characters—for example—Nikolay Stavrogin (in *The Possessed*), the consumptive Ippolit (in *The Idiot*), Versilov (in *A Raw Youth*), Ivan Karamazov, and Aleksey Ivanovich (in *The Gambler*). The question 'To be or not to be', the question of the meaning of human existence, the question of one's right to self-destruction—all these are of the utmost importance for Dostoevsky's 'Hamlets'. As to the writer himself, for him the theme of suicide is invariably associated with the image of the Prince of Denmark.

For Dostoevsky, Hamlet is juxtaposed to Othello and Falstaff. His favourite hero is Othello, who embodies a pure soul which can only be *destroyed* by evil, but never *corrupted* by it. In *The Brothers Karamazov* we read: 'Jealousy! "Othello was not jealous, he was trusting", as Pushkin observed ... Othello's soul was shattered and his whole outlook clouded simply because *his ideal was destroyed*. But Othello did not hide, spy, and peep. He was trusting ... Othello was incapable of accepting faithlessness—not incapable of forgiving it, but incapable of accepting it—his soul was as innocent and free from malice as a child's.'[36] In the world around him Dostoevsky had never found such an innocent, pure, and honest soul. That is why the image of Othello is usually invoked in connection with opposite human qualities, such as those of Mitya Karamazov, for instance.

The third attitude to life's chaos is personified by Falstaff. If Hamlet is the embodiment of the tragic nature of life, and Othello of its purity, Falstaff personifies its vileness. Falstaff feels perfectly at home in the human morass and feeds on his neighbour's vice. Dostoevsky's 'Falstaffs' are many and vary in their social horizons. There is the outwardly respectable Mr M (in *The Little Hero*); the lecherous merchant Antipov, seducer of the young (in *The Injured and Insulted*); Captain Lebyadkin (in *The Possessed*); and, certainly, Fedor Karamazov. All of this 'slimy breed', as the author calls them,[37] are parasites battening on society. That is how Shakespeare was interpreted by Dostoevsky—one of the last representatives of 'the generation of the forties', who revered and greatly admired the great English playwright.

As time passed a certain change in Shakespeare's status came about. A new generation came to the fore and its advent marked the third stage of Russian Shakespeareanism. From the 1860s Shakespeare began at last to lose his significance as an active factor in the literary process; he was becoming a part of the cultural heritage. Familiarity with Shakespeare was an essential element in one's educational background, Shakespeare was much translated, editions grew in number, wider strata of society read his plays and watched them on the stage. But the impact of a writer on the literary tradition and his popularity

[36] Ibid. xiv. 343–4.
[37] Ibid. ii. 276.

with readers are two very different things: the former is determined by the intrinsic needs of the recipient literature, the latter is dependent on the general cultural growth of the nation. We need only recall that in Pushkin's day, when Shakespeare had so powerful an influence on the course of Russian historical drama, his readers, by comparison with later time, were very few.

Frequent mention of Shakespeare and all kinds of references to and quotations from his plays in Russian literature of the second half of the nineteenth century, show that Shakespeare was firmly established in Russian culture, but this cannot serve as evidence for his actual literary influence. While the overtly acknowledged authority of Shakespeare was still unchallenged, there developed in literary circles a latent opposition to his aesthetic principles, which years later exploded in Lev Tolstoy's anti-Shakespearean revolt. The reason for this revolt was rooted in the discrepancies between two different poetical systems— Shakespeare's, on the one hand, and that of realistic Russian literature, on the other. The mid-nineteenth century witnessed the consolidation of realism in a new form which demanded the keen scrutiny of topical social issues, the handling of human nature and behaviour as socially determined, as well as the detailed and rational elaboration of sub-merged psychological motives together with a meticulous objectivity in representing the environment. Moreover, realist Russian literature of the period features a peculiar economy in the use of language—an economy derived from an opposition to the high-flown idiom of the kind employed both by the latter-day Romantics and the official press. Under those conditions Shakespeare's artistic system was conceived to be unnatural. Shakespeare's metaphorical language was the formal expression of a highly poetic structure and of a different approach to the creation of literary characters, and this seemed to be incompatible with the new aesthetic demands. Among those who, other than Lev Tolstoy, in one way or another, voiced their disagreement with Shake-speare's 'technique' were two critics of the revolutionary democratic camp—Nikolay Chernyshevsky and Nikolay Dobrolyubov, in addition to the Aleksey Tolstoy who has already been mentioned. Even Aleksandr Druzhinin, a translator and popularizer of Shakespeare, con-fessed in his diary in 1854: 'Of all the great, it is Shakespeare who escapes me—something which I have to admit with a heavy heart . . . My capa-city to understand poetry fails when I am dealing with Shakespeare's poetry . . .'.[38] It is noteworthy that such admissions are to be found in private documents, such as diaries and letters. Nobody seems to have dared to voice such opinions in public. Even Lev Tolstoy delayed publishing his anti-Shakespearean pamphlet for about half a century. Only Chernyshevsky, courageous as ever when upholding his views,

[38] A. V. Druzhinin, *Povesti. Dnevnik* (M., 1986), 314–15.

stated publicly in 1855: '. . . we should regard Shakespeare without blind veneration', as the conventions of his time 'make a good half of Shakespeare's plays incapable of giving aesthetic pleasure in our day.'[39]

The rejection of Shakespeare at the turn of the fifties and sixties had an aesthetic as well as a social resonance. By the sixties ideological confrontation in Russia had become exceedingly bitter, and literature was so intimately involved in the struggle that social significance was denied to works of art and letters which did not directly reflect the controversial political issues of the day and take sides in the general struggle. Shakespeare's objective art is not an explicitly engaged art and the implicit democratic passion which pervades his every line was unrecognized by most Russian men of letters active in the sixties. As a result, Shakespeare was labelled by them an 'art for art's sake' writer.

Such was the premise on which Tolstoy later based and developed his criticism. His essay 'On Shakespeare and drama' was published in 1906, and shocked the reading public throughout the world. Tolstoy maintained 'that Shakespeare cannot be recognized either as a great genius, or even as an average author.'[40] This paradox of a statement was backed up by a biased analysis of *King Lear* in which Tolstoy attempted to show that Shakespeare's plays are devoid of genuine dramatic tensions while his *dramatis personae* do not act consistently with the time and place they are set in, and speak 'not their own, but always one and the same Shakespearean, pretentious, unnatural, language'.[41] Further, Tolstoy proceeded to argue that Shakespeare regarded the rulers' high station as reflecting their absolute superiority over the common people, whom they despised. The universal fame of Shakespeare, he claimed, was nothing but an 'epidemic hypnosis', and he concluded by saying that 'the sooner people free themselves from the false glorification of Shakespeare, the better'.[42]

This disparaging assessment of Shakespeare by Tolstoy was partly due to Tolstoy's opposition to Shakespeare's dramatic system—an opposition that had been growing, as has been already mentioned, in realistic Russian literature since the mid-nineteenth century. Another reason why Tolstoy opposed Shakespeare was his own spiritual crisis—a crisis he experienced at the turn of the eighties, which led him to share the traditional views of the patriarchally-minded Russian peasantry. Shakespeare was thus rejected by him as part of an irreligious and therefore immoral culture, alien and hostile to the common people of Russia. Finally, this anti-Shakespeare tirade has a uniquely Tolstoyan character. It was one more manifestation of

---

[39] N. G. Chernyshevsky, *Polnoe sobranie sochinenii v 15 tomakh*, ii (M., 1949), 283, 50.
[40] L. N. Tolstoy, *Polnoe sobranie sochinenii*, xxxv (M., 1950), 217.
[41] Ibid. 239.
[42] Ibid. 271–2.

Tolstoy's immanent spirit of challenge that drove him boldly to 'tear off masks of all kinds', as Lenin put it.[43] One of these masks, in Tolstoy's eyes, was the Shakespeare cult.

Shakespeare, a genius-playwright, certainly far outdistanced his contemporaries in what he conceived to be the elements of the new drama and of what new literature in general should be. However, when nineteenth-century writers, Russian writers included, relied on Shakespeare, when trying to resolve current problems facing their national literatures, they made use not only of his strong points, but equally of those features of his 'technique' for which the imperfection of the drama of his epoch was accountable. It would be unfair to claim that nineteenth-century interpretations of Shakespeare are totally erroneous, but they undoubtedly incorporate a considerable element of modernization. Tolstoy's nihilistic ardour in rebelling against Shakespeare was a kind of historical retribution.

However, as time went on, it became obvious that Tolstoy's rejection of Shakespeare was based on a misconception. It would be wrong to assume, though, that it has left no traces. On the contrary, it has proved to be an important landmark in the history of world, as well as of Russian, Shakespeareanism. It certainly failed to blast Shakespeare's universally acknowledged reputation, and it has not impaired the response to his plays among the vast reading and theatre-going public. However, it did put an end to the uncritical adulation of Shakespeare and to the Shakespeare cult. Especially so, since Tolstoy proved that Shakespeare's methods of psychological characterization had by his day exhausted their potential, while uncritical imitation of his devices could only prejudice further literary progress. Finally, by his examination of *King Lear*, in which he stripped the great tragedy of its imagery and reduced it to a succession of ludicrous actions and remarks, Tolstoy, though unintentionally, proved the point that Shakespeare's art can exist only within its own inherent artistic and poetic system. Thus Tolstoy, whether he liked it or not, paved the way for twentieth-century interpretations of Shakespearean poetics.

*   *   *

Such, in my opinion, are the three main stages in the progress of Shakespeare in Russian nineteenth-century literature. My account has been necessarily very selective and the narrow confines of a lecture (even a long one) have compelled me to omit many facts and names, among them the works of numerous Russian writers, critics, translators, and actors, who contributed to the reputation of Shakespeare in my

[43] V. I. Lenin, *Polnoe sobranie sochinenii*, xvii (M., 1961), 209.

country. It is due to their efforts that the great English playwright and poet has become part and parcel of Russian culture. When in 1864 the three-hundredth anniversary of Shakespeare's birth was celebrated in Russia, Oxford University's Honorary Doctor-to-be, Ivan Turgenev, had every reason to declare: 'We, Russians, celebrate the memory of Shakespeare, and we have the right to do so. For Shakespeare is for us not only a famous and brilliant name to which we pay homage occasionally and from a distance; he has become part of our heritage, our own flesh and blood.'[44]

[44] Turgenev, *Polnoe sobranie sochinenii* (n. 30), xii. 327.

Ablative–Locative Transfers: Evidence from Slovene and Serbo-Croat

By DAVID C. BENNETT

1

THE term 'ablative–locative transfer' has been applied to the process whereby an expression which is assumed to have originally indicated the starting-point of a change of position subsequently comes to indicate simple location.[1] An example is provided by the Old High German and Modern German expressions meaning 'from inside', 'inside', and '(to) inside', shown in Table 1.[2]

Table 1. *Ablative, locative, and allative expressions incorporating the meaning 'inside' in Old High German and Modern German*

	Ablative 'from inside'	Locative 'inside'	Allative '(to) inside'
Old High German	*innana*	*inne*	*în*
Modern German	*von innen*	*innen*	*nach innen*

Modern German *innen* is derived from OHG *innana* but, whereas *innana* meant 'from inside', *innen* means simply 'inside' and to express 'from inside' in Modern German it is necessary to add *von* to convey the meaning 'from' (*innen* on its own can no longer mean 'from inside').

Table 2 shows similar data from Latin and Spanish but is of additional interest since it reflects ablative–locative transfers at two different stages in the history of these languages. Latin *unde* is assumed to have lost its ablative meaning in favour of a simple locative meaning, at which point it needed to be preceded by the ablative marker *de* to express the meaning 'from where'. Subsequently, however, *de* + *unde*—or at least its Spanish reflex *donde*—underwent a further ablative–locative transfer, with the result that to say 'from where' in Modern Spanish it is necessary to precede *donde* by another instance of *de*.

A revised version of a lecture given in the Taylor Institution on 26 February 1988.

[1] Cf. J. L. MacKenzie, 'Ablative–Locative Transfers and their Relevance for the Theory of Case-Grammar', *Journal of Linguistics*, xiv (1978), 129–56.

[2] Ibid. 133–4.

Table 2. *Ablative, locative, and allative expressions incorporating the meaning 'where' in Latin and Spanish*

	Ablative 'from where'	Locative 'where'	Allative '(to) where'
Latin	*unde*	*ubi*	*quo*
Spanish	*de donde*	*donde*	*adonde*

MacKenzie has shown how common ablative–locative transfers are by presenting examples from many branches and stages of the Indo-European family and from three non-Indo-European languages (Modern Hebrew, Fijian, and Sonsorol-Tobi).[3] He also considered the implications of ablative–locative transfers for the theory of case grammar—as expounded in particular by Anderson[4]—and presented a tentative explanation of how ablative–locative transfers take place. In the present paper I shall attempt to throw further light on this question by means of a detailed examination of ablative–locative transfers in two closely related languages, Slovene and Serbo-Croat. These languages are of particular interest because they represent different stages of development of ablative–locative transfers and also because they manifest ablative–locative transfers in progress at the present time.

The remainder of the paper is divided into seven sections. Section 2 shows that Slovene and Serbo-Croat have been affected by ablative–locative transfers and that they represent different stages of this process. A more detailed examination of the phenomenon in these two languages is presented in sections 3, 4, 5, and 6, and section 7 attempts to explain it. Finally, section 8 presents the main conclusions and draws attention to some unresolved issues.

2

Serbo-Croat has a number of complex prepositions in which *iz*—which on its own means 'out of' or 'from'—is followed by a simple locative preposition. They include *iznad*, *ispod*, *ispred* and *iza*, which incorporate *nad* 'over', *pod* 'under', *pred* 'in front of', and *za* 'behind' (respectively). In dictionaries of the present-day language the complex prepositions are attributed locative (rather than directional)

---

[3] Ibid.
[4] J. M. Anderson, *The Grammar of Case: Towards a Localistic Theory* (Cambridge, 1971); idem, *On Case Grammar* (London, 1977).

meanings. For example, Benson glosses them as meaning: 'above, over' (*iznad*); 'below, under, lower than' (*ispod*); 'in front of, (right) before' (*ispred*); and 'behind, in back of, after' (*iza*).[5] The corresponding Slovene prepositions, on the other hand, are ascribed ablative meanings. Kotnik, for example, glosses them as: 'from above' (*iznad*); 'from below' (*izpod*); 'from before' (*izpred*); and 'from behind, from' (*izza*).[6] Since the Serbo-Croat complex prepositions are attributed locative meanings, while the corresponding Slovene prepositions are attributed ablative meanings, it would seem that the Serbo-Croat prepositions have already completed an ablative–locative transfer, whereas a corresponding transfer in Slovene has not yet begun. However, a closer look at Slovene reveals that this language, too, has begun to be affected by the change. For instance, Gradišnik gives examples of the complex prepositions being used locatively rather than to indicate the starting-point of a movement, such as:

(1)   To je obarvana površina, izza   katere ni   ničesar[7]
       [that is painted   surface   behind which is-not nothing]
       'it's a painted surface with nothing behind it'

However, Gradišnik regards (1) as ungrammatical in Slovene and attributes its occurrence to the influence of Serbo-Croat. Instead of *izza katere*, according to him, the correct Slovene would be *za katero*. The significance of such examples, from our point of view, is that they show that the Slovene complex prepositions have begun to participate in an ablative–locative transfer.

Finally, in addition to complex prepositions, we should also consider spatial adverbs. The six Slovene locative adverbs meaning 'inside', 'outside', 'above', 'below', 'in front', and 'behind' are: *znotraj*, *zunaj*, *zgoraj*, *spodaj*, *spredaj*, and *zadaj* (respectively). Vaillant believes *zunaj* 'outside' to have developed from **iz vna* and accordingly treats the initial *z* as the remains of the preposition *iz*.[8] The *z* (*s*) in *znotraj*, *zgoraj*, *spodaj*, and *spredaj* is capable of similar explanation. By contrast, Skok treats the *z* of SCr. *odozgo* 'from above' (which will feature prominently in the discussion below) as having developed from **sъ*, corresponding to modern SCr. *s*, *sa* 'from, off' rather than *iz* 'out of'.[9] In general, I shall assume that the fricative in such words comes from an earlier *iz* in both languages, but for present purposes it is in fact unimportant which origin is correct, since in either case we should be dealing with a marker of ablativity. With regard to *zadaj* a parallel

[5] M. Benson, *Srpskohrvatsko-engleski rečnik*, 2 ed. (Belgrade, 1979), s.v.

[6] J. Kotnik, *Slovensko-angleški slovar* (Ljubljana, 1972), s.v.

[7] J. Gradišnik, *Še znamo slovensko?* (Celje, 1981), 52–3. Cf. also: idem, *Slovenščina za Slovence* (Maribor, 1967), 308–11; idem, *Slovenščina za vsakogar* (Ljubljana, 1974), 206–7.

[8] A. Vaillant, *Grammaire comparée des langues slaves*, ii. *Morphologie* (Paris, 1958), 688.

[9] P. Skok, *Etimologijski rječnik hrvatskoga ili srpskoga jezika* (Zagreb, 1971), 589.

analysis would treat the initial *z* as resulting from the fusion of the fricative at the end of *iz* with an identical fricative at the beginning of the root morpheme. Thus all six of these Slovene adverbs are likely to have undergone an ablative–locative transfer. The use of the Serbo-Croat equivalents of these adverbs is demonstrated below, using examples taken from the Serbian, Croatian, and Slovene translations of George Orwell's novel *Nineteen Eighty-Four* together with the corresponding extracts from the English original.[10] Where there is an interesting difference between the Serbian and Croatian versions, both are given; otherwise only one Serbo-Croat translation is quoted. (The words under discussion are printed in italics.) Examples (2)–(5) below involve Sln. *znotraj*, *zunaj*, *zgoraj*, and *spodaj*. As we shall see later, the situation with regard to Serbo-Croat equivalents of *spredaj* and *zadaj* is somewhat different.

(2) Srb. da će biti manje upadljiv *unutra*
        [that will be less   noticeable inside]
     Sln. da bo   manj sumljiv *znotraj*
        [that will-be less suspicious inside]
     Eng. 'that he would be less conspicuous inside'

(3) Srb. Svet je   *napolju* . . . izgledao hladno
        [world (past) outside   looked   cold]
     Cr. *Vani* . . .   svijet je   djelovao studeno
        [outside . . . world (past) appeared cold]
     Sln. Svet *zunaj* je   bil   videti mrzel
        [world outside (past) been to-see cold]
     Eng. 'Outside . . . the world looked cold'

(4) Srb. zato što je   on bio *gore*
        [because (past) he been above]
     Sln. zato, ker je   bil on tu *zgoraj*
        [because (past) been he here above]
     Eng. 'because he was up here'

(5) Cr. a bile su *dolje* baš   zato što . . .
        [and been (past) below precisely because . . .]

[10] For permission to put the English, Serbian, Croatian, and Slovene versions of this novel onto magnetic tape I am grateful to the four publishers: Penguin Books Ltd. (in association with Martin Secker & Warburg); Beogradski izdavačko-grafički zavod; August Cesarec, Zagreb; and Mladinska knjiga, Ljubljana. The cost of using an optical character reader for this purpose was covered by a research grant from the School of Oriental and African Studies, which is also gratefully acknowledged. Thanks are due, finally, to Michael Mann, of S.O.A.S., who wrote the concordance program used on the texts and who supplied invaluable additional assistance in computational matters.

Sln. in bili sta   *spodaj* zato, ker . . .
[and been (past) below because . . .]
Eng. 'and they were down there because . . .'

The data that we considered earlier indicated clearly that Serbo-Croat
has progressed further than Slovene so far as ablative–locative transfers
affecting prepositions are concerned. Examples (2)–(5), on the other
hand, might lead one to conclude that, as regards adverbs, Slovene is
ahead of Serbo-Croat. The Slovene adverbs have apparently undergone a transfer, whereas their Serbo-Croat translations seem not to
have done so.

A somewhat different picture emerges, however, from the examination of words corresponding to English *in front*. Two very similar
examples from *Nineteen Eighty-Four* are given in (6) and (7):

(6)   Eng. 'A building with . . . pillars in front . . .'

(7)   Eng. '. . . of an oval building with . . . a small tower in front'

The Croatian and Slovene translations are given below. (In the Serbian
translation there is nothing in either case corresponding to the words *in
front*.)

(6)   Cr.   Ona zgrada . . . koja   ima *naprijed* stupove
            [that building . . . which has in-front pillars]
      Sln. Poslopje . . . s   stebri *spredaj*
            [building . . . with pillars in-front]

(7)   Cr.   neke   ovalne zgrade   . . . s   malim tornjem *sprijeda*
            [of-some oval   building . . . with small tower   in-front]
      Sln. ovalnega poslopja . . . z   majhnim stolpom *v ospredju*
            [of-oval   building . . . with small   tower   in front]

Cr. *naprijed* in (6), corresponding to Sln. *spredaj*, bears no evidence of an
ablative–locative transfer. Its structure is transparent, however, and
involves the preposition *na* 'on, onto', which has coalesced with an
earlier noun stem *prijed* (Srb. *pred*).[11] Moreover, the uninflected form of
this noun stem represents the accusative case in its allative function.
Thus *naprijed* corresponds more closely to the English phrase *to the front*
than to *in front*. Example (7), on the other hand, provides us finally with
an ablative–locative transfer involving a Serbo-Croat adverb. Cr.
sprijeda contains the remains of the preposition *iz* together with the
same earlier noun stem that occurs in *naprijed*, but this time in its
genitive form (the case required by *iz*). The Slovene of (7) is also interesting. *In front* is translated here quite literally with a prepositional

---

[11] See J. Miller, *Semantics and Syntax: Parallels and Connections* (Cambridge, 1985), 80–1, for a discussion of similar Slavonic data.

phrase consisting of *v* 'in' plus the noun *ospredje* 'front' in its locative case, but this noun is derivationally rather complex. It incorporates *-spred-*, derived from *iz* + *pred*, preceded, perhaps, by the locative preposition *o* 'at'. However, in view of the fact that French *devant* 'in front (of)' is assumed to have been derived from [*de* + [*ab* + *ante*]],[12] it is possible that *ospredje*, too, incorporates two ablative markers, namely *od* + *iz*. The loss of the plosive at the end of *od* may represent a simplification of an otherwise rather complex consonant cluster.

Finally, (8) contains an instance of Sln. *zadaj* from *Nineteen Eighty-Four*. It will be seen that the Croatian translation contains a prepositional phrase rather than an adverb (and the same is true of the Serbian translation). Throughout the novel, and not only in relation to the word *behind*, it is often the case that an English adverb is preserved as an adverb in Slovene but rendered by a prepositional phrase in Serbo-Croat. As for locative uses of *behind*, it so happens that there are no examples in the whole novel where either Serbo-Croat translation uses an adverb.

(8) Cr.   Crnokosa djevojka je sjela odmah   *iza*   *njih*
          [black-haired girl (past) sat immediately behind them]

     Sln. Temnolaso dekle je   sedelo takoj   *zadaj*
          dark-haired girl (past) sat   immediately behind

     Eng. 'The girl with dark hair was sitting immediately behind'

A crucial issue that has emerged during the latter part of this section concerns the extent to which Serbo-Croat *adverbs*, as opposed to prepositions, have undergone ablative–locative transfers. This question will be taken up again below.

3

In our preliminary survey of the Serbo-Croat complex prepositions *iznad*, *ispod*, *ispred*, and *iza* no mention was made of the relationship between them and the simple prepositions *nad*, *pod*, *pred*, and *za* (other than that the former incorporate the latter). We need now to consider the relationship in more detail.

Example (9) is one of many examples from *Nineteen Eighty-Four* where the English preposition *above* is translated into Slovene as *nad* and into Serbo-Croat as *iznad*.

[12] Ibid. 78.

(9)   Srb.   Vinston je   imao . . . proširenu-venu *iznad* desnog
                                              članka

         Cr.   Winston je   imao . . . proširenu-venu *iznad* desnog
                                              gležnja

         Sln.   Winston je   imel . . . krčni-tvor   *nad*   desnim
                                              gležnjem

         [Winston (past) had   varicose-ulcer   above right
                                               ankle]

         Eng. 'Winston . . . had a varicose ulcer above his right ankle'

There are, however, many other places in the text where all three
Yugoslav versions contain *nad*; (10) is such an example.

(10)   Srb.   čak bez   krova *nad* glavom
               even without roof   over head
         Cr.   niti   krova *nad* glavom
         Sln.   niti   strehe *nad* glavo
         [not-even roof   over head]
         Eng. 'not even a roof to sleep under'

Moreover, there is a contrast in Serbo-Croat between *iznad glave* and
nad glavom, which Bugarski elucidates with the help of the labels
'detachment' and 'interrelation'.[13] Bugarski glosses *krov* **iznad** *glave* as
'the roof *above* one's head' and points out that it merely states 'relative
position', whereas *krov* **nad** *glavom* means 'the roof *over* one's head' and
implies 'protection'. There is a similar distinction between *ispod* and
pod (also discussed by Bugarski) and one may add that *ispred* and *pred*
seem to be related in a parallel way. (I suspect that the situation is
somewhat different with *iza* and *za*, but shall not embark here upon a
discussion of this pair.) Wherever interrelatedness is crucially present, it
is inappropriate to use one of the prepositions which imply separation.
This is why *pod kontrolom* in (11) cannot be replaced by *ispod kontrole.

(11)   Srb.   Držati ih   *pod*   kontrolom . . .
         Cr.   Držati ih   *pod*   kontrolom . . .
         Sln.   Držati jih   *pod*   nadzorstvom . . .
         [to-keep them under control]
         Eng. 'To keep them in control . . .'

In the same way, English *under the influence of* cannot be replaced by
**below the influence of*.

    We observe now, finally, that while it is certainly appropriate to
attribute to *iznad* a locative rather than a directional meaning in (9),
there is nevertheless a residual meaning of ablativity present, in the
form of the notion of separation.

---

[13] R. Bugarski, 'A System of English Prepositions and their Serbo-Croatian Equivalents', *The Yugoslav Serbo-Croatian–English Contrastive Project Reports 8* (1973), 3–20, esp. 15.

4

The many languages that have undergone ablative–locative transfers include French. For example, complex prepositions of the kind illustrated by *au dessus de* 'above' now have a locative meaning, though (as MacKenzie postulates) *de sus* was originally ablative:

It is highly implausible to suggest that the preposing of *de* had no semantic effect: it must be supposed, given that OF *sus* 'above' was locative, that *de sus* was originally interpreted as ablative, in the same way as the ModF speaker interprets *de dessus* as ablative.[14]

Since the preposition *de* can still have an ablative meaning, e.g. in *ce train est venu de Paris* 'this train has come from Paris', we conclude that there are some uses in the present-day language in which it is ablative and others where it has lost its ablative meaning and is merely part of a complex locative preposition.

Let us consider now also the French preposition *à*. In sentences such as *je vais à l'école* 'I am going to school' *à* translates English *to* and thus seems to have an allative meaning. As such it may be said to stand in a relationship of antonymy to the preposition *de*. It is interesting to note, therefore, that there are other uses of *à* where its meaning is locative rather than allative, e.g. *elle demeure à Paris* 'she lives in Paris', and that it thus seems to participate in an allative–locative neutralization. Given, then, that *de* and *à* are antonyms, it is natural to wonder whether there is any connection between ablative–locative transfers (which involve *de*) and allative–locative neutralizations (which affect *à*). We shall see below that Slovene and Serbo-Croat throw a certain amount of light on this issue. For the moment let us consider the allative–locative distinction in the two languages.

In Serbo-Croat some spatial adverbs have specifically allative uses (e.g. *ovamo* 'here', *napolje* 'outside') and some have specifically locative uses (e.g. *ovd(j)e* 'here', *napolju* 'outside'), but many others (e.g. *tamo* 'there', *gore* 'up, above') are used in either way. In Slovene, on the other hand, a consistent distinction is drawn between the two functions. Table 3 provides relevant examples. (*Zdolaj* also occurs in Slovene, meaning 'below', but is considerably less common than *spodaj*.)

The data in question could, in theory, have either of two diachronic explanations:

(a) The earlier state of affairs involved no distinction between allative and locative; Slovene has by now acquired such a distinction; and Serbo-Croat is at present in the process of acquiring the distinction.

---

[14] MacKenzie, 'Ablative–Locative Transfers' (n. 1), 154.

(b) The earlier state of affairs involved a distinction between allative
   and locative; Slovene still preserves the distinction; but Serbo-
   Croat is at present in the process of losing the distinction.

If explanation (a) is true, Slovene is ahead of Serbo-Croat. On the other
hand, if explanation (b) is correct, Serbo-Croat is ahead of Slovene. In
fact, however, it is clear that (b) is correct. For instance, of the various
ways of saying *where are you going?* in Serbo-Croat—*gd(j)e ideš?/kuda
ideš?/kamo ideš?*—the versions containing (Serbian) *kuda* or (Croatian)
kamo represent the older usage;[15] the newer usage involves allowing the
originally locative *gd(j)e* to occur also in directional sentences. The
situation is thus parallel to that in English, where sentences such as
whither are you going? gave way to *where are you going?*

Table 3. *Locative and allative adverbs in Slovene and Serbo-Croat*

	Slovene		Serbo-Croat	
	locative	allative	locative	allative
'inside'	*znotraj*	*noter*	*unutra*	*unutra*
'outside'	*zunaj*	*ven*	*napolju/vani*	*napolje/van(i)*
'above, up'	*zgoraj*	*gor*	*gore*	*gore*
'below, down'	*spodaj*	*dol*	*dol(j)e*	*dol(j)e*
'there'	*tam*	*tja*	*tamo*	*tamo*
'where'	*kje*	*kam*	*gd(j)e*	*kuda/kamo/gd(j)e*
'here'	*tu*	*sem*	*ovd(j)e*	*ovamo*

5

Given that we are interested not just in changes affecting Slovene and
Serbo-Croat but in the phenomenon of ablative–locative transfers in
general, one naturally cherishes the hope of being able to specify the
stages that any language passes through as it undergoes such a transfer.
From this point of view, our preliminary findings in section 2 were
somewhat disappointing. As regards Slovene, it was clear that the
adverbs *znotraj* 'inside', *zunaj* 'outside', *zgoraj* 'above', etc., have
already undergone an ablative–locative transfer, whereas the prepositions *iznad* 'from over', *izpod* 'from under', etc., have barely begun to be
affected. On the basis of the Slovene data, therefore, one might
hypothesize that whenever a language undergoes an ablative–locative
transfer, its adverbs are affected before its prepositions. Such a

---

[15] Vaillant, *Grammaire comparée* (n. 8), 709–14.

hypothesis is supported by the facts of the Romance languages.[16] We may recall, however, that although the Serbo-Croat prepositions *iznad*, etc., have already been affected, *sprijeda* 'in front' in example (7) is the only case we have observed of the same process affecting an adverb. At this point we faced the prospect of being forced to retreat into the rather weak observation that in some languages adverbs happen to be affected before prepositions, whereas in other languages prepositions are affected before adverbs. Fortunately, when we take more data into account, we find that the situation is more encouraging and that the hypothesis set up on the basis of Slovene is, after all, in agreement with the facts of Serbo-Croat. Moreover, it is possible to identify the additional factor which obscures the situation in the latter language.

A relevant consideration, first of all, is that SCr. *iznad*, *ispod*, *ispred*, and *iza* may be used not only as prepositions but also as adverbs. Thus one way of saying 'the dictionary is underneath' is: *r(j)ečnik je ispod*. Admittedly, the use of these words as adverbs is rather less frequent in the present-day language than their prepositional use, but in view of the fact that they can be used as adverbs, they provide examples of adverbs that have undergone an ablative–locative transfer.

Let us now consider the way in which one says 'above' and 'from above' in Slovene and Serbo-Croat. The Slovene word for 'above' is *zgoraj*; and to derive the expression meaning 'from above', one precedes it by the ablative marker *od* 'from', giving *od zgoraj*. In Serbo-Croat, the normal way of saying 'above' is *gore*. One might expect, therefore, that the Serbo-Croat expression for 'from above' would be *od gore*. In fact, however, the normal expression for 'from above' in Serbo-Croat is *odozgo* (and the normal expression for 'from below' is *odozdo*). As was pointed out in section 2, the *z* in the middle of SCr. *odozgo* (like that in Sln. *od zgoraj*) is the remainder of an ablative marker. Moreover, the facts of such French examples as *devant* 'in front (of)' (discussed above) and *de dedans* 'from inside' (where there are clear traces of three occurrences of *de*) force us to take seriously the possibility that *odozgo* is derived from [*od* + [*od* + [*iz* + *gor-*]]]. In this case *odozgo* has presumably undergone two separate ablative–locative transfers at different times in the past, and we may posit that at an earlier stage of its development Serbo-Croat had a word corresponding to Sln. *zgoraj*, with a similarly locative meaning. This is borne out by the examination of earlier texts. As early as 1309, *zgora* was being used in phrases such as *zgora rečen* and *zgora pisan*, meaning 'above mentioned' (literally 'above said' and 'above written', respectively).[17]

---

[16] T. Sävborg, *Étude sur le rôle de la préposition* DE *dans les expressions de lieu relatives* (Uppsala, 1941), 332.

[17] Ð. Šurmin and S. Bosanac, *Čitanka iz književnih starina staroslovenskih, hrvatskih i srpskih za VII*

Ablative–locative transfers in Serbo-Croat adverbs are thus attested from as early as the beginning of the fourteenth century. On the other hand, the locative use of the prepositions *iznad*, etc. is of more recent origin. Budmani offers the following earliest attested locative instances: *ispod*—sixteenth century (the Dubrovnik writer N. Nalješković); *iza*—eighteenth century (the Dubrovnik writer B. Zuzeri); *ispred* and *iznad*—nineteenth century (folk song collection of Vuk Karadžić).[18] Thus it is, after all, apparent that adverbs were affected by ablative–locative transfers before prepositions not only in Slovene but also in Serbo-Croat. The situation will be further clarified if we are able to explain how it is that the Serbo-Croat facts seemed at first to be the other way round. The explanation lies in allative–locative neutralizations. As we saw in section 4 above, whereas Slovene preserves a distinction between allative *gor* and locative *zgoraj*, in Serbo-Croat the word *gore* is now used in either an allative or a locative function, with the result that it is no longer the case that the normal word for 'above' in Serbo-Croat is the product of an ablative–locative transfer. While there are no grounds as yet for establishing any causal relationship between ablative–locative transfers and allative–locative neutralizations, the ablative–locative transfer involved in the early locative use of *zgora* clearly preceded the allative–locative neutralization which resulted in *gore* having both allative and locative functions. Thus the situation with regard to ablative–locative transfers has been obscured by a subsequent allative–locative neutralization.

6

In colloquial usage, as opposed to the standard literary varieties, there is ample evidence of a wave of ablative–locative transfers affecting both languages at the present time.

The Slovene words for 'inside' and 'outside', as we have seen, are *znotraj* and *zunaj*. Although they incorporate the ablative-marker *iz*, their meaning is locative. This is clear from the fact that to express the meanings 'from inside' and 'from outside' it is necessary to add the further ablative-marker *od*, as in (12) and (13). (The corresponding Serbo-Croat ablative adverbs are *iznutra* and *spolja* or *izvana*.)

(12) Srb. Partija se nije   mogla   oboriti *iznutra*
     [party   self (neg.-past) been-able topple from-inside]

---

i VIII razred srednjih škola, 5 ed. (Zagreb, 1923), 88. I am grateful to Harry Leeming, of the School of Slavonic and East European Studies, London, for drawing my attention to these examples and for considerable further help on matters of etymology.

[18] P. Budmani, *Rječnik hrvatskoga ili srpskoga jezika*, iii (Zagreb, 1887–91), 935, 959; iv (Zagreb, 1892–7), 113, 257.

Cr.   Partija se ne može srušiti   *iznutra*
      [party   self not can   overthrow from-inside]
Sln. *Od   znotraj* je ni   bilo mogoče strmoglaviti
      [from inside it (neg.-past) been possible overthrow]
Eng. 'The Party could not be overthrown from within'

(13) Srb. . . . ga . . . gotovo zagluši klicanje *spolja*
             [it   almost deafens cheering from-outside]
      Cr.   . . . se   utopio   u urnebesom klicanju *izvana*
             [(self-past) drowned in noisy   cheering from-outside]
      Sln. . . . ga je   preplavilo rjoveče vpitje *od   zunaj*
             [it (past) deluged   bellowing cries from outside]
      Eng. 'it was almost drowned by a roar of cheering from outside'

However, in colloquial usage *od znotraj* and *od zunaj* can mean simply
'inside' and 'outside'. The following example comes from the folk-song
Majol'ka, bod' pozdravljena 'Greetings, Majolika (sc. wine jug)':

(14) *Od zunaj* lepo pisana, *od znotraj* vinca štrihana
      'On the outside beautifully coloured, on the inside painted
                                                     with wine'

In fact, such uses are quite old; example (15) dates from the early
eighteenth century:

(15) vinʃke-jágode . . . katére *odsnótraj* pizhké jimájo[19]
      [grapes   . . . which inside   seeds have]
      'grapes with seeds in them'

Similarly, *zgoraj* 'above' and *spodaj* 'below' are frequently prefixed with
od in colloquial Slovene, even when the meaning is locative rather than
ablative, and the resultant *od zgoraj* and *od spodaj* are often reduced to *od
zgor* and *od spod*.
    In Serbo-Croat some speakers make a distinction in colloquial usage
between two locative adverbs *ispod* and *od ispod*, and because of the
neutralization of the allative–locative distinction (cf. section 4 above)
each can occur also in an allative function with a verb of motion such as
staviti 'to put':

(16a) Staviću ga ispod
(16b) Staviću ga od ispod

Both sentences in (16) mean something like 'I'll put it underneath'.
However, whereas (16a) may be used if something is to be put under

---

[19] Fr. Hipolit [Janez Adam Gaiger of Novo Mesto], MS Slovene version of J. A. Komenský's *Orbis
sensualium pictus* (Nuremberg, 1658) (chap. xvii). The MS is an appendix to Hipolit's MS Diction-
arium trilingue, written in 1711–12 and now in the National and University Library, Ljubljana.

one object, (16b) apparently implies that it is to be put at the bottom of a pile of things. The same speakers make a distinction also between (17a) and (17b):[20]

(17a) Stavić́u ga gore   'I'll put it up there'
(17b) Stavić́u ga od gore 'I'll put it on top'

In attempting to explain ablative–locative transfers it is obviously important to consider not only the traditional type exemplified by *ispod* in (16a) but also the latest wave of innovation illustrated by *od ispod* and *od gore* in (16b) and (17b). I shall return to them below.

7

In attempting to explain the phenomenon under discussion I shall consider three approaches. The first, proposed by MacKenzie, involves the notion of 'reconceptualization'. The second invokes a derivational cycle relating to adverbs and prepositions. The third involves a different kind of derivational cycle based on the locative vs. directional distinction. Two facts which emerged in the previous section are worth keeping in mind throughout. First, our explanation should be consistent with the fact that adverbs are affected by ablative–locative transfers before prepositions. Secondly, it makes sense to concentrate our attention on relatively recent ablative–locative transfers such as that illustrated by *od ispod* in (16b) rather than on the inner layers of the structure of a word such as SCr. *odozgo*, since the relevant details are presumably more accessible.

The mechanism which MacKenzie tentatively proposes to explain ablative–locative transfers involves the notion of reconceptualization. Referring to the situation described by the Faroese example

(18)   Fáa mjólk undan   kúnni
        [to-get milk   under (abl.) cow-the]
        'to milk the cow'

he points out that it may be interpreted in either of two ways: either the milk is got *from under the cow* or it is got *under the cow*.[21] He suggests therefore that ablative forms may come to be reconceptualized as locative even though the original morphological form of the ablative is retained:

The ablative morphology thus becomes associated with locative meaning and may, ultimately, perhaps aided by reduction of affixes, come to oust the original locative place-adverbs.[22]

[20] I am very grateful for many subtle observations supplied by Milica and Branko Brozović on details of Serbo-Croat and by Simona Bennett on Slovene.
[21] MacKenzie, 'Ablative–Locative Transfers' (n. 1), 154.   [22] Ibid.

Although (18) involves a prepositional phrase rather than an adverb, reconceptualization of the kind that MacKenzie invokes could apply equally well to adverbs. Moreover, this is a convenient point at which to venture an explanation of the fact that ablative–locative transfers affect adverbs before prepositions.

The adverbs and prepositions in question typically refer to some side of an object, e.g. the top, bottom, front, back, inside or outside.[23] Two syntactic structures are involved, illustrated by English (i) *in front* and (ii) *in front of the house*. Both are originally prepositional phrases in which the side in question (here *front*) is the object of a preposition (here *in*). The difference between (i) and (ii) is that (ii) specifies the object whose front is being referred to—by means of a genitive phrase (*of the house*)—whereas (i) treats the identity of the object as recoverable from the context. As regards present-day English, it is customary to describe *in front of* as a complex preposition, whose object in (ii) is *the house*. Thus the string of words *in front of* is well on the way to becoming fused into a single word. This process, whereby originally separate words become fused into a single word, is carried further in the case of (i') *behind* and (ii') *behind the house*, in which *behind* functions first as an adverb and secondly as a preposition. We see, then, that the adverbs and prepositions in which we are interested are derived from two different types of prepositional phrase, as in (i) and (ii). It should now be clear why adverbs (which derive from the type-(i) structure) are affected by ablative–locative transfers before prepositions (which derive from the type-(ii) structure): since the type-(i) structure is included in the type-(ii) structure, the possibility of an ablative–locative transfer affecting the latter presupposes the possibility of the same process affecting the former. There is nevertheless a mystery concerning the time at which adverbs and prepositions are affected, to which I will return in section 8.

Examples (16b) and (17b) may seem to present a problem for the explanation based on reconceptualization. Given that the normal way of expressing 'from below' and 'from above' in Serbo-Croat is with the words *odozdo* and *odozgo*, there is no need to use *od ispod* and *od gore* as ablative expressions. Consequently, the ability of the notion of reconceptualization to account for the locative (and subsequent allative) use of *od ispod* and *od gore* may be questioned. But this sort of objection can be answered. Once a pattern has been established—in this case the pattern whereby ablative markers are used locatively—it can be extended to other items without each individual item needing to undergo the same reconceptualization process.

A more serious problem for the reconceptualization hypothesis, however, is that, if ablative expressions can be reconceptualized as

[23] Spanish *donde* (cf. Table 2) is an exception.

locative, there would seem to be no reason for excluding the possibility of locative expressions being reconceptualized as ablative. Thus the hypothesis would predict transfers in either direction; locative–ablative transfers, though, seem not to occur. Admittedly, a French phrase such as *prendre* sur *le haut de l'armoire* 'to take *from* the top of the wardrobe' (literally: 'to take on the top of the wardrobe') involves an alternative conceptualization of a situation, by comparison with its English translation;[24] and similarly in the case of *boire* dans *un verre* 'to drink *out of* a glass' (literally: 'to drink *in* a glass'). However, there is no evidence that *sur* and *dans* are losing their locative meaning in favour of an ablative meaning.

As a second approach to explaining ablative–locative transfers one might start from the observation that prepositions and adverbs exhibit varying degrees of morphological complexity. Whatever the history of the Serbo-Croat preposition *pod*, it seems reasonable to regard it as being morphologically simple in the present-day language. On the other hand, *ispod*—which may function either as an adverb or as a preposition—is obviously morphologically complex; and the adverbial expression *od ispod*—as in (16b)—is yet more complex. The relationship between these forms may be tentatively represented as in Table 4, which involves a derivational cycle in which adverbs are derived from prepositions and may then themselves be used as prepositions.

Table 4. *The preposition–adverb cycle*

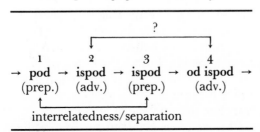

The distinction between interrelatedness and separation is shown as applying to the contrast between stage-1 prepositions and stage-3 prepositions. The analogous distinction illustrated by example (16) between stage-2 and stage-4 adverbs is left unlabelled. A parallel for the first three stages of Table 4 is provided by English *under* and *underneath*. Like SCr. *pod*, *under* functions as a preposition but not as an adverb. *Underneath* is an adverb derived from *under*, and may itself also be used as a preposition. Similarly, stages 2, 3, and 4 of Table 4 are illustrated

[24] Miller, *Semantics and Syntax* (n. 11), 71.

by English *before* and *beforehand*. In internal structure, *before*—like *underneath*—was originally a prepositional phrase (meaning 'by the front'), and—again like *underneath*—it functioned as an adverb (stage 2). But *before* can also be used as a preposition (stage 3) and *beforehand* is an adverb (stage 4) derived from the preposition *before*. In creating adverbs out of prepositions a variety of elements may be added, as is illustrated by the following pairs: *under → underneath*, *before → beforehand*, *after → afterwards*, *in → inside*, *in → within*, *in → therein*. (Miller posits a somewhat different kind of 'cycle', whereby 'nouns are downgraded to adverbs, adverbs to prepositions, prepositions to case inflections and case inflections to zero'.[25] There is certainly evidence for the progressive grammaticalization of lexical items along these lines, but one can also focus attention on the words within which the items occur and the derivational processes in which they participate, as I have done in Table 4.)

The main hypothesis built into Table 4 is that the function of *iz* in *ispod* and of *od* in *od ispod* is to derive an adverb from a preposition. However, such an analysis would call into question the validity of the term 'ablative–locative transfer': if *iz* and *od* have the morphological function of creating an adverb out of a preposition, then in this context it would be inappropriate to assume that their meaning was originally ablative. In the adverb *ispod* it would not even be appropriate to attribute the meaning of 'separation' to *iz*. Rather, according to this analysis, the meaning of 'separation' would become associated with *ispod* only with the emergence of a contrast between *pod* and *ispod*, which would depend on *ispod* being able to be used as a preposition.

It is a rather suspect measure, though, to attribute to *iz* and *od* a morphological function in the context in question without attributing to them a particular meaning. Even if the meaning of *iz* in *ispod* was not originally ablative, it must have had some meaning. One possibility is that it had a genitive meaning. This is suggested by the fact that *iz* and *od* are used to translate not only *out of* and *from* in sentences such as *I made it out of wood/I made it from wood* but also *of* in sentences such as *it is made of wood*: SCr. *od drveta je* (*napravljen*); Sln. *iz lesa je* (*narejen*). Moreover, it is worth mentioning the Slovene words *zjutraj* 'in the morning' and *zvečer* 'in the evening', which also begin with what is apparently the remains of the word *iz*. The words *zjutraj* and *zvečer* can hardly have undergone reconceptualization themselves, since they presumably never meant 'from the morning' and 'from the evening'. If, on the other hand, *z-* in these expressions were ascribed a genitive meaning, they would parallel temporal expressions in other languages, such as German *des Morgens* 'in the morning' and French *de nuit* 'by night' (literally: 'of the morning' and 'of night'), or indeed SCr. *ovoga jutra*

[25] Ibid. 78.

'this morning' (literally: 'of this morning'). Nevertheless it would still be incumbent upon us to explain the relationship between the ablative and the genitive that allows one and the same form to have either meaning.

There is, however, in any case, another problem raised by the cycle illustrated by Table 4. We saw from (17b) that in colloquial Serbo-Croat some speakers use the adverbial expression *od gore* (which contrasts with the adverb *gore*). Table 4 may imply that *od gore* is derived from a prepositional use of *gore*, but in fact *gore* functions only as an adverb.

In a study of the meaning of English prepositions carried out quite a long time ago, I employed a descriptive framework in which the hierarchy of spatial expressions shown in Table 5 featured prominently.[26]

Table 5. *A hierarchy of spatial expressions*

level 4: directional
level 3: locative
level 2: directional
level 1: locative

A simple locative expression (level 1) is illustrated by *over the table* in *my hand is over the table*. The same location can function directionally (level 2) in three different ways: as a 'source' or 'path' or 'goal', i.e. with ablative, prolative, or allative function. The three possibilities are illustrated by the sentences *I removed my hand from over the table*, *can you jump over the table?*, and *please put the lamp over the table*. A level-3 locative expression is one which contains one or more directional expressions functioning locatively, e.g. *over the hill* in *the post office is over the hill*. The location 'over the hill' in this sentence is at the end of a path leading over the hill from some known starting-point. Finally, this complex (level 3) locative expression can itself function directionally (level 4), as in *a car appeared from over the hill*.

It would seem that the same hierarchy is relevant to the question of ablative–locative transfers in Slovene and Serbo-Croat. However, there is a crucial respect in which the details are different. In relation to English, it was assumed that level-3 locative expressions necessarily contain either a path expression or a goal expression. The first kind was illustrated above with the sentence *the post office is over the hill*; a further example is: *the ticket office is through that archway*. The second kind is illustrated by *the caretaker lives to the right* or *the lamp stood well into the corner*. As regards source expressions, it was assumed that these could accompany a path or goal expression—as in *the post office is over the hill*

[26] D. C. Bennett, *Spatial and Temporal Uses of English Prepositions* (London, 1975), 50–62.

from here or *the caretaker lives to the right from the main entrance*—but that a locative expression could not consist simply of a source expression functioning locatively. Data from other languages force us to recognize just such a possibility. In Modern Greek there are two ways of saying 'in front of the house', one of which contains the preposition *se* 'to', while the other contains *apo* 'from':

(20a) brosta sto   spiti
       [in-front to-the house]
(20b) brosta apo to spiti
       [in-front from the house]

Frequently (20a) and (20b) are interchangeable, but there are also situations where one or the other would be preferred. For instance, (20a) is preferred in saying 'there is a tree in front of the house' but (20b) would be used if the location 'in front of the house' was where one intended to meet someone. A tree in front of a house is permanently associated with the house. On the other hand, if one waits for someone in front of a house, the situation involves what Bugarski calls 'relative position' but no other relationship.[27] Thus the Greek examples in (20) involve the distinction that we have already encountered between interrelatedness and separation.

In the terms of the hierarchy in Table 5, English phrases such as *in front of the house* were analysed as level-1 locative expressions.[28] Given the existence of uses of *in front of* where the 'front' of an object is 'deictically' defined (i.e. the 'front' *from* a particular viewpoint rather than its inherent front), this analysis was not necessarily adequate even in the case of the English data. The Modern Greek examples in (20), on the other hand, surely need to be treated as level-3 locative expressions, in which either a goal (allative) expression or a source (ablative) expression is embedded inside a locative expression and thus functions locatively.

Two analyses suggest themselves for the contrast between SCr. *nad glavom* 'over one's head' and *iznad glave* 'above one's head'.[29] If *nad* is not only morphologically but also semantically unmarked—i.e. if we are dealing with the absence of the meaning of 'separation' rather than the presence of the meaning of 'interrelatedness'—then *nad glavom* involves a level-1 locative expression, whereas *iznad glave* involves a level-3 locative expression incorporating the meaning of 'separation' in the form of an embedded ablative expression. On the other hand, if semantically *nad glavom* (like *iznad glave*) is marked—i.e. if its meaning necessarily involves 'interrelatedness'—then an analysis parallel to that

---

[27] Cf. section 3, p. 139 above.
[28] Bennett, op. cit. (n. 26), 81–3.
[29] Cf. section 3, p. 139 above.

proposed for Greek *brosta se* and *brosta apo* may be appropriate. Specifically, *nad glavom* may involve an allative expression functioning locatively, whereas *iznad glave* may involve an ablative expression functioning locatively, and both may be level-3 locative expressions. Bugarski's discussion invites preference for the second of these analyses.

The third approach to an explanation of ablative–locative transfers crucially involves the distinction, and interrelationship, between (a) ablative expressions as a type of directional expression and (b) locative expressions consisting simply of an ablative expression functioning locatively. I shall symbolize them as in (21):

(21a) [abl. [loc.]]
(21b) [loc. [abl. [loc.]]]

Even (21a) contains a locative expression, since what functions ablatively (or, for that matter, prolatively or allatively) is a location.[30] An expression of type (21a) occurs in a directional sentence, i.e. a sentence which describes a change of position. Its function is to specify the starting-point of a change of position. On the other hand, (21b) can occur in a locative sentence, such as Sln. *spredaj je* 'it's in front'. When such expressions as *spredaj* are first formed, with an unreduced ablative marker in them, it would seem that they specify a location as being situated *at some distance from* some side of an object (in this case the front). The meaning of ablativity present in them is that of separation. Their function, however, is to specify a location and the ablative marker that they contain does not express ablativity proper. For this reason it is susceptible to reduction, as we see from the fact that Slovene *iz* has lost its vowel.

It is important that ablative expressions proper—those of type (21a)—stand in a relationship of markedness to allative and prolative expressions (which from this point of view can be considered together), with ablative functioning as the marked term of the opposition.[31] Two aspects of the marked nature of ablative expressions are relevant. First,

(22) ablative expressions are relatively infrequent.

Directional sentences typically indicate a new location, by means of a prolative or allative expression. The earlier location—which would be indicated by an ablative expression, if present—is frequently recoverable from the preceding discourse and as such does not need to be specified. Secondly, where an ablative expression is present,

(23) ablativity is always overtly signalled.

---

[30] Bennett, op. cit. (n. 26), 18–26.
[31] Ibid. 75–7; and especially Y. Ikegami, '"Source" vs. "Goal": a Case of Linguistic Dissymmetry', in: R. Dirven and G. Radden (eds.), *Concepts of Case* (Tübingen, 1987), 125–7.

That is to say, ablative expressions consist of a marker of ablativity attached to a constituent representing a location. In this respect they contrast with prolative and allative expressions, since in many languages these two directional functions are frequently not overtly signalled—e.g. English *the ball rolled under the table* (in either directional interpretation).

The remaining points that need to be made are best clarified in relation to specific examples. Consider in this connection the Serbo-Croat examples (24)–(26):

(24)   On se izvuče   ispod   kamiona[32]
       [he self pulled-out from-under lorry]
       'he pulled himself out from under the lorry'

(25)   Alat se nalazi ispod   kamiona
       [tools self finds underneath lorry]
       'the tools are underneath the lorry'

(26)   On je   premestio alat od   ispod   kamiona
       [he (past) moved   tools from underneath lorry
           (i   stavio ga na stolicu)
           (and put   it on chair)]
       'he moved the tools from under the lorry (and put them on the chair)'

Example (24) demonstrates that ablative uses of SCr. *ispod* can still be encountered. (It thus forces a qualification of the suggestion in section 2 that the Serbo-Croat prepositions in which we are interested have already completed an ablative–locative transfer.) The reconceptualization hypothesis would treat locative uses of *ispod* as arising in directional sentences such as (24)—though not necessarily with the kind of verb that occurs in this particular example—and then being extended to locative sentences such as (25). According to the present hypothesis the locative use of *ispod* arises in locative sentences, as an instance of structure (21b). At this point *ispod* has two distinct uses, as in (24) and (25), whereupon the two aspects of the marked nature of ablative expressions—cf. (22) and (23)—become relevant. Given (22), the locative use of *ispod* is likely to be considerably more common than the ablative use. In turn, the fact that the whole of *ispod* is commonly assigned a locative interpretation creates a difficulty from the point of view of interpreting its ablative use—in accordance with (23)—as consisting of an ablative marker attached to a locative constituent. The solution to the problem is found by allowing *ispod* to occupy the locative slot in the ablative expression and inserting a separate marker

---

[32] This example is taken from Bugarski, 'A System' (n. 13), 11.

of ablativity. This is what we have in the case of *od ispod* in (26). It contains two ablative markers, but only the outermost one expresses ablativity proper. An advantage of the present hypothesis is that it provides a basis for explaining the unidirectional nature of ablative–locative transfers and the fact that the process can be repeated over and over again in the history of a language. Thus when phrases such as *od ispod* are standardly used in ablative expressions, they will also be available to function locatively, providing the language still retains the possibility of the structure in (21b) and the process then repeats itself.

One final comment is necessary concerning the presence of *od* in (26) and its absence in (24). The crucial difference between these two examples seems to be that *izvući* 'to pull out' has a rather more specific directional meaning than *premestiti* 'to move'. Since *izvući* contains the prefix *iz-* 'out', indicating a movement towards the outside, it is clear that *ispod kamiona* in (24) must indicate the starting-point of the movement. On the other hand, in view of the general meaning of *premestiti*, coupled with the fact that *ispod* takes the same case in all uses (the genitive) and the further fact that allative expressions in Serbo-Croat frequently contain no overt marker of allativity, the use of *od* as an overt marker of ablativity is needed to a greater extent in (26) and serves the purpose, for instance, of preventing the allative interpretation of *ispod kamiona* which would otherwise be a possibility. Such considerations suggest the possibility of a causal relationship between allative–locative neutralizations and ablative–locative transfers.

8

We are still a long way from a definitive account of ablative–locative transfers. I hope, however, to have shed light on some of the issues involved. The main conclusion is that the locative–directional cycle, and in particular the distinction between the structures in (21a) and (21b), coupled with two aspects of the marked status of ablative expressions, provides a better basis for explaining ablative–locative transfers than the notion of reconceptualization.

However, an important question immediately suggests itself: namely, why some languages—or some languages at particular times—are *not* affected by ablative–locative transfers. For instance, there is no evidence of an ablative–locative transfer affecting English at the present time. This is clearly related to the fact that English seems not to have locative expressions of type (21b), but this fact also requires explanation.

There are also several other topics touched on above which have not been resolved. For instance, at the time of writing I have not had access to any native speaker whose usage includes the difference in Croatian between *naprijed* as in example (6) and *sprijeda* as in example (7). Thus I have not been able to determine whether the two expressions contrast or not. Moreover, the relationship between the notions 'ablative' and 'genitive' is a further issue which requires more detailed investigation.

Finally, with regard to the distinction between adverbs and prepositions, Sävborg's discussion of the Romance languages leads one to expect ablative–locative transfers to affect prepositional uses of adverbs soon after the adverbs themselves are affected.[33] Yet in both Serbo-Croat and Slovene the prepositions seem to have lagged rather far behind the adverbs. In Slovene, the fact that the adverbs *zgoraj*, *spodaj*, etc., have a *-j* ending characteristic of other types of adverb may have inhibited their use as prepositions. However, this is not necessarily the answer, since *znotraj* and *zunaj* may by now be used also as prepositions, as in *znotraj in zunaj hiše* 'inside and outside the house'. Clearly the matter requires further investigation.

[33] Sävborg, *Étude* (n. 16), 63.

The Galoshes Manifesto: A Motif in the Novels of Sasha Sokolov

By D. BARTON JOHNSON

FOOTWEAR and feet occupy a prominent place in the Russian literary consciousness. The 'pedal digression' in *Evgeny Onegin* is one of the most famous passages in Russian literature.[1] Pushkin's arch-detractor, the radical utilitarian literary critic Dmitry Pisarev, is remembered for his observation that stitching a pair of boots is more useful than reading Shakespeare's plays.[2] Or perhaps even writing them, although Pisarev thought highly of the English playwright. Lev Tolstoy, no lover of Shakespeare, none the less seems to have taken Pisarev's advice to heart, for in the 1880s, having rejected what he now regarded as his frivolous novels, *War and Peace* and *Anna Karenina*, he took up shoe-making. Although his gifts as a cobbler were modest, he proudly presented his wares to friends. One of them, S. M. Sukhotin, set a pair of the master's boots next to a twelve-volume set of Tolstoy's writings and labelled them 'Volume XIII'.[3]

The origins of the footwear theme in Russian literature remain obscure. Afanas'ev's famous collection of fairy tales is rife with magical and mundane footwear. *Bashmaki* occur in fourteen tales; *sapogi* in six; and *lapti* in three; to say nothing of numerous *samokhody*, *bakhily*, and *cheveriki*.[4] For our purposes, however, it is appropriate to see as progenitor Gogol' with his comi-tragic hero, Bashmachkin, who is truly *pod bashmakom* 'under the boot' of all and sundry: 'It is quite evident', Gogol' says, that the name 'sprang from *bashmak* or shoe, but at what time, just when and how it sprang from a shoe—of that nothing is known. For not only this clerk's father, but his grandfather and even his brother-in-law, and absolutely all the Bashmachkins, walked about in boots, merely resoling them three times a year.'[5] This flight of fancy is quintessentially Gogolian. The same tendency to seize upon an odd

---

[1] The phrase is taken from Vladimir Nabokov, who describes the passage as 'one of the wonders of the work'. See *Eugene Onegin. A Novel in Verse by Alexander Pushkin*, tr. with commentary by Vladimir Nabokov (New York, 1964), ii. 115.

[2] William E. Harkins, *Dictionary of Russian Literature* (Patterson, N.J., 1959), 300.

[3] Henri Troyat, *Tolstoy* (Garden City, N.J., 1967), 467.

[4] A. N. Afanas'ev, *Narodnye russkie skazki*, ed. L. G. Barag and N. V. Novikov (M., 1984). See the 'Ukazatel' predmetov' in vol. iii.

[5] Nikolay Gogol', 'The Overcoat', in: *A Treasury of Russian Literature*, ed. and tr. Bernard Guilbert Guerney (New York, 1943), 130.

word or sound and let language and imagination playfully evoke lines of association which take on their own independent existence is equally the essence of Sasha Sokolov's style. Although Sokolov's more immediate stylistic forebears are Bely and Pil'nyak, Gogolian ink runs deep in his veins.[6] Sokolov and Gogol' also share the central theme of *poshlost'*. And both utilize elaborate motif systems. If the nose is all-intrusive in Gogol', the shoe pervades Sokolov's fictional universe. At the lowest level, the prominence of the motif is suggested by the sheer number and diversity of terms relating to footwear in Sokolov's novels: *bashmaki, botforty, boty, botinki (polubotinki), cheboty, chizmy, chubury, galoshi (kaloshi), gety, ichigi, kedy, klogi, lapti, mokrostupy, obuvi (obuvki), sapogi, sandalii, tapochki (polutapochki), shlepantsy, shtiblety, tapti, tufli, valenki*. The list may easily be extended with appurtenances such as socks, stockings, footcloths, gaiters, skates, crutches, and artificial legs.

Sasha Sokolov (b. 1943) is the author of three very different avant-garde novels.[7] *Shkola dlya durakov* (1976), set in the milieu of the Moscow professional classes *circa* 1960, tells of an adolescent schizo-phrenic's attempts to come to terms with the fundamental human experiences of love, sex, and death in a morally corrupt, adult world. *Mezhdu sobakoi i volkom* (1980), a tale of lethal violence, putative paternity, and possible incest, takes place in the timeless, primitive world of the remote upper Volga among hunter and fisher folk. *Palisan-driya* (1985) is an elegant parody of the many varieties of pseudo-literature that make up the bestseller list: the sensational self-serving pseudo-memoir, the adventure thriller, the pornographic novel, and so on. Its self-deluded hero, the hermaphrodite Palisandr, tells of his bizarre adventures leading to his ascension to the Russian throne in 1999. Although the three books are united by Sokolov's language-obsessed style and his playful thematic preoccupation with time and death, three novels more different in tonality and setting are scarcely imaginable. It is surprising to find a motif that is not only common to all the novels but which has a distinct thematic resonance in each. I shall examine the boot motif in each novel, relate it to one or more of the book's themes, and, finally, offer some speculations about the origin of the motif in Sokolov's creative development.[8]

    [6] Sokolov pays particular parodic tribute to Gogol' in chap. 5 of *Mezhdu sobakoi i volkom* (Ann Arbor, 1980) in a dialogue between Nikodim Ermolaich Palamakhterov and Ksenofont Ardal'onych.

    [7] *Shkola dlya durakov* (Ann Arbor, 1976), *Mezhdu sobakoi i volkom* (Ann Arbor, 1980), and *Palisan-driya* (Ann Arbor, 1985). Quotations are taken from *A School for Fools*, tr. Carl Proffer (Ann Arbor, 1977), although I have sometimes modified Proffer's translations. Page references to the Russian original and the English translation are indicated respectively by the abbreviations R and E. An English translation of *Palisandriya* as *Astrophobia*, tr. Michael Heim (New York, 1989) is forthcom-ing. For biographical and bibliographic information, see D. Barton Johnson, 'Sasha Sokolov: A Literary Biography' and idem, 'A Selected Annotated Bibliography of Work by and about Sasha Sokolov', *Canadian-American Slavic Studies*, xxii, 1989 (forthcoming).

[*See p. 157 for n. 8*]

1

The theme of Sokolov's first novel *Shkola dlya durakov* evolves from a series of antinomies: madness/sanity, freedom/bondage, and nature/institutions.[9] Madness, freedom, and nature are interdependent and closely linked with artistic creativity, as in the best tradition of high Romanticism. The oppressive institutions of 'sanity' are the boy's Moscow apartment dominated by his loathsome father, a state prosecutor; the psychiatric hospital presided over by Dr Zauze; and the school for fools headed by Perillo, the petty tyrant principal, and his deputy Sheina Trakhtenberg. Opposed to these institutions and their representatives are two of the school's teachers—the irrepressibly eccentric geography teacher Pavel (also Savl) Norvegov, who is the boy's iconoclastic idol, and Veta Akatova, the biology teacher, who is the boy's fantasized bride-to-be.

The nameless hero, Student So-and-So, and the two teachers are closely identified with nature. The boy imagines himself transformed into a water lily and assumes its Latin name, Nymphea Alba. The names of the biology teacher, Veta Akatova, respectively suggest *vetka*, 'bough', and *akatsiya*, 'acacia'. Her father, Arkady Akatov (cf. 'arcadian'), an elderly entomologist, is referred to as 'a stoop-shouldered tree'. The stressed *-ve-* of Norvegov's name foretokens the novel's prevailing deity, the *Nasylayushchii veter*, the Ill-Boding Wind, that promises to sweep away the repressive institutionalized structures of society. The positive characters are identified with the nature-filled holiday community where all have dachas.

The novel's central thematic conflicts, freedom versus repression, nature versus institutions, madness versus sanity, the individual versus the collective, unbounded circumambient time versus linear chronology, a free, spontaneous intuitive art versus an institutionalized pseudo-art are all very general, very broad abstractions. They are, for

[8] I shall use 'boot motif' as a generic term for any kind of footwear and closely related items. The data for the present study was collected by computer with the help of Nota Bene and Brigham Young Concordance programmes. I would like to express my appreciation of the technical assistance of Darl J. Dumont and Ellendea Proffer, who provided Sokolov's novels in machine-readable form.

[9] Discussions of the thematics of *Shkola dlya durakov* may be found in Alexander Boguslawski, 'Sokolov's *A School for Fools*: An Escape from Socialist Realism', *Slavic and East European Journal*, xxvii (1983), 91–7; John Freedman, 'Memory, Imagination, and the Liberating Force of Literature in Sasha Sokolov's *School for Fools*', *Canadian-American Slavic Studies*, xxii (1989) (forthcoming); Felix Philipp Ingold, '*Škola dlja durakov*. Versuch über Saša Sokolov', *Wiener Slawistischer Almanach*, iii (1979), 93–124; D. Barton Johnson, 'A Structural Analysis of Sasha Sokolov's *School for Fools*: A Paradigmatic Novel', in: *Fiction and Drama in Eastern and Southeastern Europe: Evolution and Experiment in the Postwar Period*, ed. Henrik Birnbaum and Thomas Eekman (Columbus, 1980), 207–37; Fred Moody, 'Madness and the Pattern of Freedom in Sasha Sokolov's *A School for Fools*', *Russian Literature Triquarterly*, xvi (1979), 7–32.

the most part, manifested indirectly in the conflict between the boy and his idol Pavel (Savl) Norvegov, on one side, and the nameless father together with his spiritual allies, the Principal Perillo and his deputy Sheina Trakhtenberg, on the other. The thematic conflict is also expressed on a more subtle, smaller scale. The complex, seemingly chaotic novel has an elaborate motif system that epitomizes these abstract themes. We shall show the novel's theme to be embodied in one such motif: footwear—more particularly, the opposition between footwear and its absence, between the shod and the shoeless.

Shkola dlya durakov opens with the hero's description of the dacha community railway station and its splintery, nail-embedded platform where '*bosikom ne sledovalo khodit*' (R7/E11). The narrator then recalls an earlier encounter with a barefoot Norvegov on this platform, although we soon learn that Norvegov had died some two years before this imagined encounter (R18/E26). The boy, who suffers from 'select-ive memory' as a part of his inability to understand linear time, struggles to recall Norvegov's attire. He ends by deciding that 'It is simpler to say what he was not wearing. Norvegov never wore shoes' (R16–17/E24). This assertion is challenged by the other half of the boy's personality: it was only in summer at the dacha; surely their teacher did not go to school barefoot.

The 'barefoot motif' follows Norvegov throughout the narrative. The book's most frequent image is that of Norvegov sitting in the school's toilet, warming his bare feet on a radiator. Here, Pavel (who is also Savl, the prophet of the wind) expounds his views to the narrator and tries to recall the fact of his own death and its circumstances. Student So-and-So helps his deceased idol remember how, shortly before his death, he was suspended from his beloved teaching duties at the instigation of Trakhtenberg. The schizoid boy (who always refers to himself in the plural) vows that (t)he(y) will never forget Norvegov: 'Almost sound-less, your bare feet have left an imprint in our brain and frozen there forever, as if you had imprinted them in asphalt softened by the sun, walking across it to the triumphant ceremonial march of the Julian calendar' (E186/R137).

The Julian calendar relates to another aspect of the footwear motif. The image of Pavel as a Roman legionary flickers in and out of the story (R128–9/E175–6). Faced with possible dismissal, Norvegov resolves to conform to the dictates of Perillo: to arrive at school on time, to follow the official lesson plan, and to buy and wear sandals (R146/E198). This compromise footwear gives rise in the boy's mind to the Roman legion-ary image. Pavel dies before his probation period is up, and the deceit-ful school officials bury the popular, if troublesome, eccentric with full honours. To the outrage of the deceased, they fit him out in suit and tie and, worse still, 'metal-buckled leather shoes of a kind I never wore in my life . . .' (E61/R43). He demands the return of his own clothes, his 'sandals in the style of the Roman Empire period when the aqueduct was built, I will put them under my balding head because—to spite you—I am going to go barefoot even in the valleys of nonbeing . . .' (E61–2/R43).

The thematic juxtaposition of the barefoot and the shod is explicitly posed by the narrator's prosecutor father, the quintessential institutional man. Immediately following the narrator's inner dialogue on Norvegov's footwear, the scene switches to the father on a hot summer day at the dacha. The hammocked father looks up from his paper (his fixed attribute) and grumbles 'why the hell should Pavel want shoes in weather like this. It is only poor officials like us . . . who never give our feet any rest: if it's not boots, then it's galoshes; if not galoshes, then boots—it's lifetime torment. If it's raining out, you have to dry your boots; if it's sunny, watch out or they'll crack. And the main thing is that you have to polish them every morning. But your Pavel, he's a free soul, a dreamer, and he's going to die barefoot. He's a loafer, your Pavel, . . . that's why he's a barefoot bum.' The prosecutor continues: [Norvegov] 'should thank God that I'm not his principal, I'd make him jump, . . . the barefooted tramp. The poor geographer, our father didn't have the slightest respect for him. That's what it means not to wear shoes' (R19/E25–6).

The badly paid, gloomy, hard-drinking Principal Nikolay Perillo, who bears the patronymic Gorimirovich, is an old comrade-in-arms of the hero's father (R162/E116). They served with Kutuzov, according to the boy. Perillo tries to run his school of misfits with military punctiliousness. The most hated among his regulations is the *tapochka* or 'slipper' system, which he proclaims in a classroom briefing. From a certain date each student is to bring to school a pair of slippers in a specially made, precisely labelled bag. On arrival he or she will put on the slippers, put street shoes into the bag, and leave it in the school cloakroom. The procedure is to be reversed upon leaving (R79–84/ E109–16). Student So-and-So, who thinks himself two people, inquires whether (t)he(y) will be required to have two bags, fearing the strain on their poor mother who must make the bags (R84). The boy has hysterics, and Perillo threatens to send him back to the mental institution. The Principal ends his presentation by 'clicking his heels military style' and going out.

The *tapochnaya sistema* becomes the much decried symbol of the school for fools. As the boy says, its pupils are 'prisoners, . . . slaves of the *tapochka* system' (R131/E178). On the book's final pages, a scene in a botany class, the narrator speaks of the happiness of rhododendrons for 'they know neither love, nor hate, nor the Perillo *tapochka* system'. The new regimen, incidentally, applies only to the pupils, for when

Perillo later reappears, we again hear the clicking of his boot heels (R147/E199).

Sheina Solomonova Trakhtenberg, whose eavesdropping on Norvegov's class is soon to be the cause of his suspension, presents a different dimension of the footwear motif. She has a squeaky artificial leg that lends her 'a sort of merry, dancing gait' (R106/E145). In the boy's mental landscape she is identified with the Russian folklore witch Baba Yaga, whose rhyming fixed attribute is her *kostyanaya noga*, her bone leg.

The old woman lives in the same communal apartment building as the boy and his family. Strangely enough, she is a figure of powerful sexuality. She drives her first husband, Yakov, to poison himself while betraying him with the one-armed building manager Sorokin, who hangs himself (R15/E21–2). Her present lover, an excavator-operator, amuses himself by stealing the boots from a corpse he unearths at the cemetery (R66–7/91–2). The excavator's name, Trifon Petrovich, is associated with the children's rhyme '*Tra ta ta, Tra ta ta, / Vyshla koshka za kota*' which involves a lustful female cat who toys with her lovers (RE105/143–4). This echoes another bit of popular lore associated with her first husband Yakov. Sheina is fond of borrowing from the hero, her neighbour, an old wind-up record-player that does not work. None the less he hears from her room her single recording, Yakov reciting the folk-tale '*Skirly*'. The tale is of a bear who has a wooden leg which makes a screeching sound ('*skirly*') as he walks. The bear abducts a small girl, takes her to his lair and 'does something with her there, exactly what is unknown, it's not explained in the fairytale . . .' (E145/R106). The boy has only the dimmest notion of the sex act, but the sound evokes powerful emotions. He hates to think of the tale, for it suggests images of Veta in a hotel room with an unknown man. Their activity produces the dread squeaking. The sound, which occurs in several places in the novella, is exactly that made by Sheina Trakhtenberg's prosthesis as she moves through the school corridors (R105–6/E145).[10]

One other character in the narrative is metonymically associated with footwear. The young hero has repeated fantasies of introducing himself to Veta's father, the retired and rehabilitated entomologist Arkady Akatov who owns a nearby dacha. He wishes to apprentice himself to the old scholar and, more importantly, ask for his daughter's hand in marriage. He makes his way to the dacha but becomes distracted by the delights of shouting into the resonant rain barrels standing at the dacha's corners. Looking around he sees a shabby old man watching him. The man wears a torn white robe with a rope belt, a folded paper

---

[10] The unlikely conjunction of an aged woman, footwear, and sexuality also is found in the English children's rhyme 'There was an old woman / Who lived in a shoe. . . .'

hat, and 'on his feet—look carefully at what he has on his feet, that is, how he is shod—and on his feet—I can't see very well, after all he is relatively far away—on his feet, it seems, he has overshoes. Maybe you're wrong, maybe they're sneakers instead of overshoes. The grass is too high, if it were cut down I could make a more definite statement about his footwear, but this way—you can't make it out, but hold it, now I see: they're galoshes' (E138/R101). Only after establishing the nature of his footwear does the boy start to wonder about the identity of the old man 'with galoshes on his bare feet' (E139/R101).

The figure is, of course, Akatov. But why the elaborate discussion about his footwear? A famous naturalist in his day, Akatov has spent many years in a labour camp. Now rehabilitated and pensioned off, he is a broken man, 'a stoop-shouldered old tree'. Although he is one of the nature-loving affirmative characters, his position between the barefoot and the shod is unclear. The narrator is perhaps subconsciously reflecting this ambiguity in his strange preoccupation with the old man's ambiguous footwear: galoshes, not boots, and furthermore, over bare feet. Akatov has been broken, semi-shod by Soviet institutions.

It is in the course of his imaginary conversation with his prospective father-in-law that the narrator makes one of two references to his own footwear: boots with metal clasps which he wears both at school and at home (R110/E151 and R146/E197). The description is nearly identical with that of the burial boots that Pavel rails against (R43/E61). Another telling boot detail occurs when the boy, terrified that he is about to be recommitted to the psychiatric hospital, tries to win over his mother with promises of exemplary behaviour. He will not spy upon her when she ascends the squeaking stairway at his music teacher's home. He will master a czardas on his accordion, and he will even clean his boots (R143/E193). The hero is, as he so often says, a slave of the *tapochka* system in all its variants.

The narrative contains other scattered allusions to footwear in addition to those involved in the central thematic opposition. But they too are suggestive of the boy's preoccupation with footwear. In one sequence the boy fantasizes about finding a kindly woman to initiate his sexual education in preparation for his marriage to Veta. Deciding that a post office clerk is a likely candidate, he wanders toward the post office idly reading shop-signs along the street. Each sign evokes its own associations and images: '*OBUV'*. And I read the word "*obuv'*" [footwear] as "*lyubov'*" [love] on the store' (R118/E161). So pervasive is the footwear motif in *Shkola dlya durakov* that it literally frames the novel from its foreshadowing of the barefoot Norvegov on the first page to its reference to Perillo's *tapochka* system on the last. Many of the novel's major characters are defined as metonymic extensions of their footwear, and its themes are neatly encapsulated in the shod/shoeless motif.

2

The footwear motif occupies an equally important place in Sokolov's second novel, *Mezhdu sobakoi i volkom*.[11] Both the theme and the plot of the novel grow out of the title, a Russian idiom meaning 'twilight', when all is indistinct. Originally the phrase referred to that intermediate time of day when the shepherd is unable to distinguish between his guard-dog and the wolf menacing his flock. Between dog and wolf is the controlling metaphor describing that ill-defined area between two distinct conditions or categories and comprising certain features of both. It is an indeterminate zone between fantasy and reality. The twilight zone, the world between dog and wolf, is a thematic metaphor that pervades every dimension of the novel. All traditional distinctions are called into question. There is no discrimination between past, present, and future; between the living and the dead; between father and son (if even the paternity itself were clear); between mother and mistress, and so on. Different temporal dimensions exist concurrently and some events seem to echo or foreshadow their counterparts. Contradictory versions of events are equally valid, and characters may have no recollection of each other or of earlier events. Such a universe obviously makes it impossible to offer any fully coherent account of the novel's plot, which unfolds along the remote upper reaches of the Volga. What follows is one putative sequence of events accompanied by occasional asides on alternate realities.

Il'ya Patrikeich Zynzyrella, hero and prime narrative voice, is (perhaps) murdered because he cannot tell the difference between a dog and a wolf. Il'ya, an itinerant one-legged grinder, thinks he is being stalked by a wolf. Full of alcoholic courage, he beats off the creature with his crutches. The dog, for such it is, belongs to the game-warden and dog-keeper, Yakov Il'ich Palamakhterov, who in revenge apparently steals Il'ya's crutches. The feud escalates, Il'ya shoots two of the gamekeeper's dogs, and is eventually drowned. Deceased, Il'ya tells his story through a series of letters (chapters) addressed to a state investigator.

The sorrows of Il'ya begin many years before the events that lead to his death. As a young man he meets and innocently woos a girl named

[11] Studies of *Between Dog and Wolf* include: Barbara Heldt, 'Female *Skaz* in Sasha Sokolov's *Between Dog and Wolf*', *Canadian-American Slavic Studies*, xxii (1989) (forthcoming); D. Barton Johnson, 'Sasha Sokolov's *Between Dog and Wolf* and the Modernist Tradition', in: *Russian Literature in Emigration: The Third Wave*, ed. Olga Matich with Michael Heim (Ann Arbor, 1984), 208–17; Vadim Kreid, '*Zaitil'shchina*', *Dvadtsat' dva* (Tel Aviv), xix (1981), 213–18; Gerald S. Smith, 'The Verse in Sasha Sokolov's *Mezhdu sobakoi i volkom*', *Canadian-American Slavic Studies*, xxii (1989) (forthcoming); Leona Toker, 'Gamesman's Sketches (Found in a Bottle): A Reading of Sasha Sokolov's *Between Dog and Wolf*', ibid.

Orina, unaware of her promiscuity. They live together for a time and a child, Yasha, is born, but Orina soon returns to her previous habits. Il'ya, drunk, attacks a group of her lovers, sailors, who leave him trussed to a railroad track. Orina unsuccessfully tries to free him. As the train approaches, she hysterically confuses him with a pet fox of her girlhood that hooligans had tied to the tracks. Orina is killed, and Il'ya's leg is severed. Il'ya eventually joins an artel for cripples and wanders about the countryside sharpening tools and skates, endlessly obsessed with the memory of Orina whose ghost seeks him, so that he may join her in death.

In an alternate reality, the incident on the track does not occur. Il'ya leaves the promiscuous Orina, who takes Yasha, moves away, and changes her name to Mariya (Alfeeva and/or Palamakhterova?). Orina-Mariya continues her promiscuous existence while raising Yakov, who becomes a drunken dreamer; he fancies himself to be both painter and poet while working as a gamekeeper. A second series of chapters, interspersed among Il'ya's letters, are Yakov's alcoholic account of his past and day-dreams. Yakov's poems make up a third set of chapters.

The name of the main narrator of *Mezhdu sobakoi i volkom* is a very odd one for a Russian. Odder still is that it constantly varies in its spelling: Zynzyrela (9), Zynzyrella (17), Dzynzyrela (46), Dzyndzyrella (71), Dzhynzhirela (72), Dzynzyrella (89), Dzhynzherela (166), and his putative kinsman, Zhizhirella (69). He also receives a letter to I. P. Sindirela (142). Other names receive the same treatment, e.g. the town of Bydogoshch (21), Bygodozhd' (87), Vygodoshch' (112), and Gybodoshch' (115). This variation of spelling is not a consequence of Il'ya's marginal literacy, for he spells all other words correctly. It is a feature of the world between dog and wolf, signifying the blurred nature of persons, places, states, and things. Not only is Zynzyrella's name uncertain, but so is his identity. Perhaps due to the coexisting time dimensions in the book, Il'ya Zynzyrella and his putative son (and murderer), Yakov Il'ich Palamakhterov, seem to merge. This confusion of identities also holds for Orina (Mariya) and a nameless retarded girl (or girls) loved by Il'ya and Yakov.

During their courtship Orina tells Il'ya of her girlhood, while they shelter from the rain in a beached boat. She was brought up by an old woman rag-picker. A youthful trapper (whom she later seduces) presents her with a fox cub, which is killed when hooligans tie it to the railway tracks. She takes the hide to the shoemaker who lives beneath the stairs of her building to be made into slippers. In the course of the fittings, she is seduced by him (95–6 and 106–8). Orina's story has strange echoes in Il'ya's later life. After parting from Orina, Il'ya sets himself up as a fur-dresser/cobbler (157–60). Living in a room beneath the stairs, he befriends an old woman rag-picker and her mentally retarded ward whom he seduces when she brings him an animal hide. Their assignations take place in his room and under a beached boat, but the relationship ends when the pregnant girl takes up with the local sailors (158–9). The fox-fur slippers made for Orina by her cobbler-seducer foreshadow the unknown article made by cobbler Il'ya for the slow-witted girl who is Orina's successor.

These parallel stories told by Il'ya and Orina reverberate even more oddly in Yakov's adult day-dreams about his own youth. Young Yakov has sexual fantasies about a mentally defective girl neighbour who goes with the sailors (24–5). The plot assumes a new level of complexity when we recall that Orina's son, the young Yakov, who loves the mentally defective neighbour girl, sets fox-traps (24) and that the adult Yakov makes squirrel-fur slippers (37 and 185). The circle closes. Yakov merges with both the young trapper who first presents Orina with the fox cub (and is seduced by her), and with Il'ya, his 'perhaps' father, the lover of Orina and the mentally defective girl. In a world where time means nothing, Yakov's 'beloved' may be identical with the feeble-minded girl seduced by Il'ya, who, in turn, seems to echo much of Orina's personal history. These unities are hinted at through the fantastic interconnections involving the fox and the slippers that are echoed in both Il'ya's middle name, Patrikeich (cf. Patrikeevna, the patronymic of the fox in folklore), and in his strange last name, Zynzyrella, with its evocation of Cinderella of vair (or *verre*) slipper fame. Sokolov's novel seems to borrow freely from and invert key elements of the Cinderella legend. A male Cinderella makes fur slippers for his beloved who (posthumously) seeks to be reunited with him. We may also note that some interpretations of the Cinderella tale stress the theme of incest inherent in *Mezhdu sobakoi i volkom*.[12]

If the fur slippers are central to the intergrading of Orina and the mentally defective girls, *valenki* 'felt boots' strongly hint at the relationship between Il'ya and Yakov. It is here that we find echoes of the Oedipus legend. Boots are an insistent theme in Il'ya's rambling epistolary narrative which encompasses his entire life. The theft of boots is referred to particularly often. At one point Il'ya imagines a mushroom-hunting expedition with Pozhilykh, the state investigator,

---

[12] The Cinderella tale is most widely read in the Charles Perrault version, *Cendrillon ou la petite pantoufle de verre*, in which a glass slipper plays a key role. Many other versions of the tale refer to slippers of *vair* 'squirrel skin'. The issue is much disputed among folklorists: see W. R. S. Ralston, 'Cinderella', in: *Cinderella: A Case Book*, ed. Alan Dundes (New York, 1983), 37–8, and Paul Delarue, 'From Perrault to Walt Disney: The Slipper of Cinderella', ibid. 110–14. See Alan Dundes, 'Selected Bibliography', ibid., for references to psychoanalytic readings arguing that the basic theme of *Cinderella* is incest. Typical of these is Bruno Bettelheim, *The Uses of Enchantment: The Meaning and Importance of Fairy Tales* (New York, 1977), 245–8. There is, incidentally, a well established tradition of male Cinderellas in the European folklore tradition. See Emmanuel Cosquin, 'Le "Cendrillon" masculin', *Revue des traditions populaires*, xxxiii (1918), 193–202.

to whom he addresses his letters. His companion must be sure to bring boots, although such luxuries are not for the likes of himself (49–50). He goes barefoot from Easter to the Feast of the Protection of the Virgin in the late autumn. Only when the mud freezes does he pull on his one felt boot (*valenok*), to which he attaches an ice-skate when the river freezes over. Il'ya suddenly remembers he is speaking to a state official. Where would such as he get even one *valenok*? This leads to the long, hilarious, self-justifying tale of how he stole a boot. More important, the story bears upon his relationship to his son Yakov, from whom he has been separated for many years.

Il'ya is in the hospital recovering from the loss of his leg. The hospital has an abundance of everything—cold, hunger, typhus—everything except *valenki*. For the entire ward of amputees there is but a single pair shared by all. The patients use them in rotation. Il'ya and another patient, Yakov Il'ich Alfeev (apparently identical with Palamakhterov) who lacks the opposite leg, share them, joining each other for walks about the grounds. 'Two boots make a pair', as the Russian proverb says. At length, the two are notified that they are to be discharged from the relative luxury of the hospital. The winter is harsh. They are both homeless cripples unable to make a living. Worse still, they have no footwear. The two men plot to steal the ward's sole pair of *valenki* and take French leave. On fleeing the hospital their first act is to get drunk before going their separate ways at the railway station. Il'ya, perhaps because he wishes to borrow the fare from Yakov, suggests that he may be Yakov Il'ich's long-lost father. The boot motif here would seem to serve a dual function. The proverbial idea 'two boots make a pair' supports the suggestion that the two men are related, although the point is made more forcefully (and grotesquely) by their sharing (and stealing) a single set of footwear. It also hints at the intergrading of personalities so typical of the murky world between dog and wolf. The other function is more speculative. Both father and son are lame. They do not know each other. The son is destined to kill the father. It appears that they have both loved the same woman, i.e. the mentally defective girl who shares much of her past (including the slipper episode) with Orina, the wife and mother. The parallel to the Oedipus legend is striking: father and son are lame (cf. the etymologies of Laios and Oedipus),[13] they do not recognize each other, the son kills the father, and loves (a version of) his mother. In conversation Sokolov has told me that, although he did not initially have the Oedipus parallel in mind, it struck him during and after the writing. Here again, as with the Cinderella slippers, the boot motif alludes to the novel's main theme— the world between dog and wolf with its (con-)fusion of supposedly immutable categories in nature and human affairs.

[13] Claude Lévi-Strauss, *Structural Anthropology* (New York, 1963), 214–15.

The above cases of the footwear theme relate to both the theme and subtext of *Mezhdu sobakoi i volkom*. The novel's plot also turns on footwear-related items—Il'ya's crutches. He uses them to beat off the supposed wolf and they are stolen in retaliation. Their loss is particularly distressing because the ghost of Orina is seeking Il'ya, and they are his means of escape. One of the novel's motifs is 'There is nothing to shove off with', referring to his missing crutches. His feud with the dog-keeper Yakov centres upon his efforts to secure their return. When he begins writing denunciations of Yakov, his fate is sealed. As with most things in the book, there are variant versions of the fate of the crutches, and it is by no means clear which version, if any, is correct. In one variant it is suggested that they may have been used to give weight to the empty coffin of a man drowned and swept away. In another it is suggested that since time flows at different rates in different places, Il'ya needs only to go to a place in which the theft has not yet occurred.

There are still other occurrences of the boot motif, albeit of less importance. Discharged from the hospital, Il'ya is befriended by a traveller with whom he gets drunk. In the brotherhood of alcohol the two men decide they are related and, in fact(?), the travelling rail inspector's name is Emel'yan Zhizhirella (67–73). In his drunken rambling he tells of an earlier train trip on a hunting expedition after the fabled *Zhar-ptitsa*, when his boots were stolen. There is even a poem about the theft (173). Although Il'ya accepts the gift of a set of false teeth (direct from the man's mouth), he repays this act of generosity by stealing his host's boots as he leaves (145). Other scattered references include one to Ahasuerus, the legendary cobbler who became the Wandering Jew when he refused Christ permission to rest at his shop door. The allusion may seem appropriate to Il'ya, the wanderer, but it is evoked by the worn-out boots of one of Yakov's schoolteachers (99).

The boot motif and its extensions play an unusually large role in the novel, occurring in sixteen of the eighteen chapters, including all four poetry sections. It figures heavily in the plot. Nor is it by chance that Yakov makes shoes (37, 116, 121, and 185) and that Il'ya is a cobbler. The obscure relationship between father and son, victim and killer, and the woman (women) they love is spelled out in the shoe motif: the Oedipal relation between lame father and son by the shared pair of *valenki*, and their relationship to Orina (in her many guises) by the Cinderella/Zynzyrella fur slippers. *Mezhdu sobakoi i volkom* is a novel of mythical archetypes in which Oedipus meets Cinderella.

3

The footwear motif has an equally prominent but very different role in Sokolov's third novel. *Palisandriya* 'The Epic of Palisandr' is parody on a grand scale.[14] The novel, cast in the form of a memoir, tells the fantastic adventures of Palisandr Dal'berg, 'Son of the Kremlin'. Palisandr, an orphan, is heir presumptive to the leadership of the mysterious secret Order of Watchmen (*Chasovshchiki*), an hereditary society that has ruled Russia for many generations. Great-grandson of Rasputin and grand-nephew of Lavrenty Beriya, Palisandr is a difficult lad of great charm and enormous sexual and intellectual endowments whose welfare is supervised by a Guardian Council consisting of Stalin, Beriya, Khrushchev, Brezhnev, and Andropov—all characters in the novel. The hermaphrodite hero portrays himself as a strapping youth, hairless, cross-eyed, seven-fingered, and falsetto-voiced, but nevertheless a veritable Apollo. He avoids mirrors, spending much of his hundred-year life-span sitting (fully clothed and shod) in his bath. A passive figure who sees himself as History's amanuensis, he is in fact a self-deluded graphomaniac. The novel's plot has two major strands: the traditional epic quest, in which the hero loses and regains his homeland, and the hidden tale of his hermaphroditism.

The Russian leadership is apparently subject to the authority of certain forces abroad, possibly the Freemasons. In his memoir, which unwittingly displays the author's complete incomprehension of reality, Palisandr recounts his many bizarre, and often comic, adventures and misadventures. These include his escapades with elderly Kremlin wives and widows, the *real* story of the death of Nadezhda Stalina, a childish prank that results in Stalin's death, internal exile as steward of the Government Massage Parlour (located in the Novodevichii Convent), an attempt on the life of Brezhnev (in revenge for the latter's appropriation of Palisandr's beloved, Shagane, the aged legless whore who presides over the Parlour), a pseudo-espionage venture in Western Europe (where he is supposed to neutralize the 'Masonic Cabal'), and exile abroad by forces that fear his accession to power in Russia. In the West, Palisandr (who eventually wins Nobel Prizes for both literature and leadership of the struggle for hermaphrodite civil rights) becomes a wandering bisexual courtesan—intimate with the great and near-great, entrepreneur of an international chain of massage parlours, a prolific writer of scabrous best-sellers, and the owner of the graves of all

---

[14] The critical literature includes: D. Barton Johnson, 'Sasha Sokolov's *Palisandrija*', *Slavic and East European Journal*, xxx (1986), 389–403; Olga Matich, 'Sasha Sokolov's *Palisandriia*: History and Myth', *Russian Review*, xliv (1986), 415–26; P. Vail and A. Genis, 'Tsvetnik rossiiskogo anakhronizma', *Grani* (Munich), xli (1986), no. 139, pp. 159–64; Alexander Zholkovsky, 'On the Stylistic Roots of Sokolov's *Palisandriia*', *Canadian-American Slavic Studies*, xxii (1989) (forthcoming).

Russians who have died in exile or emigration. Upon his final triumphant return to Russia to assume his rightful position, he is accompanied (Lenin-like, in a sealed train) by the remains of the exiled Russian dead.

Palisandriya, Sokolov says, is the only one of his novels to start from an idea. Real literature is being displaced by subliterary forms such as memoirs.[15] Semi-documentary works such as those by Solzhenitsyn, Svetlana Allilueva, Khrushchev, and Brezhnev come to mind. *Émigré* literature in particular is obsessed with memoirs revealing a suppressed past. Nor is the general phenomenon restricted to Russian letters. Sokolov makes a second, more fundamental, claim: history is unknowable. This is inadvertently reflected in memoirs, which ultimately show us little but the inevitably limited and often self-serving views of their authors. *Palisandriya* is, among other things, a satire on historical memoir literature. Sokolov's comically deluded memoirist-hero illustrates the absurdity of the very idea of history. Strangely enough, it is *Palisandriya*'s galoshes motif that expresses this central theme. If the footwear motif in *Shkola dlya durakov* and *Mezhdu sobakoi i volkom* requires explanation, in *Palisandriya*, perhaps because of its 'ideological' origins, its meaning is much more explicit.

The opening pages of *Palisandriya* offer a discourse on the nature of history (19–21). In his youth the fascinated hero naïvely has submerged himself in archives and primary source materials. As the years pass, however, his attitude becomes more circumspect: 'One thing inevitably replaces another, and then is supplanted by something else, and so on. And there have always been people and nations who publicly have harboured sympathy or animosity to each other; and not far off there have always been other people who write about these relationships; and also those who write about those who have written about those who have written' (20). The eyes and the mind glaze. Such thoughts preface the formulation of Palisandr's own credo concerning history.

Palisandr is the unwitting victim of an elaborate plot rigged by his rival Andropov, who wishes to remove him from the scene to clear his own path to power. To this end Andropov places a newspaper advertisement in which a royal family living abroad (who turn out to be Anastasia Romanova and her husband) expess a wish to adopt an orphan who will be their heir. As it happens, the Romanovs live near the headquarters of the mysterious foreign cabal that holds the Russian leadership in secret thrall. Andropov appeals to the lad's patriotism. By offering himself as the heir, he can penetrate the secret society and free his homeland. In order to prepare himself for adoption Palisandr

---

[15] Ol'ga Matich, 'Nuzhno zabyt' vse staroe i vspomnit' vse novoe . . .', *Russkaya mysl'* (Paris), no. 3571, 31 May 1985, p. 12. Interview with Sasha Sokolov.

conducts an exploratory correspondence with Anastasia Romanova. She has asked him about his attitude to proud Clio, the Muse of History, and to the Russian past. His answering letter (as preserved in volume XV of his juvenilia) assures her of his unwavering dedication to the ideals of the past: '"*But at the same time . . . our mundane day-to-day existence contains a circle of realia for which I nourish an equal weakness. You, perhaps, will take impartial offense at my frivolity, at the earthiness of my pre-dilections, but I cannot but reveal to You that galoshes are first among such things*." (The italics are mine. P. D.)' (20). Andropov, pretending concern that Anastasia may indeed take offence, insists on deletion. Palisandr acquiesces, but so that his conscience may be clear before the court of history he affirms to Andropov 'Yes, I love galoshes' (*kaloshi*) (21).[16]

This dithyrambic outburst introduces a veritable hymn to boots. They are integral to Palisandr's greatest pleasures. One of these is attending burials and services for the dead, where he picks up elderly women. He loves the sound of his boots (*mokrostupy*) squishing in the evening slush as he wends his way homeward. During matins and throughout the day he gratefully catches their lacquered fragrance which evokes the half-forgotten smells of Moroccan *fiacres*, Tasmanian rubber plantations, the pungent aromas of Assyrian booteries, and so on. No matter where his feet take him, his 'thoughts constantly return to them: "*Mokrostupy*!"' (21). He studies their tracks on sandy paths, admiring the blister-like and ribbed pattern of their soles. So attached is Palisandr to his boots that he is reluctant to part with them even in theatre cloakrooms, deserting the performance to retrieve them. Distressed by a cloakroom mix-up, he resolves never to attend the theatre in spite of his adoration of the arts. Only at home does his anxiety abate when, still fully clad and booted, he can settle into his bath and stage mock sea-battles in which his boots play the role of sub-merged submarines menacing paper boats (21–2 and 71–2).

Palisandr's emphatic use of the archaic *mokrostupy* for *galoshi* in the midst of his disquisition on bath-tub naval engagements evokes the latent image of Admiral Shishkov (1754–1841). Shishkov in his *Beseda lyubitelei russkogo slova* argued that foreign borrowings such as *galoshi* should be replaced by Slavonic words. The French *galoshi* must yield to the native *mokrostupy* 'wet steppers'. These terms played a central role in the famed dispute between the *arkhaisty* and the *novatory* during the second decade of the nineteenth century.[17] Admiral Shishkov's circle

---

[16] The substandard *kaloshi* which Palisandr uses for *galoshi* evokes *kal* 'excrement'.

[17] My thanks to Professor Alexander Zholkovsky for pointing out to me that *mokrostupy* and *galoshi* were key terms in the Shishkovian–Karamzinian debate. They have become standard text-book examples. See *Kratkii ocherk istorii russkoi kul'tury*, ed. Sh. M. Levin (L., 1967), 262; *Istoriya russ-koi literatury XIX veka*, ed. F. M. Golovenmenko and S. M. Petrova, 2 ed. (M., 1963), 66–8. For a detailed survey of a major aspect of the lexicon in *Palisandriya*, see Zholkovsky, op. cit. (n. 14).

was opposed by the Arzamas society headed by Karamzin and Zhukovsky. The latter group devastatingly parodied Shishkov's proposals in sample sentences such as '*Khoroshilishche idet v mokrostupakh po gul'bishchu iz ristalishcha na pozorishche*', i.e. '*Frant idet v kaloshakh po bul'varu iz tsirka v teatr*.'[18] Palisandr is much given to Shishkovian language, and his archaic usages are appropriate for one who has been reincarnated in many eras of Russian history. One suspects, however, that Sokolov's real target here, as elsewhere, is contemporary 'nationalist' writers, such as Solzhenitsyn, with their passion for cleansing Russian of foreign impurities. Once again the footwear motif serves as a thematic vehicle.

The Palisandrian Manifesto '*Ya lyublyu kaloshi*' eventually leads to a more serious disquisition—a meditation on the human condition (202–3). The youthful Palisandr is infinitely depressed by the petty vulgarity of mankind. Despairing, he contemplates suicide. He decides, however, that this is not a solution: 'Caught in the vicious circle of incarnations, we, upon each of our departures, are condemned to a return, as if to the scene of our crimes, or to the cloakroom for our galoshes' (202). As we grow older, we become hardened to human vulgarity, so that we come to prefer any indignity to a death which resolves nothing. We yield to coarse passions and reproduce our kind: 'Long live Homo sapiens! . . . And like a pair of conscientiously made galoshes slogging through the world's muck, we keep going, we never wear out' (203). This darkly sardonic vision of galoshes as symbol of the human condition throws a rather different light on Palisandr's youthful delight in them as manifestations of present, concrete, reality as opposed to an abstract, idealized past. The identification of boots with the petty vulgarity of human existence strongly evokes the Gogolian theme of *poshlost'*.

These major invocations of the footwear motif are accompanied by a host of minor ones. The most entertaining echo the history and reincarnation themes. Palisandr attempts to assassinate Brezhnev and is imprisoned in a luxurious palace, the novel's satiric version of a Gulag camp. The attempt has been motivated in part by Palisandr's hatred of Brezhnev for seducing his one true love, the legless, aged courtesan Shagane. Due to his popularity, there is much pressure on the government to free Palisandr, the universal favourite. Brezhnev's wife, Viktoriya, age seventy, arrives to negotiate a settlement.[19] Having failed to kill his rival, Palisandr decides to take his vengeance by seducing the wife and is eminently successful. During their frolics Palisandr

---

[18] Golovenmenko and Petrova, op. cit. (n. 17), 68.

[19] In one of the novel's many word-plays on the boot motif, Viktoriya argues that 'to repress a well-born orphan would be to act inhumanely and, at the same time, *sest' v istoricheskuyu kaloshu* . . .' (167). Cf. *Sest' v kaloshu* 'to get into a mess'.

becomes engrossed in Vika's black pearl ear-rings with their tiny tinkling silver bells. Formerly the possession of Catherine the Great, the ear-rings evoke memories of one of Palisandr's previous Kremlin incarnations—that of the legendary stallion who became the Empress's lover in a *ménage à trois* with her paramour Prince Potemkin. Palisandr promises the reader a full autobiography (à la Tolstoy's *Kholstomer*) of his equine incarnation, but deigns only to give a few details in a footnote.[20]

The saga of Catherine's equine lover who ends as a pair of boots is part of a small cluster of footnotes involving footwear. In a later note as Palisandr is putting on his *botforty*, 'full of the unknown', he philosophically ponders that we never really know what awaits our extremities in the dark, secret labyrinths of our footwear (233). This bit of whimsy is exceeded only by an account of a formal lecture (in Latin) in which Palisandr attempts to click his heels only to find he is wearing bedroom slippers. In a footnote he explains that his only pair of boots is under house arrest for 'systematic disobedience and a series of unauthorized absences' (272). He has personally signed the arrest order and recorded the offence in their service record.

Another episode links footwear and sex. Palisandr's sex life (in this incarnation) commences when his grandmother, smarting from a snub by her lover, avenges herself by inviting her well-developed five-year-old grandson into her bath, thus launching his lifelong predilection for elderly women. The invitation is accompanied by the command 'But take your boots off so they don't get wet' (258). Palisandr soon tires of his granny and has her pass him on to her numerous Kremlin companions. This pattern of incestuous gerontophilia also applies to the sadistic *femme fatale*, Mazhoret, whose voracious sex life has been launched by her much older brother. Because of this shared pattern Palisandr closely identifies with her, echoing Flaubert's cliché— Mazhoret, *c'est moi*. The paraphrase of Flaubert's much overworked dictum leads into a curious passage obscurely relating footwear and promiscuous literary heroines (258–9). Flaubert's words, Palisandr says, are as outworn as the felt slippers put on over shoes when entering a museum (apparently a museum of literature). Alas, few visitors take the trouble to put them on properly by wrapping the bands around their ankles. As a result, they traipse along, trailing the bands behind them and wearing out the slippers. Mazhoret, no frequenter of genteel museums, is unacquainted with such outmoded literary heroines as Madame Bovary, Manon, or Lolita. She has been exposed to less

[20] The Empress is inadvertently crushed during their love-making and the horse is held culpable. In a blatant miscarriage of justice, the valiant steed is sold to a knacker. The unfortunate animal's dappled roan hide is made into a pair of boots which are inaugurated at the Feast of the Protection of the Virgin. Their owner attends services and then, having neither confessed nor changed shoes, goes to a tavern where he drinks them away.

sedate literary models in the works of the Marquis de Sade. Palisandr quite literally becomes a prisoner in Mazhoret's palace of sado-masochism.

One last occurrence of the boot motif leads us to the character Berdy Kerbabaev, son of Shagane and apostle of the creed 'There is no death'. This imperturbable Quartermaster Captain defies tradition by wearing *valenki* rather than boots with his uniform. He is, however, on his days off, a dresser of surpassing elegance: his boots, which glitter with pearls, are particularly noteworthy. There is more than a hint that Berdy adorns himself with the pilfered attire of the dead (87). Nor is he the only such character in Sokolov's tale. The apprentice students of the crematory division of KRUBS, the Kremlin Trade School for Well-born Orphans, routinely relieve their clients of their footwear (112). As in *Shkola dlya durakov* and *Mezhdu sobakoi i volkom*, boot theft is a fixture of Russian life.

Throughout *Palisandriya* footwear is an explicit symbol of mundane, sensory reality as opposed to the grandiose, abstract pseudo-ideal of History.

4

What are the origins of Sokolov's pervasive footwear motif? To assume a psycho-sexual source would be facile. Freud and his followers inter-pret footwear as sexual symbols and boots are a well known fetish object.[21] Some of Sokolov's footwear allusions do have sexual over- or under-tones. But most do not. The allusions display great diversity of function and meaning. Is there a wider meaning that accounts for the omnipresent motif? We shall argue that its meaning arises from Sokolov's literary background.

Sokolov's adolescence coincided with a cycle of Khrushchevian cultural 'thaws' that were marked by great changes in the Soviet liter-ary scene. Long suppressed figures were, in varying degrees, rehabil-itated—Bulgakov, Platonov, and Bunin. Established Soviet writers such as Valentin Kataev began publishing prose that was radically more adventurous than their earlier work. Although Sokolov is reluct-ant to see other authors as influences on his work, he has mentioned

---

[21] Given Sokolov's fascination with footwear, it is somewhat surprising that shoe or foot fetish-ism has not found its way into his work, especially *Palisandriya*. Psychoanalytically inclined critics who have devoted much attention to Gogol''s nose motif have not entirely neglected his interest in footwear. Daniel Rancour-Laferriere, *Out from under Gogol's Overcoat: A Psychoanalytic Study* (Ann Arbor, 1982), discusses Gogol''s shoe motif in 'What it Means to be a Shoe' (89–92) and 'What Else it Means to be a Shoe' (184–6). The psycho-sexual meaning of shoes in folklore (with particular reference to Cinderella's slipper) is discussed in Alan Dundes, 'Projection in Folklore: A Plea for Psychoanalytic Semiotics', *Modern Language Notes*, lxxxxi (1976), 1516–17.

two figures that he recognizes as important in his early development: Ivan Bunin and, to a lesser extent, Valentin Kataev.[22] These two names are closely linked in Russian literary history.

Bunin, Russia's first Nobel Laureate in literature (1933), was one of the first (posthumous) beneficiaries of the post-Stalin thaw. Although an émigré and outspoken in his opposition to the Revolution, he was selectively republished as early as 1955 when a volume of his stories appeared.[23] During the following year both a volume of selected works and a *Sobranie sochinenii* in five volumes came out. Such publications continued and culminated in a nine-volume *Sobranie sochinenii* (1965–7) with an introduction by Aleksandr Tvardovsky, the editor of *Novyi mir*. This edition included, for the first time, what some hold to be Bunin's masterpiece, the semi-fictional autobiography *Zhizn' Arsen'eva: yunost'.*[24] *The Well of Days*, as it is known in English, describes, among other things, the author's young manhood in provincial Russian cities such as Khar'kov. In particular, it sets forth the author's developing aesthetic views while providing a less than flattering picture of the intelligentsia. Almost all the young journalist's friends were radical. In spite of their human diversity, all preached an identical message (227–8). Virtue resided in the People; vice, in the upper classes. 'One may or may not be a poet, but one must be a citizen', Bunin was told (231). Chekhov was despised for his 'political indifference', and Tolstoy as a religious hypocrite playing at being a ploughman or cobbler, while peasant bellies swelled from hunger (229). Bunin was often under attack for his aestheticism and for his view, both broader and more particularized, of mankind. Although more than ready to assist a needy individual, Bunin could not understand the merit of self-sacrifice on behalf of 'some eternally drunk handyman or horseless Klim (moreover not a real Klim, but a collective one)' (231). Among the circle of friends, self-appointed saviours of mankind whose disapproval tormented the young poet, he particularly recalled a spartan Rakhmetov-like figure 'in his sturdy hob-nailed Swiss boots' (232).

Bunin was one of the great masters of the Russian language, so much so that his critics (even sympathetic ones such as Milton Ehre) speak of his tendency to lapse into 'mere virtuosity, the exhibition of verbal powers for their own sake'.[25] His lengthy, sensuous descriptions, lyrical monologues, verbal density, and relative indifference to plot bring him

[22] Sokolov acknowledged his debt to Bunin and Kataev in his remarks at the 'Sasha Sokolov and the Avant-Garde' session of the annual meeting of the American Association of Teachers of Slavic and East European Languages on 29 Dec. 1984 in Washington, D.C.

[23] Information on Soviet Bunin publications is from the bibliography in James B. Woodward, *Ivan Bunin: A Study of his Fiction* (Chapel Hill, N.C., 1980).

[24] Subsequent page citations are to I. A. Bunin, *Zhizn' Arsen'eva: yunost'* (New York, 1952).

[25] Milton Ehre, 'Bunin', in: *Handbook of Russian Literature*, ed. Victor Terras (New Haven, 1985), 64. The following quotations and comments on Bunin and modernism are based on Ehre's discussion.

close to the modernist tradition. Although Bunin frequently expressed his hostility to modernism, Ehre, noting Bunin's tendency to subjugate experience to form, rightly suggests that his 'realism is closer to the impersonal aestheticism of Flaubert' than to that of the Russian tradition (64). Bunin's challenge to the sterility of Socialist Realism fell on fertile ground in the sixties and early seventies.

Valentin Kataev played a considerable role in the Soviet rehabilitation of Bunin. His *Trava zabven'ya*, which appeared in 1967 at the same time as the nine-volume edition of Bunin's collected works, is a remarkable homage to two of Kataev's literary mentors and friends—the flamboyant poet of the Revolution Vladimir Mayakovsky, and the anti-Bolshevik émigré aesthete Ivan Bunin.[26] *Au fond* about Kataev's own development as a writer, the volume is, among other things, a personal meditation on the conflict between a literature of social command and an art governed solely by personal and aesthetic inclination. Although somewhat ambivalent about both his heroes, Kataev presented an unforgettable portrait of Bunin to a new generation.

Kataev played an even more important part in the resurrection of Soviet literature in the post-Stalin years. One of the few survivors from the heyday of an adventurous young Soviet literature, he had been adroit in adapting to the politically imposed changes that had reduced that literature to a series of stereotyped formulas. With the thaw, Kataev undertook a series of literary experiments to which he assigned the whimsical name *mauvisme*: '. . . since everyone now writes so well, one must write as badly as possible in order to attract attention' was the explanation he offered his hostess at a Texas cocktail party.[27] Kataev later said that he sought to write 'badly' in the sense that Matisse painted badly, i.e. in defiance of established convention.[28] Under the banner of *mauvisme* Kataev published a series of controversial works during the sixties and seventies that reintroduced modernism into Soviet literature. The most important of these works were *Svyatoi kolodets* (1965) and *Trava zabven'ya* (1967). Hybrid in form, they are part autobiographical memoir, part surreal fantasy, part novel. Plot and chronology are displaced by associative memory as the organizing principle. The narrator often merges into observed objects and perceives the world from their points of view. Time collapses when a current image merges with a similar one of many years before. Perception and evaluations are unabashedly subjective. Although *Trava zabven'ya* deals with Bunin as a subject, its predecessor, *Svyatoi kolodets*, whose title echoes the subtitle (*Istoki dnei*) Bunin orginally gave to

---

[26] Valentin Kataev, *Trava zabven'ya* (M., 1967). Page references are to this edition.
[27] Valentin Kataev, *Svyatoi kolodets* (M., 1967), 109. Page references are to this edition.
[28] Robert Russell, *Valentin Kataev* (Boston, 1981), 115.

Zhizn' Arsen'eva: yunost', is in some ways more reminiscent of the older author. While Kataev's modernist techniques owe little to his mentor, the long, dense sentences of much of his late prose and what he terms 'stereoscopic description' at times strongly evoke Bunin's style.[29]

Kataev influenced Soviet writing of the sixties in yet another way. In 1955 he founded and until 1962 edited *Yunost'*, a literary journal for a new generation of writers and readers.[30] The so-called *molodaya proza* movement grew out of the coterie of writers that came to be associated with the magazine. Much of the 'young prose' focused upon the inner psychological world of the character (usually a youthful first person narrator), representing a major shift from the wooden heroes of much Soviet fiction. Kataev's most gifted protégé was undoubtedly Vasily Aksenov (1932–), whose *Zvezdnyi bilet* (1961) became the bible of a generation of Soviet youth. Far more significant in a literary sense, however, was *Zatovarennaya bochkotara* (1968), a surrealist work very much in the vein of the late Kataev.[31] It is also difficult to imagine Andrey Bitov's (1937–) deeply introspective prose in the absence of Kataev.[32] By establishing a link between Bunin and the rising generation and by the example of his own prose Kataev provided a context for Sasha Sokolov.

We now return to Sokolov's insistent footwear motif. The new atmosphere called for a return to specifics in the description of the real world instead of the generalities so characteristic of Socialist Realist fiction. Kataev's proclaimed 'stereoscopic vision' made objects three-dimensional, recreated them as if seen for the first time.[33] This meant attention to detail such as personal appearance, clothing, and footwear. Growing literary sophistication also meant a return to elaborate motif patterns which, in turn, might acquire larger thematic meanings in the work as a whole.

The origins of Sokolov's boot theme can be located much more specifically. In *Zhizn' Arsen'eva* Bunin describes his evolution as a writer. We have referred to his dismay at the attitude of his friends, who were so committed to the salvation of 'the people' that they were oblivious to individual reality in either life or art. The young writer wanders down a street at dusk relishing the outlines of the roof tops and noticing the

[29] Ibid. 126.

[30] Ibid. 12.

[31] Aksenov was quick to come to the defence of his mentor when Kataev's *Svyatoi kolodets* was attacked in the Soviet press. Russell, *Kataev* (n. 28), 151 n., draws attention to Aksenov's article 'Puteshestvie k Kataevu', *Yunost'*, 1967, no. 1, pp. 68–9. In personal conversation Sokolov has told me that the appearance of Aksenov's *Bochkotara* in *Yunost'* made a strong impression on him.

[32] Parallels between Bitov's and Sokolov's prose are discussed in Dzhon Fridman [John Freedman], 'Razmyshleniya nad tekstom: Iskrivlenie real'nosti i vremeni v poiske istiny v romanakh *Pushkinskii dom* i *Shkola dlya durakov*. (Nenauchnyi ocherk)', *Dvadtsat' dva* (Tel Aviv), xlviii (1987), 200–10.

[33] Russell, *Kataev* (n. 28), 113–14.

passers by: '. . . Like a detective I pursued now one, now another passerby, staring at his back, his galoshes, trying to understand, to catch something within, to get inside him. . . . To write! Yes, roofs, galoshes, backs—these were what one must write about, and certainly not for the sake of fighting tyranny and oppression, defending the downtrodden and dispossessed, producing vivid characters, broad pictures of society, of modern times, its moods and trends!'.[34] Precisely such details as galoshes lend Bunin's prose its extraordinary, life-like density. Not surprisingly, this passage is widely regarded as Bunin's aesthetic credo.[35]

Kataev's *Trava zabven'ya*, his tribute to Bunin and Mayakovsky, is also his manifesto as a writer. For Kataev, the loyal Soviet artist, Bunin's aestheticism and specificity of perception must be coupled with the social commitment of his other idol, Mayakovsky. But Kataev's portrait of Mayakovsky, although a much more flamboyant figure than the dry, acerbic Bunin, is far paler than that of the émigré master. Kataev is obsessed with Bunin's verbal mastery of the stuff of reality. Bunin's 'galoshes manifesto' obviously made a strong impression, for in *Trava zabven'ya* Kataev quotes precisely the passage just cited (206). It had long remained in his mind, for he draws Bunin's credo not from the Soviet edition, but from *Lika* (1939) which its author had sent him just after the war, before incorporating it into the final text of *Zhizn' Arsen'eva*.[36] The style of Kataev's 'stereoscopic' *mauvisme* is far closer to that of Bunin than Mayakovsky.

Kataev seems to render indirect homage to Bunin's manifesto in his *Svyatoi kolodets*, a *mélange* of dream sequences induced by the anaesthetic administered before a serious operation. In it Kataev reflects on various episodes of his life. The longest sequence centres on a trip to the United States in the early sixties. Possibly taking his cue from Bunin, Kataev introduces footwear as the major motif of the episode—a motif that is superficially humorous, but portentous in its obscure subtext. Before flying off, Kataev looks at his black, highly polished moccasins. There follows a detailed, paragraph-long description of every aspect of

[34] *Zhizn' Arsen'eva*, 314. The English translation is from Valentine Kataev, *The Grass of Oblivion*, tr. Robert Daglish (New York, 1970), 205–6.

[35] It is perhaps significant that boots figure prominently in the *émigré* Bunin's memorial sketch of his former friend and colleague, Maksim Gor'ky. Famed as the portrayer of Russia's *bosyaki* 'the barefooted ones or outcasts', Gor'ky, the patron saint of Socialist Realism, is pictured as a posturing, booted, pseudo-*bosyak*. Bunin ends his description of Gor'ky's picturesque attire with '. . . some sort of peculiar boots . . . into which he tucked his black trousers. Everyone knew how Andreev, Skitalets, and other Gor'ky disciples, imitating his "national" attire, had begun wearing high top-boots, blouses, and Russian coats. It was intolerable.' See I. A. Bunin, *Vospominaniya* (Paris, 1950), 127. Bunin's derisive portrait of Gor'ky (118–29) was not included in the otherwise virtually complete nine-volume Soviet edition of 1965–7. Incidentally, one of Gor'ky's many jobs as a youth had been as an apprentice in a shoe-shop.

[36] Kataev, *Trava zabven'ya*, 205. Woodward, *Bunin* (n. 23), 174–5, discusses the post-war inclusion of *Lika* in *Zhizn' Arsen'eva*.

their appearance (45–6). Time becomes confused during the long flight and its passage is marked by the fading lustre of his moccasins. The ageing of the shoes and their inevitable future history induces a dark foreboding in their owner (52). Some colossal misfortune lies in store. On his first morning in New York, a Sunday in August, Kataev nervously takes an early walk. He plans later to visit several art museums. His shoes are dirty, and although he is very short of money, he cannot defile works of art by viewing them in dirty shoes. This leads to a surreal encounter with a decrepit old man who offers to shine his shoes in his sidewalk place of business. They share no common tongue, and their encounter (by far the book's longest scene) is simultaneously one of incomprehension, humour, and anxiety. Although the shoeshine 'boy' cheats him (25 cents *per shoe*), the outraged Kataev forgives the sick old man and, most curiously, thinks of his first love (62–71). One of the purposes of Kataev's American journey is to see his first love, a young girl with whom he had been infatuated before the Revolution. She had married and emigrated. Their meeting is the culmination of his journey and proves bitter-sweet, as death all too obviously hovers over both. Their journey is nearly over. The shoe motif is, as Robert Russell points out, symbolic of the passage of time and the approach of death (122).[37] In *Svyatoi kolodets*, his first *mauviste* work, Kataev echoes the boot motif without reference to his early mentor. In *Trava zabven'ya*, where Bunin holds centre stage, his 'galoshes manifesto' moves from latent motif to overt theme.

Bunin and Kataev were Sokolov's acknowledged masters during his formative years as a writer. When asked what he owes to Bunin, Sokolov replies '*vizual'nost*' by which he means that 'stereoscopic vision' that Kataev argued for in the face of the featureless prose of Socialist Realism.[38] Sokolov argues that such prose achieves transcendence into another dimension, making it the highest form of art.[39] Like Bunin's, Sokolov's 'visuality' is rendered in a rich, extravagant language of great density and syntactic complexity. Most obviously, Sokolov's aestheticism, his absolute rejection of social concerns as artistic subject matter, allies him with the *émigré* master, as does a certain darkness of vision.

Striking as they are, such general parallels might link Sokolov with any number of other writers. Although Sokolov is much given to literary allusion, there are, so far as I know, no specific references to Bunin

---

[37] The motif is omnipresent in this short book. Apart from the above references, shoe allusions occur on pp. 46–7, 77, 98, and 108.

[38] Matich, 'Nuzhno zabyt' . . .' (n. 15), 12.

[39] Unpublished portion of interview reported ibid., in which he also speaks of *predmetnost'* and paraphrases Bunin's words about galoshes and other realia. The full text of the interview, which took place in January 1985, was generously made available to me by Professor Matich.

in his fiction. Sokolov does, however, mention Bunin in an important essay 'Klyuchevoe slovo slovesnosti: kak'.[40] Artists are divided into adherents of the 'What' and of the 'How'; materialists and idealists; realists and avant-gardists. He then lists his heroes: Kandinsky, Flaubert, Rimbaud, Joyce, Shostakovich, and others. Sokolov sums up his discussion with Bunin's credo from *Zhizn' Arsen'eva*, the very same quotation as that cited by Kataev: 'To write! Yes, roofs, galoshes, backs—these were what one must write about, and certainly not for the sake of fighting tyranny and oppression, defending the downtrodden and oppressed'. Sokolov has taken Bunin's injunction literally, as well as metaphorically. He writes about footwear. It is almost a signature motif.

Sokolov owes much to Bunin, although his writing is very different from that of the aesthetic realist. Sokolov sees himself as a modernist who rejects much in the realist tradition. His initial perception of Bunin was almost certainly through the eyes and pen of Valentin Kataev. *Trava zabven'ya*, in which the Bunin 'galoshes manifesto' is adduced and discussed, seems almost a textbook for Sokolov's *Shkola dlya durakov* both in general manner of composition and sometimes in matters of particular imagery.[41] The collapse of time and space, the merging of the narrator's identity with that of other characters or objects, the use of associative memory as a constructive principle—all these devices are shared by *Shkola dlya durakov* and *Trava zabven'ya*. Richard Borden specifically remarks the dissolution of the narrators into flowers. The merging of Kataev's narrator into a bignonia both triggers and frames his hybrid work. Sokolov's fool, overcome by beauty, merges with a water-lily, assuming both its identity and name *Nymphea alba*. Even in his first book, however, Sokolov goes much further along the road of modernism than his Soviet mentor.

Sokolov very consciously sees himself as a part of the Russian literary tradition. Because of his 'modernism' some of his critics have been quick to see him as 'un-Russian', a charge often levelled (more accurately) at his *émigré* predecessor Vladimir Nabokov.[42] We have traced the diffusion of the footwear motif throughout Sokolov's *œuvre* and also its diversity of meaning from work to work and even within

[40] *Al'manakh Panorama* (Los Angeles), no. 245, 20–7 Dec. 1985, pp. 30–1.

[41] For discussions of the influence of Kataev on Sokolov, see Helen von Ssachno, 'Valentin Katajew und Sascha Sokolow', in: *Sowjetliteratur heute*, ed. G. Lindemann (Munich, 1979), 208–19; Ingold, op. cit. (n. 9); Richard C. Borden, 'Time, Backward! Sasha Sokolov and Valentin Kataev', *Canadian-American Slavic Studies*, xxii (1989) (forthcoming). A more general discussion of Sokolov's antecedents may be found in Olga Matich, 'Sasha Sokolov and his Literary Context', ibid.

[42] Nabokov's *Dar* (Ann Arbor, 1975) has its own minor shoe motif in the latter part of chapter 1, where Fedor writes a poem about experiencing an absent Russia through his worn, paper-thin soles (73–5). The discomfort induced by his new shoes is one of the clues to the fact that his famous literary dialogue with Koncheyev is in fact a monologue (80–7).

the same work. Its ultimate meaning, however, lies in its extra-textual origin and history. The footwear motif is Sokolov's tribute, both conscious and unconscious, to the tradition in Russian literature represented by his predecessors—Ivan Bunin and Valentin Kataev.